FREEDOM OF SPEECH

The Supreme Court
and Judicial Review

Martin Shapiro

Classics of Law & Society Series

Quid Pro Books
New Orleans, Louisiana

Freedom of Speech

The Supreme Court and Judicial Review

Originally published in 1966 by Prentice-Hall, Inc., Englewood Cliffs, New Jersey.

Published in the 2011 *Classics of Law & Society* edition by Quid Pro Books.

Quid Pro, LLC
5860 Citrus Blvd., Suite D-101
New Orleans, Louisiana 70123
www.quidprobooks.com

The cover photograph is copyright © 1969 by Bill Irwin and is used under license with Bill Irwin Photography (*www.billirwinphotography.com*). It depicts an anti-war protest in 1969 on Geary Street, San Francisco, California.

ISBN: 1452854866 (pbk., 2011)
ISBN-13: 9781452854861 (pbk., 2011)
ISBN-13: 9781458196866 (ePub, 2011)

qp

To Barbara

PREFACE

One function that prefaces frequently serve is that of an academic gossip column in which the writer has the chance to render a few thanks and drop a few illustrious names to add some borrowed luster to his own. Perhaps it is the general reader who ought to be thanked first and most for permitting this sort of thing at all. He is excused the paragraphs that follow unless, of course, he too enjoys the columns now and then.

The original, and by now much layered over, version of this book was, in that curiously deflating phrase, submitted in partial fulfillment of the requirements for the degree of Doctor of Philosophy. When the last professorial signature goes on the approval page, partial fulfillment hardly describes the emotional state of the exhausted but triumphant dissertation writer. It is not until the next week that somebody tells him that he really must begin thinking about revising the thing for publication. Then the feeling of partial fulfillment begins.

For the first sense of triumph, however, I owe a great deal to the Department of Government at Harvard which provides graduate students with what was for me a perfect set of working conditions, conditions perhaps best characterized by a phrase borrowed from aesthetics, "psychical distance." I wish especially to thank Professors W. Y. Elliott, C. J. Friedrich, Arthur Maass, Judith Shklar, and Dean Don Price for their help both as teachers and later as colleagues. I think none of us who were at Harvard during his time will be able adequately to express our respect and affection for the late V. O. Key.

As a dissertation supervisor, Professor Robert McCloskey managed the perfect combination of intolerance for dubious prose and tolerance for ideas in conflict with his own. Professor Earl Latham of Amherst College gave me a most stimulating afternoon pointing out the errors of my ways, many of which I am afraid still remain indubitably mine some six years later. Professor Arthur Sutherland was extremely generous with his time in examining one chapter in detail, a chapter which alas has disappeared from this volume under the publisher's ax but has appeared elsewhere.

Thanks must also be given to Cornell University for granting me permission to use, in preparing Chapter One, portions of an article I wrote for the Cornell Law Quarterly (47 Cornell L.Q. 175, © copyright 1962 by Cornell University).

Finally I must thank Mrs. Dorothy Peterson for her typing chores expertly performed at a range of 6,000 miles; Mrs. Gretchen Gillem, my ideal of a librarian; my wife for very considerable editorial and research assistance (unpaid as usual); and the Samuel S. Fels Fund of Philadelphia for providing me with a year free of other responsibilities in which to complete the initial manuscript.

Martin Shapiro
1966

CONTENTS

[Page numbers after headings are retained from the original print edition, to show detailed organization and pagination, and for continuity of referencing and citations. They are inserted into the text by the use of brackets. The new pagination of this edition is shown to far right. Nonetheless, the new pagination closely approximates the original.]

Chapter Four

INTRODUCTION

ONE OF THE great continuing disputes of American politics concerns the role of the Supreme Court. Another concerns the First Amendment and freedom of speech. This book is about both; it is about both for two reasons.

First, discussions of "*the* role of *the* Supreme Court" in the abstract are misleading. The Supreme Court has many different roles, depending upon the area of law with which it is dealing. If we are to make any progress in understanding the place of the Court in American politics, we must concretely examine what the Court does and can do about each specific segment of its jurisdiction. I choose the First Amendment jurisdiction here because it provides a particularly good illustration of one of the Court's major functions, and because it provides something more than an "academic" illustration. It is always easy to be in favor of free speech when the speaker is saying something harmless or something with which we agree. The real problem of the First Amendment comes when the speaker is expressing ideas we hate or fear, or is speaking in the hope of destroying the freedom of others. That is why the two great flurries of free speech debate came in the 1920s and 1950s when Communists were speaking long and loud. We now face a period when right wing and racial extremisms are going to be very much with us. The Ku Klux Klan will wrap itself in the First Amendment as well as in its white sheets. The Black Muslims will claim the freedom of speech and association which it seems so reasonable to give to the NAACP. And a host of messianic and paranoid crusades, societies, and private armies, not to mention bevies of youthful enthusiasts, will claim that their weird visions are entitled to free expression and their mob scenes to tender loving care by the police. Thus we are again going to be faced in the most compelling way with the question of how much protection ought the courts to give to speakers whose words we despise, or whose methods deviate from orderly and responsible political action.

The second reason this book is about both the role of the Supreme Court and freedom of speech is that the debate over freedom of speech, as it has been waged by the justices and their critics, has so intermingled freedom of speech and role of the Court questions that they have become inseparable. It is impossible to discuss the First Amendment without {2} involving the political role of the Supreme Court. Indeed, I hope to show that the crucial issues in the constitutional debate over freedom of speech can only be resolved by a proper understanding of the place of the Supreme Court in American politics.

1

Thus, Chapter One concerns the conflict between the judicially modest and the judicial activists. The judicially modest recognize that the Court has always exercised the power of judicial review, that is, the power to declare statutes unconstitutional. But they feel that review is undemocratic. They seek to relieve the Court of this dilemma by having it retain the power of review while using it as little as possible. Thus, in the First Amendment area, the Court would do as little as possible to protect freedom of speech. The traditional arguments of the judicial activists, who want the Court to use its powers of review to the fullest, have never convinced the modest, for the activists just keep repeating the positive arguments for review, the validity of which the modest generally admit but feel is not enough to overcome the essentially undemocratic nature of review. After describing this debate, therefore, I seek to show that review is not undemocratic when considered as part of a realistic analysis of how American politics works. In fact, in the free speech area, the Supreme Court represents some interest groups while other government agencies represent others. The Supreme Court can actually contribute to greater democracy by vigorously furthering the interests of its groups, which are not being protected by other parts of the government, so that all interests in our society may have a voice in making policy decisions. Thus the modest can be freed of their democratic guilt feelings, and the way is paved for more active judicial enforcement of the First Amendment.

We then turn in Chapter Two to the clear-and-present-danger rule, which has traditionally been the vehicle for active judicial protection of freedom of speech. A survey of the origins and basic meaning of that rule, and its ups and downs in the doctrinal history of the Court, indicates that its basic logic has never been destroyed and that it remains the most viable available rule for the enforcement of the First Amendment.

Nevertheless, the clear-and-present-danger rule has been vigorously challenged and partially replaced in recent years by another doctrine—balancing of interests. The burden of Chapter 3 is that the balancing formula is little more than a tactical device adopted by the modest to avoid the activist implications of the danger rule. The principal virtue of balancing from their point of view is that it allows the Supreme Court to abandon totally the defense of the First Amendment without openly admitting that it is giving up the power of review. Indeed, the debate {3} pro and con over balancing is really just the newest version of the old debate between the modest and the activists. It too can be resolved by a proper appreciation of the actual operations of American politics and the political role of the Supreme Court in representing free speech interests not represented elsewhere in the government.

The final chapter of the book, therefore, begins with a consideration of the one constitutional doctrine that acknowledges this special political role of the Supreme Court, the preferred position doctrine. Under this doctrine the Court, in its free speech adjudications, maintains a special preference for freedom. I then seek to show that the clear-and-present-danger rule is still one of the best means of implementing this preference, and conclude with a survey of how the preferred position doctrine might be applied to the various free speech problems that reach the court.

Chapter One

THE SUPREME COURT AND FREEDOM OF SPEECH

SINCE WORLD WAR I the Supreme Court of the United States has been involved in a long struggle over freedom of speech. It is possible to view that struggle either as a dispute about the meaning of the words "Congress shall make no law abridging the freedom of speech," or as a continuing discourse on the philosophy of liberty. Indeed, much has been said about what the framers intended by the First Amendment and what freedom of speech means and requires in terms of the theoretical suppositions upon which our polity is built. However, the feeling becomes inescapable among students of the great Supreme Court opinions in this area that the struggle basically revolves not around the First Amendment as such, but around the question: what ought the Supreme Court to do about the First Amendment? Most of the abstract argument among the justices and their academic satraps about the meaning of the First Amendment really amounts to nothing more than a set of elaborate disguises for that question. In other words, the key issue in the debate is not the legal one of the meaning of certain words in a written ordinance, nor the philosophic one of the meaning of freedom of speech in democratic theory, but the political one of what a certain governmental institution ought to do about a certain set of demands.

The justices, of course, have never denied this. Much of the incisive judicial writing about the role of the Supreme Court in relation to other agencies of government has come out of the free speech decisions. Questions about the role of the court have been raised in nearly every free speech case for the last twenty years. Moreover, it seems that most of the difficulties the Supreme Court has had with the First Amendment as constitutional doctrine arise from the dilemmas faced by the Court as government agency. In order to understand both the Supreme Court and the First Amendment, it is necessary to begin with the Supreme Court and add the First Amendment in small doses. {6}

Judicial Modesty v. Judicial Activism

The role of the Supreme Court, particularly in wielding its power of judicial review—the power to declare statutes unconstitutional—has been the subject of one of the central debates of modern American jurisprudence. The fierceness of that debate is suggested by the difficulty of even labeling the participants without getting caught in the cross fire. One side seizes for itself the labels "judicial modesty" and "judicial self-restraint"—thus suggesting that its opponents are unrestrained and immodest. At the very least they call the other side activists. But would they consent to be called passivists? The "unrestrained, immodest activists," on the other hand, tend to introduce themselves as preservers of a traditional American institution, judicial review, thus leaving their opposite numbers in the unfortunate position of attacking American tradition. But the confusion of labeling is fortunately offset by the appearance of two clear statements by leading members of the opposing schools, Learned Hand, until his death in 1961, one of America's most distinguished judges, and Professor Charles Black of the Yale Law School.[1] These may serve to focus our examination and clarify the real points at issue.

Judge Hand finds in the Constitution as he sees it a system of separate and coequal departments, each a "Leibnizian monad." Judicial review, which breaches the walls of separation, is contrary to the whole design. Nor does the Constitution provide any specific authorization for review. The supremacy clause, while admittedly allowing a measure of supervision over state acts, is so limited and specific as to undermine rather than support the claim to a general power of review. The analogy frequently drawn between the necessity for judicial assessment of a supposed conflict between two statutes and the alleged power of the Supreme Court to examine conflicts between the Constitution and a Congressional enactment is improper. In the former instance the conflict is merely between an earlier and a later legislative judgment. Since the legislature is not bound by its own previous judgments, a judicial finding of conflict merely implements the later will of the legislature. It might be added that, although Hand does not say so here, the legislature in this situation is perfectly free to re-instruct the courts by new legislation if it feels that the Court is in error. However, when the Supreme Court invalidates a statute, it perforce substitutes its choice among competing values for that of the legislature. This usurpation will inevitably result in a general recognition of the fact that judges inject their own judicial predilections {7} into law. Once this is realized the principal source of judicial prestige is destroyed, for the real judicial sanction is the notion that courts enunciate the will of the people as expressed in the statutes and the Constitution, not the personal sentiments of the judges.

But Hand's objection to judicial interference with legislative decision does not rest primarily on a judge's self-interest in preserving the judicial myth. It is derived instead from his basic conception of the Constitution and American democracy. The Constitution neither embodies natural law in the sense of an emanation from the Divine Will nor consists of substantive instruction as to the ends of governmental activity. In other words, it is not a code of abstract rights and wrongs but simply a blueprint for the distribution of the people's political power among the several departments of government. Since this plan confides the determination of the substance of governmental policy to the Congress and the President, the only possible role for the Court is to determine whether these departments are operating within the confines established by the blueprint. If the Court attempts to decide whether other departments were "right," a judicial oligarchy "unaccountable to anyone but itself" usurps the task of the "popular assembly" and thus violates "the underlying presuppositions of popular government."[2]

Professor Black's reply to this plea for self-restraint is based on a simple line of logic. The Constitution is law. Courts apply and interpret law. Therefore courts apply and interpret the Constitution. Furthermore, when a statute conflicts with the Constitution, the Supreme Court must decide between the two laws. It cannot avoid the issue for, if one litigant pleads the Constitution and the other a statute, refusal to look to the Constitution in fact decides the case in favor of the statute and against the Constitution. As to the legal nature of the Constitution, Black argues that the Constitution looks like a law (it has a preamble, etc.), says it is a law (Article VI), was thought by the founders to be law (*Federalist Papers*), and has been considered law ever since.

Not only does the idea that the courts must look to both the Constitution and the statutes naturally follow from the legal nature of the Constitution, but, what is more, the Constitution itself suggests the same notion. Article III defines the jurisdiction of the Court in terms of cases arising under the Constitution, and Article VI requires that state courts be bound by constitutional provisions in the event of conflict with state enactments. How then could the Court carry on its duty of reviewing lower court decisions without interpreting the Constitution?

In short, although disagreeing with Chief Justice John Marshall on particulars, Professor Black finds that *Marbury v. Madison*, the famous {8} case of 1803 in which Marshall proclaimed the Supreme Court's possession of the power of judicial review, reflects both the views of the framers and the sentiment of the times, as well as the natural conclusion to be drawn from the concept of constitutional democracy. The people desired to limit themselves and chose judicial review as a practical means to that end. And the historical evolution and acceptance of review indicates popular confirmation of the original choice. Therefore, the judicially modest who oppose review are both illogical and immodest themselves: they seek to upset the choice of the people in the name of popular sovereignty and to effect through the judicial process a major alteration in the basic framework of our government.

As far as Black is concerned, the enemies of judicial review wish to effect such an alteration for insufficient reasons. Their principal fear is that judicial review is undemocratic and allows excessive judicial policy-making. But it is widely known that judges are compelled to make policy decisions in all areas of law. The fact that they do so in the field of constitutional law is, therefore, neither unusual nor prejudicial to their continued prestige. Nor is review undemocratic. Many appointive officials make important decisions in our governmental process. Popular control of the judiciary is accomplished through public opinion, the amending process, and the powers of Congress over the Court's jurisdiction and enforcement machinery.

There are, of course, internal difficulties with the positions of both contestants. Certainly Hand is guilty, at the very least, of overemphasis when he speaks of separation of powers and Leibnizian monads. It is hardly necessary to cite authorities for the proposition that both the relations between the three branches of the federal government and those between the national government and the states have involved a considerable degree of overlapping. Even if we cannot be confident that the framers anticipated such interplay between the geographic divisions of government, the phrase constitutional "checks and balances" serves to remind us that this was precisely their intention for the branches of the national government. Indeed, Judge Hand seems to assign the Court one of the most difficult possible functions when he asks it to set out the boundaries between the various spheres of governmental authority. One can hardly imagine an area more fraught with judicial policy-making than that of jurisdictional surveyor in a governmental system which tends to translate most of its policy questions into disputes over operational boundary lines.

Professor Black attempts to disarm his critics in advance by admitting that his argument, if logically fallible, charts the most natural conclusions {9} flowing from the establishment of our constitutional system. Although we can admit that political institutions do not necessarily exhibit rigorous logic, making the necessary bow to Justice Holmes' famous aphorism that the life of the law is not logic but experience, it nevertheless seems strange that an argument such as Black's, which rests entirely on the legal nature of the Constitution, should scorn the normal logical niceties of legal discourse. In fact, Black wishes to have the best of both possible worlds. His basic argument—that the Constitution is law, that courts deal with law, and that, therefore, the Supreme Court must look to the Constitution—rests on logic. When his rivals poke holes in his logic, he turns to history to demonstrate that his argument has been proved by experience. And when it becomes apparent that the historical picture is not entirely clear, he reverts to his logical argument as a guide to the most reasonable interpretation of history.

A similar double shuffle occurs in his discussion of the policy-making role of judges. He argues that judges make policy in all legal areas. Constitutional law, like other law, thus requires both legal and policy decisions. Legal decisions require lawyers. Policy decisions require wise men. Therefore constitutional decisions require wise lawyers. Enter the Supreme Court. Even granting for the sake of argument that the Constitution equals law, the rest of his argument seems to rest simply on semantic and logical error. Thus logically the dual nature of constitutional law does not, even within Black's terms, require wise lawyers but *either* wise lawyers *or* legally expert wise men. Again Black might argue that his choice follows naturally if not necessarily. But it seems to follow naturally only because of the choice of words. Everyone knows where to find lawyers. They have a certificate which says "learned in law." Wise men are not so easy to identify. Therefore it seems "natural" to start with lawyers and then hope to find wise ones. But let us substitute a word as definite as "lawyers," say "philosophers," for wise men. Then it naturally follows that we start with philosophers and hope to find legally knowledgeable ones. Now the certificate of the philosopher is the Ph.D. and you are most likely to find legally knowledgeable Ph.D.'s among—but enough of this daydream of a political scientist. The point is that Black's conclusion on the issue is neither logical nor natural but simply verbal.

This becomes even clearer when we look at the policy equals wisdom part of his theorem. Now in this country the "natural" equation is not policy equals wisdom but policy equals politics. Then what we need is political lawyers. Enter not necessarily the Supreme Court but perhaps the Supreme Congress. Indeed, it seems rather strange in our day to assume, as Professor Black does, that the law-administering lawyer called {10} judge is better or even as well suited to mixing policy and law as the law-making lawyer called Congressman. Thus on probably the most crucial problem of the modesty debate, the policy-making role of judges, Black provides no convincing solution even within his basic line of argument.

All in all, when following the struggles of the champions of modesty and activism, one gets the curious impression that for all the blows and counterblows there is really no solid contact. This impression persists largely because the modest seem to have no very firm position—they roll easily with the punch but cannot deliver a knockout blow themselves. In fact the modest seem to have no more than a set of problems and hesitations which mark a dilemma rather than a solution to the problem of judicial activity.

The problems begin at the beginning, with the Constitution itself, for the work of the founding fathers, in spite of its monumental dignity, is repeatedly reduced to the rather undignified position of being an answer to a riddle. The riddle of course is, what is a law and not a law? The Constitution must in some way be a law. As Black points out it even says it is. Nevertheless a document which paints in such broad strokes as "The Congress shall have power to lay and collect taxes . . . borrow money . . . regulate commerce with foreign nations, and among the several states . . . coin money . . . declare war . . . [and] make all laws which shall be necessary and proper for carrying into execution in the foregoing powers. . . ." is obviously not law in the same sense as the Federal Rules of Procedure or the Criminal Code. Nor is it just a law. The British Constitution may be just a law in the sense that a later lawmaker may modify or replace the work of an earlier. But the American Constitution, with its elaborate amending provisions and its extraordinary origin in a series of ad hoc representative bodies, is certainly not the same thing. Indeed, the historical absurdity of actually describing the British Constitution as just a law indicates the general difficulty of subsuming "constitution" under "law." Thus the American Constitution is not so law-like in terms of detail and precision that it can automatically and naturally be applied by the courts as can the bankruptcy statutes. But at the same time it is neither so imprecise nor so low in legal status that the courts can in good conscience ignore it in the face of subsequent Congressional legislation which seems to contravene its provisions.

Other clues from the nature of the Constitution are available. Its appeal to and obvious derivation from the theory of popular sovereignty have led to the suggestion that it was conceived of as a law emanating directly from the people. It would thus displace the sovereignty of {11} the ordinary legislative bodies and subject them to the controlling popular will which it enunciates. The extensive research indicating the higher or natural law content of the Constitution is too familiar to require parading again here. The difficulty is that the commanding position of the Constitution, whether expressed in popular sovereignty or natural law terms, does not necessarily demonstrate the validity of review. Indeed, this very conception of the Constitution suggests that enforcement by all branches of the government and/or directly by the people through their right of revolution would be more appropriate than the rather narrow and technical enforcement available through the courts.

However, when we find such eminently modest judges as Justice Jackson, Justice Frankfurter, and Judge Hand all concluding that review is logically and realistically imminent in the notion of a written constitution,[3] we might expect finally to have arrived at some unquestionable support for judicial review derived directly from the Constitution. But alas it is the activists who reject this argument, insisting that its written-ness is the least important characteristic of our constitution and has no connection per se with review.[4]

Nor does the specific wording or the intentions of the drafters solve the problem raised by the unique nature of the document taken as a whole. Judge Hand was probably too cavalier in dismissing the Suprema-cy Clause of the Constitution as looking more against than toward re-view,[5] but his tone of indecision seems properly chosen. However, Pro-fessor Herbert Wechsler,[6] seconded by Professor Black,[7] has made a brave effort to derive review from the Supremacy Clause of the Constitution. He argues that the Clause, which provides both that the Constitution shall be supreme over state laws and that state judges shall be bound by the Constitution, requires state courts to decide the constitutionality of state statutes. Article III of the Constitution gives the Supreme Court jur-isdiction over all cases arising under the Constitution. Hence, it was ob-viously intended to give the Supreme Court appellate jurisdiction over the state courts. If the Supreme Court was to exercise such jurisdiction, it must have had the duty of examining the same range of issues as the lower courts whose findings it was to review. Thus it must have been empowered by the framers to determine the constitutionality of statutes. Since the Constitution does not require the creation of any inferior feder-al courts, all constitutional issues might have arisen in the state courts so that the Supreme Court must have been intended to review all such is-sues. And it could hardly have been the purpose of the framers to give the Supreme Court less authority over the lower federal courts than over the state courts. Therefore the establishment of lower federal {12} courts could not reduce the scope of the Court's appellate jurisdiction.

This argument, while ingenious, hardly seems decisive. In the first place, the Constitution does not specifically give the Court appellate jur-isdiction over state proceedings. Wechsler must even here operate one step removed from the Constitution and rely on the Judiciary Act of 1789 in which Congress did provide such jurisdiction. And his argument may be turned on its head to suggest that the Act of 1789 was itself unconsti-tutional. For how can a court which has not specifically been given access to the Constitution review the work of courts that have? But more fun-damentally, the problem is that the Supremacy Clause only concerns conflicts between state statutes and the federal Constitution. Therefore, even giving Wechler's argument the fullest play, it can only prove that the Supreme Court was intended to decide the constitutionality of state statutes. Given the combination of strong central government and sepa-ration of powers favored by many members of the Convention, this is not an unreasonable conclusion. The presence or absence of lower federal courts is, of course, irrelevant. Wechsler's argument that their absence would have thrown all constitutional issues to the state courts, and thus to the Supreme Court for review, merely assumes what is to be proven: that conflicts between federal law and federal constitution were conceived as proper issues for the courts. Certainly the creation of lower federal courts could not give the Supreme Court any more power to declare federal statutes unconstitutional than it originally had. The actual wording of the Constitution thus leaves us exactly where we began, with a strong suggestion of review but no clear-cut case.

The intentions of the framers have been so dissected and centrifuged that it hardly seems worthwhile to perform the laboratory work again here. Suffice it to say that no one has made out an absolutely clear case for review on these grounds, but most authorities agree that some kind of review was intended by some members of the Convention. Professor Crosskey, who has made the most exhaustive modern study of the problem, has overwhelming proof that the Convention did not intend review. The trouble is that his evidence has not overwhelmed most of the authorities who have considered it, so that at most his researches add to the ambiguity of the problem.

In short, the Constitution itself, the theory behind it, and the intention of the framers all suggest some sort of judicial review but are neither clear nor decisive about it. The modest are not seeking to ignore or refute the data; indeed, it seems that their modesty is largely derived from a consciousness that the Constitution speaks rather loudly but not very well for review. The problem is not that the activists say that the {13} Constitution requires review and the modest say the Constitution forbids it; it is, rather, that the modest agree with most of the things that activists have to say but, because of the ambiguity of the data, are not totally convinced. The result is not a debate which someone can win, but a running conversation in which one side expresses its self-satisfaction and the other bleats out its doubts.

If the modest experience some tension over the initial authorization for review, they are even more disturbed by the problem of its compatibility with the democratic system. As we shall have occasion to note a little further on, much of the trouble here stems from a rather naive view of democracy and particularly of the democratic character of legislatures. Nevertheless, it is true that Supreme Court justices are not directly responsible to the people in the sense that elected officials are, and it is equally obvious that government by nine specialists, appointed for life and at least theoretically insulated from the political process, smacks of something other than democracy. But the nagging fear of the modest is less usurpation by the Court than abdication by the people. Professor James Bradley Thayer of the Harvard Law School set down the foundations of modern judicial modesty in his famous *Harvard Law Review* article of 1893.[8] Ever since, the modest have cautioned that excessive activity by the courts would reduce the responsibility of the people for their own affairs and thus weaken democracy. If the people were to foist many of their governing responsibilities on the courts, they would lose the education by experience which is essential to popular self-government. Because the Congress constitutes the people working out their own salvation through the political process, the Supreme Court must leave it the widest possible responsibility. There is a good deal more to say on this subject and we shall return to it later, but it must be admitted that reliance on the judicial process to the complete exclusion of the rest of the political process would greatly change our system of government. This rationale of the modest does contain at least a kernel of truth. Having emphasized the undemocratic features of review, the modest do not, however, reject it out of hand. First of all, the historical evidence as to whether the Court has ever for very long thwarted the will of the populace is so mixed that it is bound to shake any extreme position. Did the post-Civil War Court thwart popular desire to regulate its own vital affairs through democratic government? Or did it uphold a concept of individualism which was the popular consensus of the day? If there is the period of 1933 to 1937 in which the Court seemed to be thwarting the New Deal program, there is also 1937 to 1942 in which {14} the Court yielded every Constitutional point necessary to the carrying out of President Roosevelt's plans. The interpretations and polemics fly at a great rate but convince hardly anyone that the Court ever quite justifies the *ad horrendum* arguments which are so pleasant to the pen and so unlikely to correspond with reality.

Of course, the problem of the democratic nature of review is finally and decisively affected by our first area of discussion, the nature and origin of the Constitution itself. First of all, if any constitutional authorization for review can be found—and there does seem to be some—then the courts can hardly deny in the name of deference to the people a task bestowed upon them by "We the people. . . ." And, more basically, if the Constitution suggests, as it most certainly does to most authorities, that the founders wanted something less than pure and unlimited democracy, it hardly behooves the Court under the guise of modesty to espouse an unbridled democracy.

In the final analysis, the modest cannot totally reject review because of their democratic scruples. Nor can they, in view of those scruples, rest content with judicial activism. The result is not a firm position but a nervous uneasiness. Witness Justice Frankfurter:

> The reason why from the beginning even the narrow judicial authority to nullify legislation has been viewed with a jealous eye is that it serves to prevent the full play of the democratic process.

The fact that it may be an undemocratic aspect of our scheme of government does not call for its rejection or its disuse.[9]

Of course the proponents of review have made much of the historical acceptance of that institution by the American people. And the modest would, I think, be the last to deny the traditional role of review.[10] But, as Judge Hand's work clearly shows, they are troubled by the suspicion that the popular purchase was the result of fraudulent advertising. It is not necessary to dredge up a theory of Marshallian usurpation to justify this suspicion. For if the people have been led by the Justices themselves, or for that matter by Fourth of July oratory, into believing that the Supreme Court merely puts the Constitution on top of a statute and lops off whatever sticks out over the edges, they have accepted the form but not the substance of review. This is not to say that popular acceptance means nothing, but only that it cannot mean too much. Thus the modest Justices are left with the feeling that history has given them the power of review, but—presumably not being followers of Voltaire—they cannot rest easy with a prize perhaps won by trickery. It can hardly soothe the {15} democratic conscience to employ a history of popular support in defending a policy-making function which the people never knew they were giving away. The judge who feels that review has been unavoidably thrust upon him by a long continued error in popular understanding may, like Judge Hand, seek to limit the error and point out the misunderstanding. Again, it is not that the modest abandon review, it is that they cannot in good conscience fully accept it.

It is precisely this policy-making element in review that is the real sticking point for most of the modest. Judicial caution can, to be sure, be traced, at least among some of its principal proponents, to Professor Thayer. However, there can be little doubt that its principal impetus has come from the realist school of jurisprudence which has dramatized the role of personal predilection in the judicial process. Just as the people's ignorance of the realist canons vitiates their acceptance of review, the acceptance of those canons by many judges has shaken the Court's self-confidence.

It is all very well to say, as Professor Black does, that policy preference are an inevitable part of all legal decision-making, so that their presence in constitutional adjudication is nothing extraordinary. But to the modest, already uncertain as to the democratic authorization and constitutional legitimacy of review, the argument that they cannot avoid policy-making under the guise of review is less likely to be comforting than to drive them completely from the field. Yet, as we have noted, the Court does not, in the light of history, feel justified in making such a retreat. The Court, therefore, must remain in the policy-making realm while engaging in endless self-flagellation for its unavoidable sin.

Perhaps the Justices can console themselves with Professor Freund's aphorism: "If anything more is needed to assure a disinterested judgment than a bias against bias, it is perhaps a bias against bias against bias." But one suspects this is just a more elegant repetition of T. R. Powell's notion that the Court would not invalidate a statute unless it were "too damned raw." And this leads directly back to the personal prejudice which is the bête noire of the modest. The point is that unless the policy-making function of the Court can be linked with some special justification for review, there is not much comfort in stressing the inescapability of personal judgment. A recognition of the inevitability of sin has not proved a particularly successful means of tranquilizing the transgressors.

Thus the modest find that the Constitution is law but not quite the same sort of law as a normal statute, that the intentions of the founders and subsequent history justify review somewhat but not entirely, that{16} the Court and review are neither wholly compatible nor incompatible with majoritarian democracy, and that judicial policy-making is an unavoidable but not completely laudable element of constitutional adjudication. To all this Professor Black replies for the activists that the Constitution is law, that the Court is democratic, that review has the sanction of the founders and of history, and that the Court must make policy decisions. To the modest it can only seem that the activists deal with the dilemma of review by firmly impaling themselves on one of its horns.

It is little wonder then that what we find among the modest is not a direct attack on the proponents of review but a kind of intellectual schizophrenia. Judge Hand denies that any specific provision of the Constitution and *most particularly* the Bill of Rights, justifies review, but he then drags it back in by a rule of statutory construction which is admittedly a lawyer's artifice. Professor Thayer approves review by fashioning a rule of administration which could be logically met by any statute passed by any but a totally guileless Congress. Justice Jackson attacks the cult of judicial activism while writing a totally activist opinion in the Second Flag Salute Case which we shall return to presently. And Justice Frankfurter, who, in spite of acknowledging the legitimacy of review, would usually go to almost any lengths to find a Congressional enactment constitutional, was the sole justice in one famous labor relations case to hold the statute involved unconstitutional.[11] He tops it all off with the following eulogy of John Marshall.

> The courage of *Marbury v. Madison* is not minimized by suggesting that its reasoning is not impeccable and its conclusion, however wise, not inevitable. I venture to say this though fully aware that, since Marshall's time and largely, I suspect, through the momentum of the experience which he initiated, his conclusion in *Marbury v. Madison* has been deemed . . . indispensable. . . .[12]

If the hosts of the modest are to be delivered from their dilemma, some role and rationale for the Supreme Court must be found which will preserve review but limit it sufficiently, giving it the amount of special justification needed to meet the qualms and suspicions which have been aroused. More particularly, if the Court is to continue in the free speech area, some formula must be derived that will ease the tension between libertarianism and modesty which is so striking a characteristic of the contemporary constitutional scene. Both Justices Holmes and Brandeis were simultaneously libertarians and champions of judicial modesty in the face of the democratic commands of the legislature. "The legacy of {17} Holmes and Brandeis" is still the outstanding intellectual heritage of current judicial thinking. Quite basically we are still paying the price of the potential conflict between the democratic and libertarian values of those two great justices.

Judge Hand provides the most vivid example of a Holmesian caught between the advantages of review in the speech cases and the general democratic objections to review. His view of the Bill of Rights is thus another sign of the modesty dilemma. After trying to strike a balance he simply chooses to impale himself on the opposite horn from Professor Black.[13] The great irony of constitutional law today is that the very judicial group which is most concerned with the preservation of freedom and the democratic process has thought itself into near paralysis. The problem is to find some means of helping those who favor free speech to overcome their qualms about exploiting judicial support—to add a new dimension which will reharmonize the libertarian and democratic ideas which Holmes and Brandeis themselves thought were compatible.

The Supreme Court and the American Political Process

The first step, it seems to me, is to reunite two bodies of data which are separated with the most amazing perversity in the structure of constitutional discussion. While the political role of the Supreme Court is widely, albeit often shamefacedly recognized, all real knowledge of politics seems to disappear as soon as the discussion turns to constitutional law. We hear the most starry-eyed political naiveté from the very persons who are most clearly perceptive about law itself. The legal fraternity, while it has abandoned most of the fictions which previously protected the power and dignity of the Court, insists on returning to the clichés of the high school civics book when describing the political process.

It is not that many of the modest do not know better. Judge Hand has spoken of the legislature as a vehicle for group struggle.[14] Certainly Professor Latham, a distinguished political scientist, is the last person who could be accused of political naivety.[15] But the former, nevertheless, insists on talking about the democratic legislature and the undemocratic court, and the latter contributes to the endless discussion of whether the Court has historically thwarted the will of the majority without pointing out that nearly every interest in society is a group and, therefore, a minority interest.[16] But there is also the school which, eyes firmly fixed on a political court, is so entranced by the undemocratic ogre it thinks it sees that it never gets a chance to look at real politics.[17] Even among the activists there is much talk about democracy and free government {18} and majority rule without much awareness of the political complexities which lie behind the tags.[18]

We must take a closer look at the "democracy" with which the modest, in revulsion to judicial activism, have armed the "political" branches. It might be best to begin with the favorite son of the modest, the Congress. The major problem is, of course, that judges and others who should know better keep talking about Congress as if it were a unified body, but even when Woodrow Wilson wrote that "Congressional government is committee government,"[19] it could hardly have been news that Congress rarely acts as a whole. Indeed, when Wilson wrote *Congressional Government* the immense power of the Speaker, particularly his power over committee assignments, provided greater over-all control of the committees than presently exists. Congressional policy is today largely made in the crosscurrents of clashing committee jurisdictions, not by an orderly implementation of the will of any Congressional majority. The shaky history and the sporadic use of the discharge procedure which theoretically allows a Congressional majority to extract bills from the committees' clutches and bring them before the whole House signal the continued dominance of the committees.

Nor can this dominance be considered as simply a routine division of labor, for the committees are not microcosms of the Congress as a whole. They have distinct and separate characters to match their independent power. The seniority rule insures that the chairmen will be from those particular geographic areas where one party or the other is permanently in the majority. The preponderance of southern Congressmen in key committee chairmanships is an old story. And more important, since committee assignment is now largely a matter of personal preference, at least once a minimum of seniority has been accrued, many of the most important committees tend to be packed by particular interests. The agriculture and interior committees whose memberships are comprised almost entirely of representatives from farm constituencies and westerners are prime examples.

This means that committees tend to establish and maintain a point of view far different from Congress as a whole. And these special viewpoints combined with the great power of the committees turns Congress into a feudal domain with various special interests glowering at each other from their own strongholds. The Rules Committee and the Appropriations Committees in both Houses are, of course, special domains, less influenced by special interests perhaps, but with institutionalized interests of their own which are derived from and implemented by their guardianship of the key fords in the legislative landscape. {19}

The party leaders are thus placed in something like the position of a feudal monarch. They rarely penetrate very deeply into the committee's business, so that they tend to get problems which have already been stamped with the views of the special jurisdictions. Nevertheless, the leadership, or at least its very top levels, seems to have important powers because of its central and mediating position. It is probable that committee chairmen and other representatives of special groups can rarely hope to attain their legislative ends without at least the passive approval and often the active intervention of the leadership.[20]

This leadership, however, tends to act interstitially so that its responsibility for any particular decision is difficult to trace. Moreover, it attains its position not by direct popular election, but by the complex internal politics of the two Houses. Once established it can normally maintain itself regardless of the state of public opinion. Here again it is not just the independent power and lack of responsibility to the nation as a whole which makes the party leadership "undemocratic." It is the mode of their accession to the throne—only those reach the top who have the staying power of a safe constituency.

The winds of constituency pressure play upon this complex Congressional power structure. But what could be more democratic than representatives heeding the views of their constituents? The difficulty is that, because Congressmen hold widely unequal positions of power which vary from issue to issue, particular constituencies hold immensely disproportional influences on certain questions. It is not being suggested that Representative Vinson of Georgia, for instance, consciously yielded to pressure from his constituents in formulating defense policy as the chairman of the Armed Services Committee. His constituents probably had no particular views on most issues. The point is that the tremendous power wielded by the chairman of such a key committee could be put to use through the normal give and take of politics to yield his constituents great influence in areas which did concern them. Visualize, if you will, a suicidally bent Pentagon attempting to shut down Fort Benning, the largest military installation in Georgia.

One last horrible can be added to the parade—lobbying. Lobbyists tend to exercise their influence selectively. They concentrate on those Congressional fiefs and fief holders who are either most powerful in the area of their interest or some other area which can be traded off at a profit to the special interest involved. The lobbyists are most effective when they are able to help a Congressman who is in a particularly favorable position to pursue their mutual interest. The lobbyists thus recognize, and reinforce by whatever influence they wield, the fragmentation {20} of Congress' power and the concentration of the resulting subject oriented fragments in the specialized committees.

There have, of course, been many attempts to provide a democratic rationalization for the twisted patterns of Congressional lawmaking. Probably the most popular has been Professor Holcombe's notion of majorities of the moment.[21] Holcombe argues that individual Congressmen, largely unconstrained by party discipline and operating from independent power bases both in their constituencies and in the Congressional apparatus, come together to form a majority on a given issue and then break up and re-form along different lines on each succeeding issue. Now if all Congressmen were roughly equal and representatives of roughly equal constituencies, and if voting went on in a political vacuum free of trading and jockeying for position, this theory would seem to satisfy the most ardent majoritarian.

But first of all, the majority of the moment is formed only after a bill leaves committee, i.e., it acts on whatever issues and formulations these clientele oriented and seniority dominated bailiwicks choose to hand on to Congress as a whole. Secondly, it is formed by a body of representatives who are profoundly aware of the complex power structure of Congress and the fact that the success of their own special endeavors depends largely on the favor of certain key committees, their chairmen, and other Congressional leaders. The majority's votes are then partially a declaration of the members' views on the issue at hand and partially a calculation of the relative power of the various seigneurs on whom they depend. The result is that the majority of the moment in Congress has no necessary connection with the majority opinion of the nation as a whole.

The rash of new literature on Congress that has been appearing in the last few years[22] emphasizes that the Congress is essentially a social system, and that a major consideration embodied in each policy that this system produces is its own continued smooth operation. Most Congressmen are as concerned with getting along with one another as in representing the views of a majority of their constituents or in pursuing their vision of the public interest. The Congress has evolved an elaborate set of formal and informal rules and societal rewards and deprivations to insure that new members learn the cardinal rule that "you must go along to get along" and to constantly reinforce this learning among the older hands. Congressmen tend, consciously and unconsciously, to filter the communications reaching them from the outside and their image of the real world—to filter, in short, their feel for what the people need and want in such a way as to conform to the rules of their immediate society at a minimum psychic cost to themselves. They tune their images of {21} the real world—and hence their policy views—to meet the demands of internal cooperation. Where Congressmen have, and know they have, little hard knowledge of most of the problems that confront them, or even of the state of public opinion, it takes no conscious dissimulation to adopt from among rival images of reality that which will make it easiest to act in harmony with one's colleagues.

The principal beneficiaries of this ethos are, of course, the old hands who occupy the principal points of influence within this social system: committee chairmen, senior minority committee members, party leaders, the members of key committees. For deference to the smooth functioning of a social system inevitably becomes deference to the most influential members of that system. An excessive challenge to any of their interests must be viewed not only as a threat to each of them as an individual but as a source of dysfunctional conflict in the system as a whole. The leaders in turn insure that future leaders are recruited from the rank of those properly deferrent to the existing system. Thus, each new set of leaders carries on and reinforces the deferential and cooperative norms that it has learned from its predecessors. A challenge in the name of majority rule or public interest to those norms is viewed as a challenge to the interests of the most influential members, to which they are likely to respond with all the considerable force they command.

In a social system of this sort, the sum total of societal acts, that is the legislative program as a whole, must be constructed so as to defer to the interests and views of each Congressman sufficiently to retain his loyalties to the system. And varying quantums of deference must be awarded to each Congressman, graduated according to the level of his influence within the system.

In short, Congress is not simply a reflector or neutral channel for majoritarian sentiment but an independent political institution which trims its legislative program to its own requirements for institutional self-preservation as well as to the winds of public sentiments. Given the widely differing internal influences of various Congressmen, and the fact that these differences do not neatly vary with the proximity of the individual Congressman to majority national sentiment, there is no reason to believe that the self-preservation demands of Congress are likely to correspond to the demands of the majority, or that each social interest is likely to receive that degree of attention which its numerical strength in the population might warrant. What Congressmen need to adjust their own relationships satisfactorily will not necessarily correspond at any given moment with what the broader society needs to reach a satisfactory adjustment for itself. The product of Congress, like the product {22} of all other American political institutions, is some sort of uneasy and constantly changing compromise between what is necessary for the institution's survival and what its constituents want.

In the debate over the role of the Court less attention is usually given the President than Congress. But if we are to place the Court somewhere in the structure of American government, it would be ridiculous to ignore the Presidency and the Executive branch generally, particularly at a time when they have become the principal source of legislation. At first glance the President seems to fit the democratic myth. He is elected by and represents the people of the United States—the majority that the judges are not supposed to thwart. But when we look at the nominating conventions which actually determine who the people get to choose, we again find a complex structure of political powers, and the occupation of key positions by individuals who represent narrow interests rather than the people of the nation. The conventions have been vigorously defended as the necessary arenas in which various groups and interests can compromise their differences and carry on the political process which might otherwise fly to pieces under the pressures of American political diversity. We need not decide on the adequacy of this defense, but we should note its value in showing that here again the process does not proceed entirely in terms of the voice of the people and majority rule. The conventions allow diverse and conflicting interests an opportunity to further their programs and compromise their differences. It is because a majority is sometimes not clearly evident that smoke filled rooms are necessary.

Nor need we decide whether the electoral college is a good or bad thing to understand that it is not inspired by pure democratic majoritarianism. Its existence tends to favor certain kinds of candidates and emphasize the claims of certain constituencies (e.g., the marginal states and particularly the key cities in marginal states) and, conversely, to effectively disenfranchise many citizens (e.g., Southern Republicans). It therefore provides still another complexity of government from which certain groups gain tactical advantage over others.

The Presidency itself, then, can hardly be understood in simplistic majoritarian terms. It does not even provide the comfort of direct responsibility to the people, the absence of which so often troubles the Supreme Court. Not only is the President secure for four years—a time period in which he could do immeasurably more damage to the nation than could the Supreme Court in fifteen—but in many instances he may also wield nearly dictatorial powers. {23}

When we turn from the Presidency itself to the Executive branch even less of the voice of the people comes through. Many of the great executive departments are, and were frankly intended to be, clientele agencies representing not the majority of the nation but special interests. Even those departments like State and Defense, which do not have the readily identifiable constituencies of the Commerce and Agriculture Departments, have their particular representational chores. Indeed, many of the problems of the State Department stem from its function of championing foreign interests. The other departments have learned from State's sufferings. They not only find themselves captured by special interests but fling themselves willingly into the traps in order to gain the independent grass roots political support which makes their life vis-à-vis Congress and the other departments so much easier. Where no special interest group exists, the departments may feel compelled to create one as the Department of the Army did in organizing the Association of the United States Army to counter the power of the Navy League and Air Force Association.

It must be reemphasized that it is these interest-wedded departments and the independent regulatory commissions, whose tendencies to be captured by the industries they regulate is notorious, which are the major sources of law today. They provide the bulk of legislative proposals which get before Congress. And they create and administer their own vast system of administrative law and rule-making whose value allegedly lies in the expertise, i.e., in the specialized and interest oriented activities, of the bureaucrats.

The parochialism of the executive branch naturally is not confined to the department level. One of the most distinctive features of American government is the close relations between bureaus and their equivalent Congressional committees—called by one commentator "government by whirlpool."[23] Since the bureau generally drafts initial legislation and the committee has paramount powers over the bill once it reaches Congress, these alliances are of tremendous importance. They tend to protect subordinate, and frequently group dominated, segments of government from whatever democratic and broadly popular control one might expect from Congress as a whole and from the President.

Both the clientele aspects of the departments and the phenomenon of government by whirlpool lead to the same kind of selective lobbying in the executive branch as in the legislature. Groups desiring particular goals seek out those agencies which are best equipped and most willing to help them. In odier words, executive policy is made less through {24} general debate over major premises by politically responsible officials than by the interaction of interest groups and bureaucratic subdivisions.

The Presidency, which at least theoretically is supposed to impose some order and general direction on the executive branch, has been fighting back against all these divisive forces, but it has enjoyed only partial success. In the process the President has developed a new series of semi- independent power centers largely grouped in the Executive Office of the President. The Council of Economic Advisors, the Bureau of the

Budget, and the National Security Council have all, in varying degrees, developed their own institutional and personal interests, clienteles, and constituencies so that they tend to divide and obscure the responsibility for decision-making at the same time they seek to impose order on the lower echelons.

Thus what really emerges from an examination of Congress and the Presidency is not a simple picture of democratic, majoritarian bodies, voicing popular will and responsible to it, but an elaborate political structure in which groups seek advantage through maneuvering among the various power centers. The results are not necessarily the enunciation of the will of the majority of the American people, but often of compromises among competing interest groups. Professor Truman, in a widely known study of American government, has characterized the system as one of "political interest groups" with "shared attitudes toward what is needed . . . observable as demands or claims upon other groups . . . through or upon . . . the institutions of government," and "potential" or "unorganized" interest groups representing widely held interests and expectations about the "rules of the game." The political process then proceeds through the "access" of organized interest groups to the various organs of government roughly within the boundaries set by the general values of society.[24]

But these groups cannot be conceived as simply portions of the population acting on the elected or appointed officials. Politics is a two or perhaps a three way street. Government agencies themselves, in order to further their programs or the programs of the groups they represent, seek to create support among other governmental and non-governmental groups. In this process of building, rebuilding, trading, and borrowing political strength, clear questions for majority decision often simply do not emerge.

Thus, in the real political world it is senseless to carry on examinations of any branch of government in simple terms of the voice of the majority or "democratic" and "undemocratic" labels. There are undoubtedly many instances in which the policy decisions of American government {25} reflect and/or result from majority sentiment, but there are many instances in which they do not. The role of the majority and of public opinion in American politics and the relation of the general will to the many particular wills are complex and difficult to understand, but what is quite obvious is that there can be no automatic and blanket equation of Congress or the Executive branch with the voice of the people. The remarkable thing about discussions of judicial modesty is that they tend to proceed blithely ignoring all the things that the discussants actually know about the other two branches, for what I have said here is hardly a new or startling interpretation of the governmental process. If we are going to talk about the real Court vis-à-vis the "political" branches, let's talk about the real Congress and the real Executive, too. And while we're at it, we might as well give up the cliché of three equal and cohesive branches and attempt to view the Court's actual position as simply one of the numerous institutions of the central government. Perhaps a look at the real world will help to break up the theoretical dilemma which the modest have constructed for themselves. The decisive question is, then, what is the role and relative weight of the Supreme Court in the national government as it in fact operates today?

The "Power" of the Supreme Court

It has been a curious feature of the debate over the Court that some of the modest have been arguing that it is too strong to leave unrestrained while others have been warning that it is too weak to rely upon. Careful examinations of the Court's actual accomplishments do not yield much support for the hypothesis that review is an extremely strong power in our system of government.[25] Indeed, that school which has found review a weak reed seems to have most of the evidence on its side. But if the Court is weak, why worry about whether it exercises self-restraint or not? A helpless "undemocratic" body should not bother the majoritarians very much.

Friends of the Court, remembering Chief Justice Hughes' vivid metaphoric reference to decisions of the Court that severely damaged its prestige as "self-inflicted wounds," may worry that it will overestimate its strength and take on opponents too big for it. But, in fact, the Court has not historically suffered emasculation. However, the major impetus for the warnings of judicial weakness seems to be the fear that dependence on the judiciary will rob the people of the awareness that they themselves must be the ultimate defenders of their own freedom. Judge Hand, for instance, contends that no court can save a people who have {26} lost the desire to defend their own liberties and that none is needed to protect the rights of those who feel responsible for their own defense. Thus, the protection of liberty must be assigned to the popular branches of government.[26] Professor Freund has pointed out that this argument is based on a false dichotomy between a people either lost beyond saving or secure beyond the need of help. There are no such people. The question is not whether the courts can do everything or nothing. It is whether they can do something.[27]

Curiously enough, Judge Hand's plea for modesty because of the weakness of the Court, while resting on a "realistic" appraisal of the dangers to and defenses of the democratic process, also seems to be derived from an overly formalistic approach to government. He fears that the defenders of freedom will ignore Congress when hospitably received by the courts. If the Supreme Court is not equal, neither is it separate: no one is confronted with the choice of the Court or Congress. There is no more reason to assume that a group interested in freedom of speech will, when confronted by the whole panoply of government, stop with the Supreme Court than there is reason to believe that the railroads will stop with the Interstate Commerce Commission. And if some groups are overly naïve about politics, the answer is to instruct them, not to narrow the available avenues of approach.

It would also probably be best at this point to lay the ghost of old '37 which continues to haunt discussions of judicial power, for much of the fear of the Court's power undoubtedly stems from the New Deal experience. In the first place, the principal anti-New Deal decisions held statutes unconstitutional not under the due process clause, but because of undue delegation of legislative power to the executive and/or the intervention of the central government in local affairs contrary to the canons of federalism. And even the modest have generally insisted that the Court must continue its role as umpire of the federal system and surveyor of the boundaries between the great departments of the central government.[28] Indeed, one of the principal arguments against broader review has been that the Court must save its strength for these functions which are uniquely its own.

And I think it must be admitted by any contemporary observer that the New Deal period did exhibit a startling change in the balances between the states and the central government and between Congress and the President. It is hardly strange, then, to find that a court concerned with the continuity of constitutional development found some difficulty in approving what frequently has been labeled a revolution. In any event, it seems illogical to use the Court's actions of the 1930s to justify a theory {27} of modesty which restrains the Court from doing anything now except precisely the kinds of things which it was doing then.

It may be true that the Court was in fact protecting certain business interests, not constitutional balances. But if we are going to be realistic, it might be just as well to recall that immediately after his election President Roosevelt had a blank check from Congress, so that all the rhetoric about bowing to the will of the legislature comes down to bowing to Mr. Roosevelt, a somewhat less attractive judicial posture—at least to those not emotionally involved with the New Deal. Furthermore, as Mr. Roosevelt's supporters have so frequently pointed out, the President and not the Court won the fight, so that the very situation cited to prove the Court's excessive power demonstrates just the reverse.

Finally, the specter of the thirties inspires a distrust of activism based on the fear that a contemporary active court may return to excessive protection of property and consequently to frustration of rightful governmental activities. But such a fear in view of the present economic powers of the government borders on psychosis. Indeed, it may well be that property is now one of the underprotected interests of our society.

If the critics of the Hughes Court, which opposed the New Deal, were inspired by a grasp of real political issues and an understanding of what the Supreme Court actually did and could do, then there would be all the more reason for them not to stop the real world at 1937 and turn the New Deal experience into a myth which prevents examination of our present problems. Certainly that period, like all historical periods, can teach us something. But its message is not so decisive or unambiguous as to serve as the final word. There is no more sense in importing, either consciously or unconsciously, the partisan emotions of 1937 into 1966 than those of 1900 into 1937.

Of course, the principal complaint arising out of the experience of the thirties was the alleged lack of democratic restraints on the Court. The consequences of the New Deal fight tend to prove just the reverse, but the general problem deserves some examination. Professor Black has pointed out that, due to a quirk in American thinking, appointments for life seem very long indeed, but that in fact the average post-Civil War Justice sits only thirteen and a half years.[29] Since over the whole history of the Court the President has had the opportunity of appointing a new Justice on the average of once every twenty-two months, it seems unlikely that the Court could long hold out against entrenched majority sentiment. President Roosevelt's problem with the Court, which occurred largely because no justice died or retired between 1933 and 1937, was thus a statistical aberration, and the sudden and radical shift in the {28} Court's position in late 1937 after new appointments were made simply represents a variation in the more gradual change to be statistically anticipated.[30]

It is impossible, it seems, to avoid Mr. Dooley's famous aphorism, "The Supreme Court follows the election returns," in any discussion of the Court, and it should be said here that, even aside from the high turnover of the Justices, the Court does, indeed, follow the election returns, at least in terms of broad responses to popular desires. Certainly the segregation decisions indicate that public opinion is an active influence on the Court. Paradoxically enough, it is the very non-elective and formally non-political character of the Court which accentuates its sensitivity to public opinion. We have noted that other institutions of the central government tend to rest upon relatively independent and cohesive clienteles either geographically defined or oriented to specific socio-economic interests. These governmental institutions actively foster and strengthen their clienteles in order to enhance their positions vis-à-vis other agencies. The Court lacks the means and opportunity of developing the grass roots support available to the elected official. And it lacks the opportunity to continuously control the kind of active bounty-creating program which serves to focus special interest support on the bureaucrat. Thus, lacking any unified body of special supporters the Court lacks an anchor against the shifting winds of national political sentiment.

Several commentators have pointed out that the Court's duty to square its decisions with reason and authority is the key to its accountability and responsibility to the public.[31] Professor Black has made a great deal of the Court's function of providing constitutional legitimization for acts of the legislature.[32] But the Justices' work might just as well be viewed as a continuous attempt to convince the public that the Court's decisions are constitutionally legitimate. The necessity of justifying every decision publicly is a restraint placed no few other government officials. If it is naïve to believe that the Court can be wholly limited by a self-interpreted Constitution, it is certainly equally naïve to believe that the Justices are totally unrestrained by provisions to which they must continuously and publicly pay homage. Indeed, it is the most modest among the judges who constantly prove that the courts sincerely feel bound by constitutional obligations.

The greatest restraint on the Court is, of course, the judicial process itself. It has become a truism that case by case determination limits the Court to occasional and negative intervention in the governmental process and excludes many vital areas entirely. Even where the Court {29} does act it does so largely on the sufferance of Congress. And this is true not only in the fields of statutory interpretation and the conflict of state with federal law, but in the determination of the constitutionality of acts of Congress itself. The amending process is always available, and a determined Congress has rarely found that it cannot, by deft and persistent redrafting, eventually accomplish its end. Professor Peltason has concluded after an examination of the place of courts in the political process that "judicial interpretation of the Constitution is not necessarily any more final than interpretation of a statute."[33]

Finally, the Court is restrained by its very eminence and the resulting high degree of public exposure. When the Court decides, it decides a specific case, its opinion is a specific document, and that document records the state of nine specific men. In contrast, most government decisions are made through a process of bargaining in which there are many participants, so that no one is ever quite certain who did what. Who is held to a higher standard of democratic responsibility—the Supreme Court, or the Chairman of the Rules Committee with his files in his coat pocket, or the

Chief of the Fish and Wild Life Service preparing a program proposal which will pass through the Bureau of the Budget, two legislative committees, two appropriations committees, a conference committee, and the President before the new fish hatchery gets built? Any one of these participants anywhere along the line may have fundamentally changed the fish hatchery, but exactly which one can the citizen blame if he doesn't get the hatchery he wants? Each will typically say that it wanted what was best, but had to compromise on something less to get the others to go along. Even if all the proposals for attaining a more responsible Congress and a more responsible Executive branch were adopted, neither branch could come close to the standard of clear responsibility for decision-making set by the Court.

If the problems of the Court's general power and responsibility are not so simple as they are sometimes made to appear, neither are its relations to Congress. Since Judge Gibson of the Pennsylvania Supreme Court first attacked Marshall's position in 1825, the opponents of review have argued that Congress can make determinations of constitutionality as well as the Court. But Judge Gibson's argument is an early specimen of the formalistic approach which seems to plague examinations of review. It is perfectly true that Congress is officially a separate and equal branch of government and that logically it is equally bound by and has equal access to the provisions of the Constitution. But it is also true that the decision-making process in Congress is so complex and fractionalized that even if the members of Congress sincerely desired {30} to make a final and "official" determination of constitutionality, they would find it difficult to do so. Congressional statutes, as we have noted, are the product of a series of marginal adjustments and compromises among various semi-independent groups. It is nearly impossible to interject black and white questions like constitutionality into the early stages of such a process. And when the process has been so nearly completed that a bill reaches the final debate and voting stage, so many commitments have already been made that the interjection of a constitutional issue would not only be futile but in many instances appear to be a traitorous repudiation of pre-established agreements. It is, therefore, highly probable that considerations of constitutionality could only take their place among the multitude of other considerations which acquire various weights at various stages of the negotiations depending on how important they appear to any given legislative power holder. This not only means that constitutional questions would be given very little weight but that, on the few occasions they were decisive, the constitutional decision might well be made by something less than the whole Congress. If some people find it undemocratic and irresponsible to allow the Supreme Court to decide constitutional questions, I fail to see how their desires will be satisfied by transferring that function to the Chairman of the Committee on Small Business or the Minority Whip.

Now the above discussion has even assumed, in order to make the inherent problems of the legislative process clearer, that something called a constitutional issue can clearly and independently exist. But we have learned—indeed, the modest have taught us—that questions of policy inevitably are intermingled with questions of constitutionality. Therefore, even when a Congressman has sincere constitutional misgivings, his complaints would be likely to appear to his colleagues as simply part of the rhetoric of political debate, a holier-than-thou mode of pushing his policy preferences. And it is hard to resist the temptation to suggest, in spite of the paucity of evidence, that nine times out of ten his colleagues would be right. In any event, the policy content of constitutional questions must inevitably tend to push them back into the mainstream of the legislative process. Therefore it may be concluded that the nature of the legislative process, combined with the nature of constitutional issues, makes it virtually impossible for Congress to make independent, unified, or responsible judgments on the constitutionality of its own statutes.

I think these objections to Congressional determinations of constitutionality are inherent in the nature of American government. But, in fairness to Judge Gibson, it has been developments since his day which {31} have made his position totally untenable in terms of the real workings of our government. The most important of these has been the work of the modest themselves, who have evolved a large body of doctrine, such as the rule of reasonableness, to be applied to calculations of constitutionality. These formulas implicitly, and often explicitly, rest on the fact that it is the Court, not Congress, which does the calculating. However, they have become so much a part of American lore that they now seem to adhere to the process of constitutional determination itself. Even if Congress now took over most or all of the responsibility for formal constitutional review, we would undoubtedly find that debates on constitutionality still would ring with citations of Thayer and Holmes proving that a bill was not unconstitutional unless no reasonable man could find it otherwise. The result, given the pressures of politics, would probably be that Congress would bind its own power of constitutional review by the very chains with which the modest have bound the Court in order to free Congress, and the Constitution would indeed become simply a pious hope.

The problem illustrates the principal difficulty of shifting the responsibility for review from the Court to Congress. We cannot, after all, make arrangements de novo. The Congress has traditionally decided on the merits of a bill and left the final constitutional issues to the Court. It has for a very long time enjoyed the relative freedom of decision-making which comes with such a shift of final responsibility. There is no reason to believe that Congress will give up that freedom just because the Court divests itself of that responsibility. This is particularly true when the Justices' resignation is accomplished not by a formal transfer of authority but by a series of modest proposals in the form of judicial opinions which Congress is free to ignore. The result is what one commentator has called the "circular pass" in which Congress throws the constitutional issues to the Court and the Court laterals them back to the Congress. In the process what is likely to occur is disappearance of that constitutional awareness in American political life which judicial review has done so much to create and constantly re-enforce.[34]

Reviewing both the historic role of Congress and its actual mode of operation, it seems impossible to transfer to it a constitutional task which it has not, cannot, and will not undertake.

Thus, abstract arguments about the power of the Court and democracy and the constitutional duty of Congress together with emotional appeals to the New Deal experience simply becloud the picture because they fail to place the Court in its actual political environment. Even the most cursory glance at American politics indicates that Congress and the {32} Executive are not simple, direct bearers of majority sentiment while the Court goes its independent and autocratic way. There are many elements of anti-majoritarianism and irresponsibility in the "political" branches and a rather high degree of responsiveness to popular sentiment in the Supreme Court. In fact, if we must stick to clichéd visions, the most popular and most justified vision today is of Congress as the home of special interests, and the President as the voice of the people—a voice, incidentally, surrounded and often muted by a vast bureaucracy which is itself the home of all sorts of particularistic and partial visions of the public interest.

Now the lawmaker, whom the modest so reverently endow with democracy's banner, is none other than precisely this combination of bureaucracy, President, and Congress, for quite obviously, all three are major participants in the shaping of our laws. In short, the lawmaker to whom the nasty old undemocratic Supreme Court is supposed to yield so reverently because of his greater democratic virtues is the entire mass of majoritarian-anti-majoritarian, elected-appointed, special interest-general interest, responsible-irresponsible elements that make up American national politics. If we are off on a democratic quest, the dragon begins to look better and better and St. George worse and worse.

Indeed, it might be well to examine the dragon a little further. In the broadest sense, the whole debate over Supreme Court strength and weakness has a wonderland quality about it. Fear of the Court's strength and the accompanying plaints about democracy seem to stem largely from a view of the Court as one of three great independent, equal branches. If the President and Congress are elected and the Supreme Court is not, and all three have an equal voice, then the Court must abdicate in the name of democracy. In fact there are not three branches of government but many centers of decision-making which range from more to less "democratic" and from greater to lesser power, depending on the particular issue involved. The Supreme Court has no more to say on weapons development than the Forest Service does on admiralty law.

In short, the question, Is the Court too weak to operate without democratic restraint, or too weak, simply obscures political reality. It is like asking whether the Bureau of Land Management is too strong or too weak. The Court, like all agencies of the central government, inevitably exerts more influence on some issues than on others, depending on the nature the problem, the political alignment of other groups, the amount of popular support it can command, and so on. Therefore, no conclusions about the role of the Court can be made on the basis of abstract and static calculations of its power. {33}

This is precisely what Professor Dahl, in a famous and frequently reprinted article on the Supreme Court, finds when he concludes that the Court is usually a part of the general political alliance—that is, of whatever relatively long-term coalition of cooperating interests happens to be dominating the government during any given period. Therefore, it cannot normally expect to oppose the alliance on major issues with any hope of permanent success. But, as one of the affiliated power groups, it can influence subordinate decisions within the established general policy orientation. The Court can only hope to intervene successfully on major questions when the alliance is unstable on a key issue and when the Court's actions represent a "widespread set of explicit or implicit norms held by the political leadership; norms which are not strong enough or are not distributed in such a way as to insure the existence of an effective lawmaking majority but are, nonetheless, sufficiently powerful to prevent any successful attack on the legitimacy powers of the Court."[35] In view of the group nature of much of the political process, it is actually impossible to speak of Court actions in terms of majority v. minority. In the simplest terms, the Court is least likely to block a real legislative majority on a major issue and most likely to succeed against a fragile or transient majority, or on a minor issue.

Professor Latham, in a historical survey, found that the Court has traditionally aided minority groups: the Federalists, the defeated states after the Civil War, big business, and the judges themselves. He concludes that the Court "has been in a strategic position to cast its weight this way and that *when the balance could be tipped*."[36]

How far do these descriptions meet our expectations about the Court as an agency within the political system of the national government? First of all, it is evident that the Court, like other participants in the policy-making process, in fact generally makes marginal contributions. The degree of its influence on any given matter depends on the constellation of other forces acting on that issue. Indeed, the similarity of its problems and techniques to those of other agencies is striking. Over a large range of its activities it is bound closely by statutory authorization and finds its discretion largely in interpretation. Even in its narrow area of policy initiation, it can be largely checked by the later actions of Congress. The problem of "access," which Professor Truman in his well known work on American government, mentioned earlier, finds crucial to group relations with all governmental agencies, takes up a large part of the Court's time. And its discretionary certiorari powers allow the Court to take as much tactical advantage of this problem as do the legislative committees of Congress. Like the committees, {34} the Court's expertise within its specialized field can be used to influence other segments of government. To be sure, it lacks some of the opportunity which other agencies have of direct access to its fellows, but it compensates for this through its greater access to the public and particularly to the legal profession which carries its messages swiftly to the governmental bodies it wishes to reach.

The Supreme Court and the Under-Represented

The court does seem to represent certain groups—in other words, to have a clientele. Dahl and Latham agree that the Court may be viewed as defending groups or "minorities." But precisely what groups make up the clientele of the Court? What interests find that the Court can provide them with influence and services which they cannot find in as great a measure elsewhere in the government? Here we must return briefly to Truman's concept of "potential" or "unorganized" groups. Groups by definition are based on a shared value. Some of these groups are organized with a high degree of interaction among their members, with formal instrumentalities, and so on. Others, although based on a relatively specific and strongly held value, are for various reasons not organized. A particularly significant variety of unorganized group is that based on a widely shared interest or expectation about the rules of the game which has been described in terms of a "systems of belief," a "general ideological consensus," or a "broad body of attitudes and understandings regarding the nature and limits of authority." These interests may be loose and ambiguous. Nevertheless, sufficient disturbance to them will eventually call forth political action, but, more immediately, it will bring to the surface the expectation that those government functionaries who are violating the rules will be restrained by other agents of government. It is this phenomenon which provides the "balance wheel" in the American system of government.[37]

It seems to be precisely these potential groups which Dahl is talking about when he says that the Court may only intervene on major issues in behalf of widely held but politically unfocused norms. The notion of the Court as the conscience of the community also makes sense in this light.[38] It is true that Latham tends to see particular minority groups as the Court's clientele, but Professor Peltason finds that it is not the specific nature of these minorities but their general interest in obtaining representation denied them by the legislature which turns them toward the Courts.[39]

It may well be argued that in relying on Truman's notion of potential {35} groups—a concept which itself has been subject to severe criticism—I am leaning on the weakest reed in the "group theory" of politics. It has been frequently said that in seeking to explain all political phenomena in terms of the interaction of special interest groups, group theory fails to acknowledge the role which general public sentiment and/or majority will play in political decision-making. Truman's "potential group" is, in a sense, an attempt to shoehorn an essentially non-group phenomenon into a group theory. Even acknowledging that all political behavior cannot be explained in terms of interest group interaction, a great deal of it can be, and it precisely at the intersection of group activity and general public sentiment that the Supreme Court plays an important political role. I continue to use Truman's "potential group" terminology because it seems to me particularly convenient for calling attention to this role of the Court.

Nevertheless, it is probably useful to note other formulations of the problem that Truman subsumes under potential groups. Elmer Schattschneider, a prominent political scientist, in a leading critique of group theory,[40] has argued that rival groups do not in fact allow their relative initial strengths to settle policy questions, but frequently seek to broaden the arena of discussion, each side enlisting more and more groups under its banners. This process often ends in one or both of the group alliances appealing to the general public for a final measure of support. The broadening of areas which Schattschneider refers is frequently accomplished by shifting disputes from one government agency to another. A group which finds itself losing before an executive bureau may appeal to a Congressional committee whose somewhat broader scope may provide new allies to redress the balance of power. The group defeated at the committee level may appeal to the Congress as a whole, etc., etc. At each stage more groups may be enlisted and, more important for Schattschneider, greater public awareness may be generated and general public opinion become a more and more important element in the calculus of relative political strength. Appeal to the Supreme Court is precisely such an agency shift designed to overcome an initially unfavorable balance of group forces, and such appeal will often occur precisely because the initially disfavored group seeks to overcome an intergroup defeat by tapping general public sentiment embedded in the Court. This is, of course, precisely what happened when Negroes overcame the seemingly permanent group imbalances in Congress and the southern state legislatures by obtaining Supreme Court support.

Truman's "potential groups" can also be translated into notions of "hard" and "soft" majorities. Particularly in legislative bodies, one frequently {36} finds that an overwhelming majority entertains certain sentiments, but few members hold those sentiments strongly enough to be willing to sacrifice certain other crucial interests. A determined minority may then prevent the majority from effectuating its desires by threatening in turn the crucial interests of each category of members composing the majority. Again as an example, the mildly pro-civil rights sentiments of a majority of northern Congressmen might be thwarted for many years by a group of adamantly anti-civil rights southerners. For many years it was just not worth it to many northerners to get civil rights legislation which they mildly wanted at the expense of losing essential southern support for a dairy subsidy, an urban renewal program, or a highway bill, which at any given moment some of them desperately needed. Here again the Supreme Court may be able to express public sentiment which cannot find a "hard" majority elsewhere.

It may then be concluded that the Court, like other government agencies, can have a clientele. Therefore, two crucial questions emerge in evaluating the political desirability of judicial review. Is the Court contributing to the over-all effectiveness of our system of government by representing interests which otherwise would be unrepresented? If so, is the Court's influence strong enough to make that representation worthwhile? On the first issue it has been argued here that the Court's clientele are precisely those interests which find themselves unable to obtain representation from other agencies. There are of course various reasons for this inability. "Potential" interest groups generally lack the impetus for organization because the values they espouse are too amorphous to promote a high rate of personal interaction. Thus, a group built on the value of a tuna fish tariff is likely to enlist a higher degree of immediate political activity than one proclaiming the desirability of fair trial. The tuna fish group is, therefore, much more likely to have available to it the financial and personal resources necessary to gain successful access to a Congressional committee or an executive bureau than is the fair trial group.

The Supreme Court is peculiarly fitted to represent these potential groups. Of course, if the value is completely amorphous the courts can be of no help. But in a complex society such as ours, it can, I think, be assumed that this rarely occurs. There will almost always be some marginal organized group (The American Civil Liberties Union, the Jehovah's Witnesses, etc.) to actively champion any widespread social sentiment, if only as an incident to its main purpose. The American Civil Liberties Union consciously acts as the representative of the public interest in free speech. The Jehovah's Witnesses demand free speech in {37} order to carry on their religious activities. Neither group, however, is likely to have much success with Congress or the Executive—the one because the constituency it represents is too unfocused to swing much political weight, the other because its main line of activity makes it politically unpopular. It is, of course, most likely to be politically weak groups, cut off from the normal political modes of protecting their interests, which are most likely to appeal to general social values.

It is these marginal groups, who champion potential groups and find it impossible to gain access to the "political" branches, which the Court can best serve. Here the modests' dilemma of a Court which is both political and nonpolitical ceases to be a dilemma and becomes a unique contribution to American government. The Court's *proceedings* are judicial; that is, they involve adversary proceedings between two parties viewed as equal individuals. Therefore, marginal groups can expect a much more favorable hearing from the Court than from bodies which, quite correctly, look beyond the individual to the political strength he can bring into the arena. The Court's *powers* are essentially political. Therefore marginal groups can expect of the Court the political support which they cannot find elsewhere. Thus, through a judicial-political court, the potential interest group, via the marginal group, can achieve the political representation which makes a practical reality out of the values it espouses.

Highly organized groups may also turn to the Court, not because they are unsuited to gain access to other agencies, but because, having gained access along with other groups, they lost the political battle. Pressure groups will naturally attempt every governmental avenue which seems promising. If the Court is to make its maximum contribution to the governing process, it should probably devote its major energies to those groups which have little other access to government. It need not act as the last resort of forum shoppers who have been defeated elsewhere. In fact, this desired emphasis seems to accord with the actual power situation, for the Court is capable of major influence precisely when it does represent widespread potential groups, and it can at most offer only minor advantages to organized interest groups which have already failed in their more proper sphere. If the Hughes Court is to be criticized, it is on exactly these grounds: it attempted to make a major intervention against the governing alliance in favor of an organized pressure group which had been defeated in its own customary arena precisely because it was acting contrary to widely held popular sentiment.

But even the comparative abilities of different potential interest groups in capturing Congressional or Executive support may vary widely. {38} Truman has pointed out that government officials themselves usually share the broad values of society, so that potential groups almost automatically have some members inside the governing instrumentalities.[41] But certain of these broad values are likely to be over-represented and others under-represented in the legislative and administrative processes. Congressmen and bureaucrats, whose everyday concerns are likely to be highly attuned to the welfare and security values which are at the heart of most governmental programs, naturally tend to be responsive to those general values. Immediate problems, and the need to provide positive governmental programs to solve them, inevitably tend to outweigh long range values such as individual freedom. The potential groups oriented to increased national security or increased public welfare are, even without direct access, likely to find sufficient satisfaction in Congress and the Executive. They need little help from the Court.

Here again the Court exhibits the characteristics of other agencies of government. It is subject to lobbying by a wide range of groups, some of whom find it an essential, others merely a supplementary, source of representation. It will, on occasion, give marginal assistance to nearly any interest. But if it wishes to act effectively in the long run, the Court must reserve its major efforts for its particular clientele.

If the Court is a clientele agency, we would expect it to follow the pattern of other clientele agencies in acting to create and reinforce its own supporting interests. Here the widely held notion that the Court acts as an educator, particularly in the civil rights field, begins to make sense in a political context. Professor Swisher notes that the Court's power "depends on its ability to articulate deep convictions on the part of the people in such a way that the people who might not have been able to articulate themselves will recognize the judicial statement as essentially their own."[42] In other words, the Court's opinions must be designed to bring the widespread sentiments, or as we have put it, certain of the potential groups in society, to the fore. From this strengthened position these groups then support the Court.

Judicial modesty poses a particular threat to this process of interacting support between agency and clientele. For other agencies have learned that they must not only support the values of their supporters, but also tout the particular ability of the agency to serve those values. These two factors become inextricably mixed in agency enunciations, so that it becomes impossible, for instance, to separate the desirability of flood control from the necessity of an active Corps of Engineers. And this is a politically if not logically sound mixture. The strength of the {39} agency, or at least some agency, is essential to the satisfaction of the group interest. Thus the modest opinion, with its praise of the value to be protected and its disavowal of the Court's ability to do the job, is politically suicidal.

The suicide is largely by means of self-fulfilling prophecy. For the more the Court announces its impotence the less group support it receives and the more impotent it becomes. Conversely, the less agency protection the group interest receives the less capable it becomes of politically meaningful action. Thus modest professions of lack of judicial power ignore the real world in which political power comes to those who seek and construct it. We have long since tired of Presidents who proclaim a program but refuse to engage in the cultivation of political support which can make that program a reality. It is time we lost patience with the Justice who proclaims his faith in the value of speech but cannot bring himself to face the political realm in which that value must be protected.

There is something to the argument that the Court must profess some limitations for fear that intervening always and everywhere will result in a dribbling away of its power. Insofar as this means that the Court should not exert itself excessively in the interest of groups on the margins or outside its clientele, it represents sound political counsel. But it must be borne firmly in mind that the building of a clientele is a continuous process. The Justice who retreats in case after case, husbanding his strength for the really big one, may find when the time comes that he has retreated right off the battlefield. For the Court, like other political instrumentalities, cannot expect to retain its strength without the constant and routine recruiting of support which other politicians call fence mending. The Court has only one means of mending its fences: the opinions it issues. If these opinions do not continuously demonstrate the Court's willingness to act in favor of its supporters, it cannot expect to find much support left when it finally does act.

Judicial Modesty and the American Political Process

The concern of the judicially modest has been to differentiate what the Supreme Court might properly do from the legitimate functions of other branches of government. Their difficulty, it seems to me, is that the differentiation has been based on an abstract and artificial view of the American governing process. The Court must indeed attempt to perform its own, not some other institution's, tasks. But what is and is not its own must be determined in the light of actual political arrangements. {40} In that light, the Court can best define its special function as the representation of potential or unorganized interests or values which are unlikely to be represented elsewhere in government.

This approach should release the modest from the dilemma which has led to their hesitancies about judicial activity. That the Constitution is both law and not law is relatively unimportant when judicial review rests not on the question of law and Constitution but on the role of the Court as one clientele agency among many. That review has, and perhaps has not, been historically accepted is less significant than the historical acceptance of a system of national government in which power is fragmented among many agencies including the Court. That the Court is democratic but not entirely so is largely meaningless in a system of government where there are many power holding institutions, each varying somewhat from the others in the degree of democracy in their selection and their direct responsibility to the people. That the Court deals with law but also with policy is hardly a critical point in a situation where the judicial, administrative, and legislative processes are carried on simultaneously within many of the agencies of government.

However, the general, almost instinctive, reluctance to admit that the Supreme Court does and should inhabit the political sphere is tied to other factors as well as the issues of democracy raised by the judicially modest. It just seems wrong somehow for courts and judges, any courts and judges, to be mixed up in politics. It seems wrong, I think, because of three closely connected and widely entertained confusions about the nature of courts and their work.

The first of these involves an anachronistic vision of what courts do. When we think about courts, we still basically think of a dispute between Joe and Tom as to where the boundary line runs or who really owns the horse. Now in such disputes, we don't want the judge to be thinking about how many votes Tom has, or how much Joe could contribute to the next campaign, or which one has more friends. In short, no politics. The trouble, however, lies in building up a philosophy about courts, and particularly the Supreme Court, as if the Joe-Tom situation was the typical one with which courts deal. The fact is that Joe and Tom never get to the Supreme Court. It is the NLRB and the State of Wisconsin who get there. And the dispute is not over who owns the horse, but over whether the ICC abused its discretion in not granting a certificate of convenience to Long Haul Truck Lines, Inc.

For a series of historical and ideological reasons, public law was the poor relation of American jurisprudence for a very long time, and most people—including lawyers—still hold a basically private law view of {41} our legal system, especially when they are thinking in general and rather fuzzy terms about the "nature" of law and courts. Informed by such a vision, it makes perfect sense to attempt to isolate judges and judging from political considerations. But once we recognize that the overwhelming weight of business in the federal courts and particularly in the Supreme Court is public law business concerning the activities of governmental agencies and the furtherance of public policy, then it becomes natural to think of the courts as political. To persons raised under Continental legal systems, which have always recognized the important role of public law, the statement that courts are government agencies pursuing public policies does not seem nearly so shocking as it almost invariably does to Americans.

The second confusion that inhibits American recognition of the legitimate political role of courts is a confusion not about the nature of law but about the nature of institutions. Somehow, at least when dealing with courts, it is widely believed that a given institution can perform only one function, and more particularly that courts can perform only the single function of deciding whether party X or Y is legally right. Taking on other functions would fatally interfere with this primary, or inherent, or correct function. If the Supreme Court were to begin functioning as the representative of free speech interests in the First Amendment area, it would suddenly become incapable of deciding whether Tom or Joe owned the horse.

Now in fact this is just not the way political institutions work. Actually, such institutions take on and slough off various and often logically contradictory functions. The British Parliament, which had been a court, became a representative body and is today primarily a location where two political parties negotiate—not with one another, but each internally. Nor does this essentially "party" rather than "governmental" function of Parliament mean by some iron rule of unity that the Commons must automatically give up all governmental functions. Actually, it still retains a few, particularly in the supervision of the bureaucracy.

The American Presidency is, of course, the prize example of a single institution which over time has acquired many different functions, some of which are directly in conflict with those intended by the founders to be its "proper" ones. How can the President be the illustrious head of state and symbol of unity, and also the dynamic, free swinging leader of a partisan political party? How can any single person charged with the incredible task of taking care that our entire enormous body of laws be faithfully executed also be responsible for bringing forth a whole program of proposed new legislation before each session of Congress? {42} How can the Chief Diplomat and Commander and Chief properly carry out his responsibilities when he also has to worry about whether a cut in the corn subsidy will lose him Nebraska in the next election? Yet Americans do not find it particularly strange that he must do all these things. Examples of multiple function in American government could be multiplied endlessly from the Bureau of Standards to the House Judiciary Committee.

It has not been our custom to limit our governmental institutions to a single function. Instead, they have tended to agglomerate functions on a pragmatic basis, even though some of those functions appear mutually conflicting. Why should we assume that the Supreme Court is incapable of doing what every other institution of government has done? There is no reason to believe that if the Justices took on the task of representing certain interest groups not represented elsewhere, they would suddenly be struck incapable of deciding whether it was legally Joe's horse, supposing someone should ever again ask them such a simple question.

The third confusion beyond the confusions about the nature of public law and the nature of institutions concerns the word "justice." Justice is, of course, a difficult word about which scholarly debate has always raged. I follow Professor H. L. A. Hart, a leading English student of legal philosophy, in believing that when the literate Englishman or American speaks about justice in the context of law and courts, he means that equals should be given to equals, and unequals to unequals, i.e., Aristotle's distributive justice.[43] It is for this reason that most persons would want "courts of justice" separated from politics, for politics is partisanship, partiality, and tit for tat, and what is desired is a court which will coolly and impartially weigh the equalities and inequalities of the litigants.

As Hart points out, however, the rub comes in deciding which qualities of the parties are to be considered and which ignored in deciding which party is more and which less equal in a given dispute. When X, a black man, comes to court for a vote equal to that of Y, a white man, are the colors of the two litigants a relevant quality to be measured in deciding whether X is equal to Y and, therefore, entitled to an equal vote? What if X is from the city and Y the country? Distributive justice can be impartially and mechanically accomplished only when, in the given category, there is a clear and definite rule as to what qualities are to be measured and what weight is to be given to each. In order to attain the ideal of distributive justice it is essential that society make such rules. It is precisely the making of these rules that we call politics. {43}

The rules themselves, of course, we call laws. It is the political process which decides what is equal and what is unequal, or more crudely, who is to get what. Justice and politics, therefore, are not incompatible; they are inseparable. There is, therefore, no a priori reason why courts of justice should be totally separated from politics. Indeed, since a completely articulated set of rules for distributive justice never exists, the courts themselves must inevitably on occasion create the rules that define distributive justice in order to do justice. This is only the old and true argument about the inevitability of judicial lawmaking in another guise, but it is a necessary reminder that doing justice is not so different from doing politics after all.

In summary then, there is a kind of ideal type of what courts are or ought to be lurking almost unconsciously in the back of many people's minds, a type prescribing that the judge devote his whole energy to impartially weighing the equalities and inequalities of Tom's and Joe's claim to the ownership of the horse under a fixed and definite law prescribing what equalities and inequalities are to be measured when considering horse ownership. This vision constantly interferes with a natural and unrestrained acceptance of the political role of the Supreme Court. It does so because it pretends to be both a general description of what all courts do at all times and a general prescription of what they should do, from which any deviation is atypical and suspect. In fact, it is a highly specialized description of one particular kind of judicial activity which is far removed from the actual work of the Supreme Court. It is necessary to abandon this romantic vision in order to see that the Supreme Court is one of many multiple function government agencies concerned with public law, i.e., public policy, and with both the creation and the application of the rules of distributive justice.

In short, the dilemma of majority and special interest, power and responsibility, policy and administration, which the modest discovered when examining the Court, is not so much a dilemma as a set of outer limits within which all American government, not just the Supreme Court, operates. Therefore, that dilemma need not paralyze the Court any more than it paralyzes the rest of the government. More specifically, it need not prevent those interested in freedom of speech from using the Court just as they would any other government agency, particularly when it is one of the means best suited to their purpose. There is no reason why one interest group should deny itself the advantages offered it by a politically system which is fully exploited by all other interest groups. A politically realistic assessment of American government leads to the {44} conclusion that neither the defenders of free speech nor the Supreme Court should have any qualms about undertaking as much activity as the current constellation of governmental forces allows them.

Having cleared away the hesitancies of judicial modesty, it is possible to proceed to the problem of what level of protection the Supreme Court ought to give freedom of speech. One of the earliest solutions to that problem, and the one around which most of the debate has centered, is the clear-and-present-danger rule. Consequently, having finished with the general controversy over judicial review, we will get down to the specifics of the Supreme Court and freedom of speech with an examination of this central doctrine of First Amendment interpretation.

NOTES to Chapter One

1 Learned Hand, *The Bill of Rights* (Cambridge, Mass., 1958); Charles L. Black, *The People and the Court* (New York, 1960).

2 Hand, *op. cit.*, pp. 3-4, 73-74.

3 Learned Hand, *The Spirit of Liberty* (New York, 1952), pp. 274, 277; Robert H. Jackson, *The Supreme Court In the American System of Government* (Cambridge, 1955), p. 26; Felix Frankfurter, "John Marshall and Judicial Function," *Harvard Law Review*, vol. 69 (1955), p. 219.

4 Black, *op. cit.*, p. 28.

5 Hand, *The Bill of Rights*, p. 28.

6 Herbert Wechsler, "Toward Neutral Principles of Constitutional Law," *Harvard Law Review*, vol. 73 (1959), p. 1.

7 *The People and the Court*, pp. 6-7.

8 James Bradley Thayer, "The Origin and Scope of the American Doctrine of Constitutional Law," *Harvard Law Review*, vol. 7 (1893), p. 129.

9 *West Virginia Board of Education v. Barnette*, 319 U.S. 624, 667 (1943) (dissent).

10 See, e.g., Frankfurter in *Rochin v. California*, 342 U.S. 165, 173 (1952).

11 *Textile Workers Union v. Lincoln Mills of Alabama*, 353 U.S. 448, 460 (1957).

12 *Frankfurter, op. cit.*, p. 219.

13 *The Bill of Rights*, pp. 69, 71-74.

14 Chief Justice Stone's Conception of the Judicial Function," *Columbia Law Review*, vol. 46 (1946), p. 697; see also *Daniel Reeves Inc. v. Anderson*, 43 F.2d 679, 682 (1930).

15 See his *The Group Basis of Politics; a study in Basing-Point Legislation* (Ithaca, 1952); *The Politics of Railroad Coordination* (Cambridge, 1959).

16 See Earl Latham, "The Supreme Court and the Supreme People," *Journal of Politics*, vol. 16 (1954), p. 207.

17 See, e.g., Wallace Mendelson, "Mr. Justice Frankfurter and the Process of Judicial Review," *University of Pennsylvania Law Review*, vol. 103 (1954), p. 318.

18 See, e.g., Eugene V. Rostow, "The Democratic Character of Judicial Review," *Harvard Law Review*, vol. 66 (1952), p. 193. {45}

19 *Congressional Government*, preface to the original edition reprinted in the Meridian edition (New York, 1956).

20 David B. Truman, *The Congressional Party* (New York, 1959), pp. 99-133, 245-47.

21 Arthur N. Holcombe, *Our More Perfect Union* (Cambridge, Mass., 1950), pp. 149-91.

22 See especially Donald Matthews, *U.S. Senators and Their World* (Chapel Hill, 1960); Raymond Bauer, Ithiel de Sola Pool, and Lewis A. Dexter, *American Business and Public Policy* (New York, 1963); Robert L. Peabody and Nelson W. Polsby, eds., *New Perspectives on the House of Representatives* (Chicago, 1963).

23 Ernest Griffith, *Congress, Its Contemporary Role* (New York, 1956), pp. 37ff.

24 David Truman, *The Governmental Process* (New York, 1951), pp. 33-34, 264-65, 510-14. The literature on the group nature of politics is by now immense. For summary and critique see Stanley Rothman, "Systematic Political Theory: Observations on the Group Approach," *American Political Science Review*, vol. 54 (1960), p. 962; Robert A. Golembiewski, " 'The Group Basis of Politics,' Notes on Analysis and Development," *American Political Science Review*, vol. 54 (1960), p. 962.

25 See John P. Frank, "Review and Basic Liberties," and Willard Hurst, "Review and the Distribution of National Powers," in Edmond Cahn, ed., *Supreme Court and Supreme Law* (Bloomington, 1954).

26 *The Spirit of Liberty*, pp. 272ff.

27 Paul A. Freund, "The Supreme Court and Civil Liberties," *Vanderbilt Law Review*, vol. 4 (1951), p. 552.

28 Hand, *The Bill of Rights*, pp. 29-30; Jackson, *The Supreme Court*, p. 61.

29 Black, *The People and the Court*, p. 180.

30 Robert A. Dahl, "Decision-Making in a Democracy: The Supreme Court as a National Policy-Maker," *Journal of Public Law*, vol. 6 (1957), pp. 284-86.

31 Alpheus Mason, *The Supreme Court From Taft to Warren* (Baton Rouge, 1958), p. 212; Charles P. Curtis, *Law As Large As Life* (Boston, 1959), pp. 99-100.

32 Black, *The People and the Court*, pp. 56-87.

33 Jack Peltason, *Federal Courts In the Political Process* (New York, 1955), p. 8.

34 Frank, *op. cit.*, p. 134; Rostow, *op. cit.*, p. 208.

35 Dahl, *op. cit.*, p. 294.

36 Earl Latham, "The Supreme Court As a Political Institution," *Minnesota Law Review*, vol. 31 (1947), pp. 227-28. Italics added.

37 Truman, *The Governmental Process*, pp. 511-14.

38 John Roche, "Judicial Self-Restraint," *American Political Science Review*, vol. 49 (1955), pp. 763-64; Charles P. Curtis, *Lions Under the Throne* (Boston, 1947), p. 197; Samuel Konefsky, *Legacy of Holmes and Brandeis* (New York, 1956), p. 295; Alpheus T. Mason, *Supreme Court From Taft to Warren* (Baton Rouge, 1958), p. 213.

39 Peltason, *Federal Courts*, p. 11.

40 Elmer Schattschneider, *The Semi-sovereign People* (New York, 1961).

41 Truman, *The Governmental Process*, pp. 513-14.

42 Carl Swisher, *The Supreme Court In Modern Role* (New York, 1958), pp. 179-80.

43 *The Concept of Law* (Oxford, 1961).

Chapter Two

THE CLEAR-AND-PRESENT-DANGER RULE

SINCE THE LEADING cases of the 1920s, the Supreme Court's treatment of freedom of speech has been dominated by two alternative approaches, clear-and-present-danger and balancing. Both of these formulas purport to be concerned with the nature of freedom of speech as such, but at crucial moments they both actually become ideological weapons in the struggle over the political role of the Supreme Court. Nevertheless, the debate on and off the Court has been conducted so much in terms of a philosophy or theory of the First Amendment, or the essential meaning and function of freedom of speech, that it is necessary to develop some stance toward this order of question before examining the clear-and-present-danger and balancing formulas in their political contexts. In short, it is time to devote some attention to the First Amendment half of "The Supreme Court and the First Amendment," without, however, losing sight of the fact that the crucial problem is not the First Amendment but what the Supreme Court ought to do about the First Amendment.

Professor Thomas I. Emerson, who has for some years held a dominant place in the legal analysis of civil rights, has recently assayed a "general theory of the First Amendment" that suggests most of the philosophic highlights.[1] He acknowledges the difficulty of constructing a viable theoretical defense of freedom of expression as an absolute value or end in itself or even as a specially reserved right of the individual. He proceeds in spite of the difficulty, but in the end his long matured, careful, and scholarly presentation proves more than anything else that such a defense is impossible. He finally leaves us with Locke and the individualism of the Enlightenment. For better or worse, the whole rationalist, natural law-natural rights substructure of this individualism has been so savagely pounded by Hume, Nietzsche, Freud, et al., that hardly anything remains. It may some day be possible to reconstruct a rational individualism that will gain something like universal assent—Professor Emerson cites some of the tentative moves—but today is not the day. It seems a great mistake to support freedom of speech on a philosophic foundation in which {47} every major philosopher of the last 150 years has gleefully punched holes; to do so invites a philosophic debate in which the proponents of freedom of speech are bound to lose and the audience is likely to mistake still another logical destruction of the Enlightenment for a successful refutation of libertarian values themselves.

FREEDOM OF SPEECH

It would be far better, I think, from both the scholarly and tactical points of view, to begin with the recognition that there is no currently accepted political philosophy that will provide the kind of firm basis for political judgment that the eighteenth century enjoyed. We live *After Utopia*[2] and at *The End of Ideology*.[3] Questions of freedom of speech will have to be considered as questions of political prudence or short term goals or posited preferences, not as philosophy, simply because there is no agreed upon philosophy to which we can turn. But it is well to emphasize that both the proponents and opponents of judicial enforcement of the First Amendment live in the same world of philosophic indeterminacy.

The libertarian sometimes attempts to escape this dilemma by pleading that if freedom of speech cannot be fully defended at the level of philosophy, it is at least firmly rooted in the American ideology. Appropriate bows are then made to Messieurs Hartz and Boorstein,[4] two noted scholars who have shown the dominant place of the liberalism of Locke in our intellectual history. The difficulty is, of course, that while we may all in a general way be Lockians, the liberal tradition in America is neither so strong nor so internally consistent as to provide an impregnable fortress for freedom of speech. If it could, we wouldn't have to be writing books about whether the First Amendment ought to be enforced or not. It is essentially fruitless to argue that freedom of speech ought, or ought not, to be respected because of American tradition when the tradition is actually a continuing dispute over whether free speech ought to be respected. Here again both libertarians and anti-libertarians face the same infirmity.

Therefore, I do not think there is much profit in an elaborate philosophical or historical preface to a discussion of the clear-and-present-danger rule. The issues lie at some intermediate level between what is and what ultimately ought to be—at the level of what we might call political prudence. If this seems a vague and unsatisfactory level, it is nevertheless the level at which most political decisions have to be made. Disguising the vagueness with outdated philosophy and incomplete intellectual history does not help very much.

This chapter concerns itself, then, not with the grand questions of philosophy, but with the intermediate ones of judicial doctrine. My {48} purpose is to describe the origin and evolution of the clear-and-present-danger rule, partly because it is difficult to understand the current controversies over freedom of speech without being aware of this background, and partly because I wish to argue that the clear-and-present-danger rule represents a politically sound middle ground between balancers and absolutists which contains the virtues and avoids the pitfalls of each.

Beginning at the concrete beginning then, the clear-and-present-danger rule developed out of reaction to the bad tendency test which was used in most American jurisdictions and was supposedly carried over from the English law of seditious libel. Under the bad tendency doctrine, utterances were punishable whenever they had a reasonable tendency to undermine governmental stability at some future date. Theoretically, the bad tendency test punishes only speech that will result in criminal action at some later date. But the question becomes whether anything in the speech has a tendency to inspire bad action at any point in the future, no matter how remote. Thus, in practice, the judge focuses on the content of the speech, for it is never difficult to imagine the possibility that speech you intensely dislike may eventually contribute in some unspecified way to action you intensely dislike.

Justice Holmes presented the clear-and-present-danger test in *Schenck v. United States*,[5] decided in 1919. "The question in every case is whether the words used are used in such circumstances and are of such a nature as to create a clear and present danger that they will bring about the substantive evils that Congress has a right to prevent." Although the clear-and-present-danger test was rather vaguely and, in the context of the whole decision, hesitantly stated in the *Schenck* case, it gained new force and precision some months later in Holmes' dissent in *Abrams v. United States*.[6] The *Abrams* dissent has been so much quoted that it need be only briefly commented on here. Holmes rejects the government's contention that the First Amendment left the common law as to seditious libel in force, and thus rejects the bad tendency doctrine which has generally been a part of that law. He repeats the *Schenck* test. "I do not doubt for a moment that . . . the United States constitutionally may punish speech that produces or is intended to produce a clear and imminent danger that it will bring about forthwith certain substantive evils that the United States constitutionally may seek to prevent."[7] The utterance in question may not be punished since it is not of the variety which "imminently threatens immediate interference with the lawful and pressing purposes of the law."[8]

Abrams, although its wording is frequently similar, represents a {49} profound change from the earlier decision, for it is the first case in which the specific facts surrounding the utterance in question are examined in the light of the clear-and-present-danger test. In *Schenck* the Court asked, can a particular category of speech interfere with the war effort? In *Abrams* Holmes asks, does this particular speech interfere with some specific phase of the war effort? It seems obvious that unless the second approach is adopted, the clear-and-present-danger test, which is largely meaningless when applied to the general situation rather than to the specific circumstances, is practically indistinguishable from the bad tendency test.

Another aspect of this shift from the general to the particular is apparent in the treatment of "intent." While Holmes had been satisfied with a constructive intent in *Schenck*, much of his *Abrams* dissent is taken up with a demand that specific intent be shown. The problem of intent is a complex one, but it seems evident that, in this case at least, Holmes is attempting to isolate the speaker's actual intent as one of the circumstances surrounding the speech which must be considered in order to determine whether a clear and present danger exists. The majority, as in *Schenck*, is satisfied to infer the intent of the speaker from the general tendency of the speech.

The majority's reply to Holmes' attempt to make "clear and present danger" more than a piece of judicial phrase-making came six years later in *Gitlow v. New York*.[9] Justice Sanford, speaking for the Court, confined the danger test to a formula for statutory construction in determining when speech was so inflammatory that it might be punished under statutes proscribing action. Deference to legislative findings of danger would be substituted for judicial examination by means of the clear-and-present-danger test when the statutes were aimed directly at speech. The *Gitlow* majority had at least recognized the continuing force of the test in some instances, but Holmes and Brandeis were not content with this Pyrrhic victory. In a dissent by Holmes, they reemphasized the general validity of the test.

In 1927, with the Court again using the bad tendency test, Brandeis, apparently hoping to avoid relegation of clear-and-present-danger permanently to the dissent, wrote a concurring opinion in *Whitney v. California*[10] which again presented the clear-and-present-danger rule as a test by which the Court could challenge the constitutionality of an abridgment of speech unless it were justified by the threat of substantial injury to society. The creators had finished their work but, although their effort had received much public acclaim, the judges were as yet reluctant to award any prizes. {50}

Exactly what did "clear and present danger of a substantive evil that Congress has a right to prevent" mean to Holmes and Brandeis? "Clear" was never precisely defined but was probably a reference to the "probable effect" of the speech.[11] Considerably more effort was directed at "present." In Holmes' movement from the general to the precise in *Abrams* a "present" danger becomes a danger which "imminently threatens "*immediate* interference with the lawful and pressing purposes of the law."[12] Brandeis also employs an imminence formula in his *Whitney* concurrence, and both Justices in one decision or another suggest that abridgment of speech may be tolerated only in an emergency.[13] Put somewhat differently, a "present" danger seems to be one that threatens to culminate in a substantive evil before the democratic process or the normal police instruments of the democratic state have sufficient time to successfully counter the threat.

Professor Meiklejohn, a distinguished philosopher and commentator on the First Amendment, has noted two schools of interpretation flowing from the Holmesian doctrine of "substantive" evil. One, basing itself on *Schenck*, would allow the regulation of any substantive evil; the other, relying on post-*Schenck* decisions, requires that the evil be serious.[14] Holmes, however, had spoken in *Schenck* of things that "are such a hindrance to its [the nation's war] efforts that their utterance will not be endured. . . ." [15] And in *Abrams* he had specified that the purpose of government with which the speech interfered must be not only "lawful" but "pressing."[16] Therefore, the requirement that the evil must be serious in order to justify regulation of speech, added by Brandeis in his *Whitney* concurrence, seems only a logical elaboration and clarification of the *Schenck* doctrine, not a modification of it. The quite early use of "emergency" language by Holmes and Brandeis indicates that the *Whitney* concurrence does not represent a new departure. Indeed, one observer insists that *Whitney* simply cleared up the ambiguities of the emergency doctrine by distinguishing the elements of imminence and seriousness which that doctrine as first stated tends to confuse.[17]

But how serious was serious enough for Holmes and Brandeis? Brandeis said, "The fact that speech is likely to result in some violence or in destruction of property is not enough to justify its suppression. There must be the probability of serious injury to the State."[18]

The statute in question proscribed the advocacy of the use of sabotage and violence as a means of accomplishing a change in industrial ownership or any political change. In this context Brandeis' statement may simply have meant that doctrines which result in only occasional and random violence and, therefore, have no marked effect on any public interest {51} may not be proscribed. It is impossible to tell what he might have said if confronted by speech which had a substantial and persistent effect on some real public interest other than national security. It can only be concluded that Justice Black is substantially correct when he sums up the cases as yielding "a working principle that the substantive evil must be extremely serious and the degree of imminence extremely high before utterances can be punished."[19] The clear-and-present-danger formula, at least as enunciated in the twenties, is not capable of any more precise description.

There were two bases for the clear-and-present-danger test as formulated by Holmes and Brandeis. The first is a philosophy of individualism and democracy which has usually been set out under the rubric of "the market place of ideas." The relevant passages by the two Justices are worth quoting at some length.

> Persecution for the expression of opinions seems to me perfectly logical. If you have no doubt of your premises or your power and want a certain result with all your heart you naturally express your wishes in law and sweep away all opposition. To allow opposition by speech seems to indicate that you think the speech impotent, as when a man says that he has squared the circle, or that you do not care wholeheartedly for the result, or that you doubt either your power or your premises. But when men have realized that time has upset many fighting faiths, they may come to believe even more than they believe the very foundations of their own conduct that the ultimate good desired is better reached by free trade in ideas—that the best test of truth is the power of the thought to get itself accepted in the competition of the market, and that truth is the only ground upon which their wishes safely can be carried out. That at any rate is the theory of our Constitution. . . . We would be eternally vigilant against attempts to check the expression of opinions that we loathe . . . unless they so imminently threaten immediate interference with the lawful and pressing purposes of the law that an immediate check is required to save the country. . . . Only the emergency that makes it immediately dangerous to leave the correction of evil counsels to time warrants making any exception to the sweeping command, "Congress shall make no law abridging the freedom of speech."[20]

> To courageous, self-reliant men with confidence in the power of free and fearless reasoning applied through the processes of popular government, no danger flowing from speech can be deemed clear and present, unless the incidence of the evil apprehended is so imminent that it may befall before there is opportunity for full discussion. If there be time to expose through discussion the falsehood and fallacies, to avert the evil by the process of education, the remedy to be applied is more speech, not enforced silence. Only an emergency can justify repression. . . . Moreover, even imminent danger {52} cannot justify resort to prohibition of these functions essential to effective democracy, unless the evil apprehended is relatively serious. Prohibition of free speech and assembly is a measure so stringent that it would be inappropriate as the means for averting a relatively trivial harm to society. . . . The fact that speech likely to result in some violence or in destruction of property is not enough to justify its suppression. . . . Among free men, the deterrents ordinarily to be applied to prevent

crime are education and punishments for violations of the law, not abridgments of the rights of free speech and assembly.[21]

The market place theory has been attacked on several grounds. The most direct assault is by those who question the pragmatic philosophy behind it. But Holmes' definition of truth as what he could not help believing is simply an epigrammatic statement of the historical distaste of Americans for rational system-building, and their consequent vision of truth not as universally demonstrable but individually felt. Pragmatism is largely a rejection of formal systems, and a transfer of the search for truth from the philosophers to the citizenry, and thus to their interaction over time. To urge that pragmatism is not philosophically defensible is finally to urge that it is no more defensible than any other modern philosophy. Until pragmatism's attackers come up with a new philosophy which is technically beyond reproach and universally persuasive, Holmes' free trade of ideas seems better suited to modern uncertainties than do the philosophies of those who point out that no philosopher—including Holmes—has yet had the last word.

Edward S. Corwin, one of the most distinguished modern students of constitutional law concludes that Holmes' doctrine is simply that the ultimate good desired and the triumph of destiny are one and the same thing and that the function of free speech is to forward that triumph no matter what it may be.[22] Similarly Walter Berns has argued that Holmes' insistence on allowing ideas to contend without limitation in the market place may lead to the triumph of some non-democratic ideal, and since the libertarians would not be willing to subscribe to this non-libertarian ideology, their whole argument is self-contradictory.[23] Both Corwin and Berns err, it seems to me, because they use an absolutist concept of truth where it was never intended. The libertarians do not argue that the market place of ideas is a temporally limited process with a fixed product, truth; rather, they insist that it is an infinite process with never more than tentative results. Holmes may indeed find that "the proximate test of excellence" is "correspondence to the actual equilibrium of forces in the community,"[24] but the test is *proximate* and "equilibriums" are rarely stable for very long. Nor does the refusal of the libertarian to offer {53} in advance full loyalty to the result of the process, no matter what it may be, render him inconsistent. On the contrary, if it is insisted that results are always tentative then there is every reason not to support them unreservedly.

Similarly, the frequent complaint that the libertarian abandons all absolutes but one, the belief in progress, and then builds his whole non-absolute system on that one absolute, is not necessarily correct. The fundamental position may again be a disbelief in any complete truth and the consequent objection to any ideology being forced upon one as a final truth. In other words, the market place notion does not depend on the idea that the truth will win out by democratic choice, but on the tentative conviction that there is no absolute truth and the deduction or willful positing from this conviction that adjustment between rival partial truths is better (more pleasing) than adherence to one fixed mixture of truth and falsehood.

This emphasis on tentativeness goes far toward solving the practical dilemma which is always posed to those defending the market place notion. What if the democratic process threatens to yield a Hitler? Or what if the decision of the market place is to limit speech, as it is, for instance, when a statute punishing speech is passed by the legislature? The first problem, of course, never appears clearly or all at once. There is no single moment at which the observer can say, today is the day to stop this total-itarian movement by limiting its political freedom. In the real world, any and every speaker can be accused of being totalitarian or contributing to eventual dictatorship. The problem is always one of degree, of when we can be sufficiently certain that a real threat to democracy is involved. Therefore, the supposedly simple solution of denying the protection of the democratic process to those who wish to destroy democracy is not available. Everyone who wishes to deny any group the right to speak can shelter himself behind such a plea. If we destroy the freedom of the al-leged erstwhile dictator very early in the game, we have chosen a present and sure limitation on democracy rather than risk an eventual and possi-ble one. Surely this is to lose by forfeit. Of course, if we wait too long our loss may be even greater. But, certainly we must wait long enough to discover whether the utterance does in fact threaten totalitarianism. A democratic government is then faced with a series of decisions about timing and methods—in short, with politics. At this point defenders of the market place do not shelter themselves in abstraction. They offer a political rule of thumb for making the continuous and tentative timing decisions necessary to keep the market place open. That rule is the clear-and-present-danger test. {54}

A similar situation occurs when a statute limiting free speech is passed. The believer in the market place is not compelled to like the stat-ute just because it is the result of a free trade in ideas. By limiting that trade, the statute itself tends to be self-preserving and thus upsets the system of tentative decisions which he is defending. What can he do about the statute? He can use whatever is left of the democratic process to bring about its alteration. It is hardly inconsistent for him to use the democratic process to change decisions which that process has previously made. Indeed, that is the core of his philosophy. To be sure, if he again loses in the market place, there is something of a dilemma, but the di-lemma is consistent with the market place rationale itself. For if truths are never absolute, no political rationale is likely to totally eliminate the chance of self-defeat. It is hardly profitable to criticize the market place theory because it does not offer absolute guarantees of success in the real world. Neither do any other philosophies.

The most serious objection to the market place rationale has been an empirical rather than a theoretical one. The vision of the market to which rational consumers come and choose the ideas of most value has been seriously shaken by evidence from the social sciences which emphasizes the irrational elements of politics. But if the idea behind the market place is not so much that the truth will always or eventually enjoy the greatest consumer demand, but that the consumer must be free to choose and the seller free to advertise whatever product he will because there can be no agreement on what is best, then the irrationality of politics is simply a support to the market place theorem. It indicates all the more vividly that there can be no agreement as to what is best.

Another empirical argument was offered by counsel for the government with some success in *Dennis v. United States,* a case of the 1950s involving Communist leaders with which we will deal at length shortly. He argued that Justice Holmes had delivered his opinions within a background of open speech in the metaphoric market place, and thus the clear-and- present-danger rule could not have been intended to apply to the clandestine and subversive propaganda techniques of which we have only recently become aware. However, it was precisely because of fear of clandestine activity and subversion that the cases in which Holmes devised his formulas had arisen. Certainly Justices who had witnessed the Russian Revolution and were constantly hearing that an anarchist, or syndicalist, or Socialist, or Communist conspiracy was about to topple the nation, or the State of California, could hardly have been unaware that clandestine speech existed. And while the cases themselves dealt only with public utterances, there is no particular reason to believe that {55} private conversation was excluded from protection. Justice Holmes did not say auction hall, he said market place. He must certainly have been as aware as are modern commentators that a quiet talk between salesman and customer was as essential a selling device as a public advertisement. It could hardly be claimed that Justice Brandeis was unaware of the uses of privacy.

Yet certain kinds of clandestine speech do not at first glance seem compatible with the market place formula. What of secret speech which does not seek, even in the long run, to win over the majority in the market place, but instead is preliminary to revolutionary force which intends to shut the market place down? We have already dealt with this problem insofar as it concerns public speech. But can we afford to allow the secret revolutionist to bide his time and build his organization until the proper moment? The answer lies in the basic faith which inspires the market place and clear-and-present-danger formulas. The revolutionist is not allowed to bide his time to succeed, but to fail. If our government is basically sound, we have nothing to lose and everything to gain by granting the revolutionist time, for in the long run a sound democratic government cannot be subverted.

If such an appeal to faith is not convincing, a more practical argument probably is. The distinction between private speech intended to convince and private speech as a device for eventually overcoming those who will not be convinced is too difficult and potentially repressive to be left to governments. Such a surrender would be more truly suicidal than the risks involved in Holmes' approach. There is no need for such suicide. The very nature of subversive speech reduces the difficulty of dealing with it. Subversion is indeed a special problem, but its uniqueness is not that it cannot be handled under the Holmesian speech formulas, but that it can so easily be handled under the regular criminal law with no reference to speech. If the "subversives" actually intend to force rather than convince others they must perform countless acts, *not speeches*, which are either normally criminal or can be made so by statute. Indeed, even speech when closely enough related to an overt act might be prosecuted as conspiracy to act. Any follower of the self-laudation of the FBI must be somewhat confused by any claim that there is nothing to punish Communists for but their abstract speech. Have Mr. Philbrick et al. worked all these years in vain?

While the market place rationale served as the philosophical basis for the clear-and-present-danger rule, the rule's immediate source seems to have been the law of criminal attempts. Holmes had introduced attempts language into several earlier non-attempts cases in order to find some {56} logical tool for handling borderline situations.[25] The *Schenck* case involved what was in effect an attempts statute, and Holmes seems to have seized the opportunity to bodily import the law of attempts into the free speech area. Both as a scholar and judge he had dealt extensively with 'his legal doctrine. A comparison of his earlier writings with the *Schenck* rule indicates the indebtedness of the clear and present danger rule to his previous work:

> . . . the act must come pretty near to accomplishing that result [a "substantive evil"] before the law will notice it. . . . Every question of proximity must be determined by its own circumstances . . . , the gravity of the crime, the uncertainty of the result and the seriousness of the apprehension. . . .[26]

An attempt . . . is an act expected to bring about a substantive wrong by the forces of nature. With it is classed the kindred offense where the act and the natural conditions present or sup-posed to be present . . . [are] so near to the results that if coupled with an intent to produce that result, the danger is very great.[27]

. . . preparation is not an attempt. But some preparation may amount to an attempt. It is a question of degree. If the preparation comes very near to the accomplishment of the act, the intent to complete it renders the crime so probable that the act will be a misdemeanor. . . .[28]

. . . the considerations being . . . the nearness of the danger, the greatness of the harm and the degree of apprehension felt.[29]

But the character of every act depends upon the circumstances in which it is done. . . . The question in every case is whether the words used are used in such circumstances and are of such a na-ture as to create a clear and present danger that they will bring about the substantive evils that Congress has a right to prevent. It is a question of proximity and degree.[30]

Holmes makes the link between the two doctrines perfectly clear in his dissent in *Shaeffer v. United States.* "The test to be applied as in the case of criminal attempts and incitements, is not the remote or possible effect. There must be a clear and present danger."[31] References to attempts or incitements were also made in *Abrams* and in *Sugarman v. United States.*[32]

The attempts rationale for the clear-and-present-danger formula is important for three reasons. First, it serves to emphasize the "present-ness" requirement in contrast to the old bad tendency test. It is not enough that a logical connection between word and illegal act exists. The speaker may not be punished until his words come "very near"[33] to the accomplishment {57} of the substantive evil, just as a would-be arsonist be punished when he lays the tinder and buys the matches, but only when he prepares to light one. Secondly, the doctrine reminds us that free speech cases are usually matters of criminal law, not simply policy debates over the relative merits of free speech and other social interests. The rules of decision in speech cases must be formulated with due regard to the traditions of our criminal law. There seems to be no reason to treat the allegedly criminal speaker more harshly than other criminals. It must be remembered, therefore, that the law should not intervene against the speaker until the last possible moment. Not until then will the high de-gree of probability necessary in criminal law be attained and the greatest possible time have been allowed for the potential criminal to change his mind and abort his preparations. It is not the state of mind evidenced by the preparations but their immediate results with which the law concerns itself.

Thirdly, Corwin and other observers who have sought to emphasize intent as an alternative to the clear-and-present-danger standard seem to have misunderstood Holmes' line of argument. Intent is not an alternative to the clear-and-present-danger rule, but a subordinate part of that rule.

> Attempt and intent . . . are two distinct things. Intent to commit a crime is not itself criminal. . . . The law only deals with conduct. An attempt is an overt act. . . . The importance of the intent is not to show that the act was wicked; but to show that it was likely to be followed with hurtful consequences.[34]

> . . . an overt act, although coupled with intent to commit the crime is not punishable. . . . But. . . if the preparation comes very near to the accomplishment of the act, the intent to complete it renders the crime so probable that the act will be a misdemeanor.[35]

A preparation is punishable "where it is so near to the result that if coupled with an intent to produce that result, the danger is very great."[36]

In other words, "intent" is not an alternative standard, but simply one of the elements to be considered in determining whether a clear and present danger in fact exists. Holmes' preoccupation with intent in the early cases resulted from the fact that the government had failed to conclusively establish that there was a very great danger to be immediately anticipated from the speech at issue. Thus, without strong proof of intent there would be insufficient showing of the probability of an evil to warrant punishment under the clear-and-present-danger test. Even in dealing {58} with intent Holmes was insisting that the law acts not to punish evil thoughts but to prevent substantive evils.

The effort of Justice Holmes and Brandeis to establish the clear-and-present-danger formula as a rule of decision seemed in the early 1930s to have failed, although it may have been one of the elements which made the Court more sensitive to civil rights issues. In the ten years from *Whitney* in 1927 to *Herndon v. Lowry*[37] in 1937, the Court acted to protect civil rights in several important cases, but clear-and-present-danger was mentioned only once. The Court instead relied on prior restraint, vagueness, and due process arguments.[38]

While no more than four Justices (Murphy, Rutledge, Black, and Douglas) were consistent supporters and there was never complete agreement on its meaning, the doctrine was used frequently between 1937 and the early 1950s.[39] The Second Flag Salute Case[40] seemed to make the test compulsory for all free speech cases and *Taylor v. Mississippi*[41] tended to confirm that impression. *Thornhill v. Alabama*,[42] by applying the test to a statute specifically aimed at advocacy, seemed to complete the work begun in *Herndon v. Lowry*[43] of burying the *Gitlow* distinction between statutes aimed at action and those specifically punishing advocacy. *Thornhill v. Alabama, Carlson v. California*,[44] the Second Flag Salute Case, and the dissent in *United Public Workers v. Mitchell*[45] indicated not only that the rule would be used as a test of whether speech could be prosecuted under a statute aimed at acts *a la Gitlow* and as a test of whether specific prosecutions under a broadly worded statute aimed at advocacy were valid, but also that it would become the standard for judging the constitutionality of the statute itself. Indeed, the *Thornhill* decision went so far as to declare that a statute so broadly drawn that its routine application would violate individual rights might be held invalid on its face regardless of the justifiability of the particular prosecution at issue.

Although the prior restraint doctrine was still in use, the clear-and-present-danger test was employed to allow the Court to deal with subsequent punishment cases. Both the high degree of imminence and the extreme seriousness of the danger which the test required were stressed.[46] Thus the Court found that street litter, the disturbance caused by doorbell ringing, and verbal abuse were not sufficiently serious evils to justify limitations on freedom of speech.

At the same time the Court was redeveloping the clear-and-present-danger test, it, or rather the same set of four Justices, created the preferred position doctrine as an essential foundation for that test. The Roosevelt Court had inherited from Justice Holmes a combination of judicial modesty and concern for freedom of speech and belief. The {59} Court required an excuse for judicial activism in an area with which it was particularly concerned, but an excuse which would leave its abdication in the economic realm unchallengeable. The preferred position doctrine was the logical result of the Court's attempt to have the best of both worlds. It not only served as a relatively clear means of delimiting two bodies of subject matter which the Court would treat quite differently, but was accompanied by a rationale which could justify the difference in treatment.

The doctrine, as first enunciated by Justice Stone in the famous footnote 4 to the *Carolene Products* decision of 1938,[47] contains three basic ideas. First, when legislation on its face violated specific provisions of the Bill of Rights, the normal presumption of constitutionality would be weakened or totally lacking. Second, the judiciary has a special function as defender of those liberties necessary to the operation of the democratic process. Third, the Court must offer special protection to minorities and unpopular groups who, in the nature of things, are unlikely to be able to protect themselves through the normal political processes of a democracy.

Justice Rutledge, however, offered the strongest statement of the doctrine:

> The rational connection between the remedy provided and the evil to be curbed, which in other contexts might support legislation . . . , will not suffice. These rights rest on firmer foundation. . . . Only the gravest abuses, endangering paramount interests, give occasion for permissible limitation . . . where the usual presumption supporting legislation is balanced by the preferred place given in our scheme to the great, the indispensable democratic freedoms secured by the First Amendment. . . . That priority gives these liberties a sanctity and sanction not permitting dubious intrusions.[48]

In short, the normal presumption of constitutionality for legislation, which is the backbone of judicial modesty, is to be set aside where First Amendment rights are involved. The Court would then be free to substitute its own constitutional judgment via the clear-and-present-danger rule. This preferred position doctrine was to be found closely brigaded with clear-and-present-danger throughout the forties.

However, the Court was also using other doctrinal tools in the speech cases. The intent standard, which we have argued is an essential part of the clear-and-present-danger test, but which may be used independently, was applied in *Taylor v. Mississippi*,[49] *Bridges v. California*,[50] and *Hartzel v. United States*,[51] all of which demanded specific intent. The Court also introduced the alternative means formula, which it had used successfully in the commerce sphere, as a supplement to the clear-and-present-danger {60} test. This formula demanded that legislatures use the means to their ends least obstructive to political liberties.[52] The more modest "reasonable basis" test, however, remained in use in spite of the attacks of the libertarian four. Generally speaking, where the restriction was on the time, place, or manner of the utterance as opposed to its content, the Court contended itself with examining the reasonableness of the statute rather than applying the clear-and-present-danger rule.[53]

Thus, even when the Court's sensitivity to freedom of speech was at its height, certain exceptions to the clear-and-present-danger test continued to exist. In these instances the applicability of the First Amendment was admitted, but the reasonableness test was substituted for that of clear-and-present-danger. The Court went even further in certain other cases. It found that some varieties of speech were not worthy of any First Amendment protection. It argued that the First Amendment was clearly not absolute and, in spite of its wording, must be read as excepting such traditionally punishable common law crimes as libel. By analogy it extended these categories of exception to include utterances whose mode of delivery and content constituted them "fighting words" which threatened an immediate breach of the peace.[54]

Such exceptions from First Amendment protection indicated, as did the use of the reasonableness rule, a reluctance on the part of the Court to apply the clear-and-present-danger doctrine to all situations, for the exclusion of certain speech from the First Amendment was obviously a device for avoiding the necessity of using this formula. Dissatisfaction with the rule and with the preferred position doctrine was brought to a head by Justice Frankfurter's long campaign against them. He attacked the preferred position during the 1940s in the First Flag Salute Case[55] and in *Kovacs v. Cooper*.[56] His dissent in *Bridges v. California*,[57] although it does not entirely reject the clear-and-present-danger standard, argued that it was not universally applicable. "A trial is not a 'free trade in ideas,' nor is the best test of truth in a courtroom 'the power of the thought to get itself accepted in the competition of the market.' "[58] He continued his attack in dissents in the Second Flag Salute Case,[59] *Bridges v. Wixon*,[60] a concurrence in *Pennekamp v. Florida*,[61] and a dissent in *Craig v. Harney*.[62] He not only argued that Holmes had never intended clear-and-present-danger as a general rule,[63] but, as he had suggested in defending his *Gobitis* decision, that the Court must take a more modest position on First Amendment questions.[64]

At the same time that Frankfurter was insisting that precise calculation of the allowable limits on free speech under the clear-and-present-danger test was impossible, the Court, with Frankfurter as a principal participant, {61} was laying the groundwork for a potentially even more delicate calculus to replace clear-and-present-danger. Frankfurter for the Court had written in *Gobitis* that national unity was "an interest inferior to none in the hierarchy of legal values,"[65] and a later majority had argued that some utterances were of so little value that they were clearly outweighed by the State's interest in maintaining order.[66] Here, then, is the first suggestion of that hierarchical structure in which good speech will be offered more protection than bad, evident in the Communist cases of the 1950s.

The clear-and-present-danger test also appeared on shaky ground in a relatively new problem area, that of the "hostile audience." When is the state justified in stopping a speaker whose utterance results in antisocial behavior not by his supporters but by his opponents? While the clear-and-present-danger test had been applied to public speech, it did not provide a ready solution to this problem, for, even if a clear and present danger of riot existed, should a speaker whose words do not urge violence be punished for the unlawful actions of others, particularly when the actions are directed against him?

Paradoxically enough, however, the weakness in the clear-and-present-danger rule exposed by the hostile audience cases is that it may not give enough protection to freedom of speech, so that these cases can hardly be used as ammunition by the opponents of judicial activism.

Two such cases reached the Court in the late forties and early fifties. In both the Court held that the police might arrest the speaker when a clear and present danger of riot existed. In both the Court used a set of technical legal blinders that obscured the real facts. A realistic application of the clear-and-present-danger rule might have resulted in exactly opposite conclusions in the two cases. For in the earlier one, *Terminiello v. Chicago*,[67] the speaker was freed under the clear-and-present-danger rule in spite of every sign of incipient riot, and in the latter, *Feiner v. New York*,[68] the speaker went to jail in a situation where the threat of riot was a patently trumped up device for shutting up a "radical."

This seeming contradiction is actually a trophy of Frankfurter's increasingly successful war against the clear-and-present-danger rule and the preferred position doctrine. In *Terminiello* the clear-and-present-danger forces were still strong enough to protect the speaker, even though the logic of their own doctrine ran against them. *Feiner* is one of the first signs of the dominance of the Frankfurter position in the fifties: the clear-and-present-danger test still nominally survives, but it is here used for the first time to send a speaker to jail. Moreover, the {62} opinion is full of deference to administrative authorities and trial courts, concern for the other interests with which speech interferes, and all the other devices of the modest for escaping judicial responsibility for enforcing the First Amendment.

Even earlier *American Communication Association v. Douds*,[69] the first major opinion on Cold War inspired legislation, had signaled the change. Chief Justice Vinson takes up Justice Frankfurter's cry that the clear-and-present-danger test was not intended to be applied mechanically to all First Amendment cases. He then notes that the statute in question, which barred Communists from the leadership of unions in the communications field, was not aimed at advocacy of political doctrines but at political strikes in the communications industry, an evil which Congress has a right to prevent under the commerce power, and a relatively serious one. In addition, the abridgment of speech is minor and only incidental to a reasonable commerce regulation. Therefore a rigid application of the clear-and-present-danger test would be incorrect. There is no need to show that the evil is either extremely great or imminent: ". . . not the relative certainty that evil conduct will result from speech, but the extent and gravity of the substantive evil must be measured by the 'test' laid down in the *Schenck* case."[70] In short, the clear-and-present-danger test is reduced to a means of determining how serious the evil is, and the seriousness of the evil is then balanced against the degree of abridgment of speech.

While the decision is somewhat obscured by its stress on the special circumstances involved, the general rule seems to be that where the social interest in preventing the evil is greater than the interest in protecting the speech the regulation is valid. This weighing technique, adding a new dimension to the *Chaplinsky* suggestion that the merits of the utterance be weighed in deciding what degree of protection it should be offered, represents a movement back to the bad tendency test. For if the evil be sufficiently horrendous or the speech sufficiently lacking in value, regulation might be valid even though the danger was remote. In this light, the return to the reasonable basis test under the guise of judging a commerce regulation is significant, for there is a close relation between the reasonableness and the bad tendency tests. Vinson also attacks the very rationale of the clear-and-present-danger rule as applied to Communists. He notes that such men can call political strikes without speech or advocacy and without the opportunity for counter-advocacy, so that the market place rationale cannot be used in their defense.

Dennis v. United States represents the culmination of judicial dissatisfaction with the clear-and-present-danger standard.[71] The test {63} foundered on two separate but neighboring shoals: first, the reluctance of the Court to apply "present" to tightly organized groups with long-term continuity, and secondly, unwillingness to concede that the market place rationale is applicable to clandestine speech.

Dennis involved prosecution of Communist Party leaders under the Smith Act, a federal law which is aimed at groups seeking to violently overthrow the government. Dennis had been convicted of conspiring to advocate the overthrow of the government by force and violence. The Communist Party, unlike the rather loosely organized and vacillating groups to whom the rule was originally applied, is supposed to be methodically building day by day toward the eventual revolution. Requiring the government to intervene only after the party has done all its preliminary work seemed foolishly naive in the face of recent experience, and the "present" standard seemed to require such a delay. Thus the trial judge, dissatisfied with the test, but feeling, as indeed did nearly all the judges concerned with the case, that the test could not be completely abandoned, modified it to allow punishment if the defendant's speech was designed to bring about the danger (i.e., revolution) not immediately but "as speedily as circumstances would permit."[72] Judge Hand in the Court of Appeals altered "present" to "probable." "Given the same probability, it would be wholly irrational to condone future evils which we should prevent if they were immediate; that could be reconciled only by an indifference to those who come after us."[73] While Hand attempted some verbal maneuverings to save Holmes' reputation, it seems obvious that he believed that the test was an aberration unsuited to the real world. Justice Vinson, in adopting Hand's test for the Supreme Court, emphasizes the same difficulty with the old rule. "[It] cannot mean that before the Government may act, it must wait until the *putsch* is about to be executed, the plans have been laid and the signal is awaited. . . ."[74]

But the whole "realist" argument about "present danger" and subversive groups dissolves with the first actual look at reality. The plain fact is that the government had been unable to get even an indictment for any seditious acts or even for a conspiracy to commit a seditious act. Thus the Court, in order to avoid the imminence requirement, had to assume a factual situation for which the government could not even offer sufficient proof to sustain an indictment. The most striking feature of the Court's treatment of the imminence requirement is the obviousness with which it was willing to put aside the Holmes-Brandeis rationale in order to "get the Communists," come what may. Brandeis had demanded no restriction while there was still time to call the police. The trouble in {64} this case was that the police had been called but hadn't found any evidence of wrong-doing. The prosecution was instituted under the advocacy provisions because there was not sufficient evidence to meet the normal requirements of the criminal law of sedition. Thus, paradoxically, the defendants were convicted in an area where they were protected by the supposedly rigorous demands of the First Amendment *precisely because* they could not be convicted in an area under the routine protections of criminal law.

Similarly, the notion that the clear-and-present-danger test is not applicable to the Communist Party because its appeal cannot be refuted in the market place is, in the light of the factual situation, nonsense. American members of the Communist Party are not locked up in party ghettos. Neither are the persons whom the party attempts to recruit. They are subject to the same mass communication appeals as the rest of us. It could not be seriously argued that Communism has spread its doctrines so secretly that no one has been sufficiently aware of their presence to refute them. The very evidence of advocacy which the government offered were books by Communist authors available at any large book store. It is perfectly clear that the Communist doctrines can be and have been successfully assailed in the market place of ideas.

Judge Hand and his supporters on the Supreme Court were not willing to stop with attacks on the appropriateness of the "present" standard. Hand offered and Vinson approved the following substitute for that standard: ". . . whether the gravity of the 'evil,' discounted by its improbability, justifies such invasion of free speech as is necessary to avoid the danger." This formula, like the clear-and-present-danger test itself, seems to have its origin in Holmes' concept of the law of attempts.

> Every question of proximity must be determined by its own circumstances. . . . The gravity of the crime . . . and the seriousness of the apprehension, coupled with the great harm likely to result . . . would warrant holding the liability for an attempt to begin at a point more remote from the possibility of accomplishing what is expected than might be the case with lighter crimes.[75]

But a reading of the *Abrams* dissent and *Whitney* concurrence makes clear that in Holmes' and Brandeis' view the correct policy was to intervene in most instances not at all, and where extremely serious evils were involved only when there was a clear and present danger. The *earliest* intervention they felt desirable, no matter how serious the evil, was only at the point where a clear and present danger existed. {65}

When Judge Hand's formula is examined in the light of the facts of the case, its real divergence from the Holmes-Brandeis concept becomes clear. The government had offered no evidence that revolution in the United States was imminent or even probable in the foreseeable future. The trial judge was apparently unconvinced that Communist revolution was probable here in the immediate future. While the Circuit Court and the Supreme Court made some rambling comments on the international scene, neither was willing to allege that revolution was likely in this country within any reasonable duration of time. Thus, Judge Hand's test amounts to this: The Court will determine what the tendency of the speech in question is, i.e., what the evil to be eventually anticipated from it is. If that evil is sufficiently serious, i.e., if you dislike the consequences sufficiently, the speech may be restricted no matter how remote these anticipated consequences. In practice this means that any radical political doctrine would receive little or no protection, since it would always appear as a threat to the nation and thus as the most serious of all possible evils. This is simply the remote bad tendency test dressed up in modern style. The test is even more extreme than bad tendency for it considers the gravity of the evil discounted by *its* improbability—not the improbability that the speech in question will bring the evil about, but that it will occur from any cause. The majority in *Gitlow*, from whom Holmes dissented, would have had no difficulty in concurring in *Dennis*.

Justice Frankfurter, concurring, continued his attack on the clear-and-present-danger test both in its traditional and modified forms. He insisted both that the Court was not suited to predicting the likelihood of revolution and that judges had no right to interfere with the legislature's judgment in this field unless there was no reasonable basis for that judgment.[76] Most significant was the almost casual statement that "On any scale of values which we have hitherto recognized, speech of this sort ranks low."[77] Combined with similar suggestions in other cases,[78] this approach seems to enforce Hand's discounting formula. But here less protection is offered not only when the anticipated *acts* are sufficiently despised but when the content of the *speech* itself is disapproved.

Seven Justices accepted some form of clear-and-present-danger, but only four supported Hand's interpretation. Black and Douglas supported the traditional test, although they insisted that First Amendment protection went even beyond it. Justice Jackson favored the preservation of the test for dealing with street corner orators, but rejected it in instances where subversive organizations were involved. Justice Clark did not {66} participate.

Walter Berns has concluded that *Dennis* is the first case in our history in which "it has been declared unlawful to hold certain ideas concerning the common good."[79] While this seems to be a bit of wishful thinking on Professor Berns' part as to the actual legal conclusion,[80] *Dennis* does seem to be the high point of the attack on the libertarian position. The clear-and-present-danger test was so seriously modified as to be put in total jeopardy. The preferred position doctrine was ignored by the majority and attacked by Justice Frankfurter in spite of strident cries by Justice Douglas.[81] The Court ignored the Thornhill Rule and the alternative means approach. Justice Frankfurter demanded and the Court came very close to a rule of reason.

Prosecutions under the Smith Act continued, and in 1957 the Supreme Court finally consented to full review of a Smith Act conviction in *Yates v. United States.*[82] More important, it attempted to reinterpret the *Dennis* decision so as to place renewed emphasis on the distinction between teaching an abstract doctrine and incitement which produces sufficient likelihood of danger to warrant restriction: ". . . mere doctrinal justification for forcible overthrow . . . even though uttered with the hope that it may ultimately lead to violent revolution, is too remote from concrete action to be regarded as the kind of indoctrination preparatory to action which was condemned in *Dennis*."[83]

The Court does, however, seem to reject the immediacy requirement. But, although it was not mentioned, *Yates* certainly did not altogether do away with the clear-and-present-danger test. First of all, in distinguishing between abstract teaching and advocacy, the Court insisted that a danger of actual violence exist. Secondly, it demanded that this danger be shown to be clearly related to the actual conduct of the accused. Thirdly, while dropping the immediacy requirement, it required that the action of the accused (i.e., advocacy) be presently occurring, that a relatively large, cohesive, and action-bent group presently exist, and that present circumstances are such as to justify reasonable apprehension that action will occur. In fact, *Yates* seems to establish a special category within the clear-and-present standard. There must be a clear danger of a substantive evil but, when a subversive group is involved, evidence of the presentness of its organizational effectiveness may be substituted for the presentness of the danger.

The history of the clear-and-present-danger doctrine subsequent to *Dennis-Yates* is rather vague and quickly told. In *Beauharnais v. Illinois*,[84] while the majority did not use the test, Justice Jackson in concurrence sought to preserve it for the street corner orator situation. When the Court was in the process of using every possible delaying tactic to avoid {67} deciding *Scales v. United States*,[85] the case testing the constitutionality of the provisions of the Smith Act which made membership in the Communist Party illegal, one of the questions they thought of for reargument was whether the clear-and-present-danger test was applicable. But the final opinion issued in 1961 does not really discuss the question. Indeed, the only language directly applicable to the issue is ambiguous.[86] Justices Black and Douglas in their minority opinions eventually abandoned the test for a more absolutist position. Justice Frankfurter et al., therefore, had no reason to specifically attack it any longer. It has never been specifically rejected by a majority of the Court. The modest did continue their attack on the preferred position doctrine and a six man majority rejected it in *Ullman v. United States*.[87] The preferred position doctrine they rejected, however, was not the preferred position doctrine that Stone and Rutledge had enunciated, but the reformulation that Justice Frankfurter had designed in order to attack it more easily.

Several cases in recent years, however, have actively involved the danger test. In *Wood v. Georgia*,[88] a sheriff who criticized the activity of a county court was found guilty of contempt under an indictment and instruction to the jury which charged that certain of his activities constituted "a clear, present and imminent danger" to the Court's proceedings. In the face of Justice Harlan's expressed doubts about the danger rule, and his introduction of balancing language, a five man majority directly and repeatedly invoked the rule as it was enunciated in *Bridges v. California*, and subsequent cases, and stressed the requirements of seriousness and imminence. But by so insistently placing *Wood* squarely in the line of contempt cases that employ clear-and-present-danger as the decisive test, the Court may be indicating that it is espousing clear-and-present-danger not as a general test of First Amendment rights, but as the test which has been consistently followed in the particular area of contempt by publication.

In *Kingsley International Pictures Corporation v. Regents of the University of New York*,[89] the Court did not quite invoke the danger test but, nevertheless, hinted at it pretty strongly.

> Advocacy of conduct proscribed by law is not, as Mr. Justice Brandeis long ago pointed out, a justification for denying free speech where the advocacy falls short of incitement and there is nothing to indicate that the advocacy would be immediately acted on.[90]

This language keeps the substance of the test alive but may or may not be a deliberate attempt to avoid the language. The significance of this {68} decision for the survival of the danger rule is also uncertain because the state action in this instance, at least as construed by the Court, was so clearly aimed directly at the expression of ideas itself that no rule, clear-and-present-danger or otherwise, for testing borderline situations was necessary. Thus the absence of the rule may be explained as a deliberate avoidance of it by the Court, or simply as the realization that it was not necessary to invoke it here.

We encounter the same difficulty in *Edwards v. South Carolina*.[91] Here a group of Negro civil rights demonstrators was convicted of disturbing the peace where "there was no violence or threat of violence on their part, or on the part of any member of the crowd watching them,"[92] where there was ample police protection, and where there was not even any material obstruction of traffic or other ill effect. There were no threats of violence or hints of incitement to riot as in *Feiner*, and no "fighting words" as in the *Chaplinski* case. There was not even an allegation of violation of a time, place, or manner regulation—such as a law regulating traffic which might have brought the case under the reasonableness rule. The Court might well have ended its opinion with its statement that

> . . . they were convicted upon evidence which showed no more than that the opinions which they were peaceably expressing were sufficiently opposed to the views of the majority of the community to attract a crowd and necessitate police protection. The Fourteenth Amendment does not permit a State to make criminal the peaceful expression of unpopular views.[93]

But the Court did not end there; instead, it went on to the following lengthy quotation from *Terminiello v. Chicago*.

> A function of free speech under our system of government is to invite dispute. It may indeed best serve its high purpose when it induces a condition of unrest, creates dissatisfaction with conditions as they are, or even stirs people to anger. Speech is often provocative and challenging. It may strike at prejudices and preconceptions and have profound unsettling effects as it presses for acceptance of an idea. That is why freedom of speech . . . is . . . protected against censorship or punishment, unless shown likely to produce a clear and present danger of a serious substantive evil that rises

far above public inconvenience, annoyance, or unrest. . . . There is no room under our Constitution for a more restrictive view. For the alternative would lead to standardization of ideas either by legislatures, courts, or dominant political groups.[94] {69}

The Court, then, squarely rested its decision on the language of *Terminiello.*

This opinion, written by Justice Stewart, is joined by every Justice except Clark, and reaffirms the clear-and-present-danger rule not in isolation, but in the full libertarian context of the original Holmes-Brandeis rationale. Is this a full renewal of commitment to the clear-and-present-danger rule? It seems to be, but it is necessary to pay close attention to the factors making for ambiguity. First, this is not a borderline case. The state action was so blatantly unconstitutional, and is one of such a long series of blatantly unconstitutional state actions, that it would have been struck down under any test. Courts may well reach for any handy test under such circumstances without evidencing any real commitment to whatever test they choose. The crucial issues are found in the borderline cases, and the real impact of the clear-and-present-danger test is on precisely those cases. Moreover, the conflict between balancing and clear-and-present-danger that has been so important in recent years does not occur in this case because balancing would have led to exactly the same results. In this situation there was no state interest that could be balanced against the infringement on speech in order to justify it. If hard cases make bad law, easy cases like *Kingsley* and *Edwards* leave one with the uneasy feeling that the Court's omissions and commissions of doctrine may not mean too much, since any of the available doctrinal stances would have lead to the same decision.

However, even assuming that the rule was consciously and deliberately introduced into *Edwards* as a first step toward reviving it, it may also be true that the fact situation of *Edwards* was consciously chosen in order to revive the rule on a limited basis. Justice Jackson, it will be remembered, had wanted to keep the rule for street corner orators. The Court may now be suggesting that the rule is to be applied, but only where non-subversive, street corner orators are involved.

Several more aspects of the case should be noted. The Court might well have chosen to reverse the conviction on the no evidence rule of *Thompson v. Louisville.*[95] It apparently preferred not to avoid the First Amendment issues, as it might have done if it felt reluctant to use the danger rule. Secondly, after having apparently decided the case specifically on the clear-and-present-danger rule, the Court decided it all over again specifically under the void for vagueness doctrine. Does this mean that a majority could not be found for the clear-and-present-danger rule alone? Finally, Justice Clark, dissenting, specifically and repeatedly invokes the clear-and-present-danger rule and stresses both its imminence and gravity requirements. {70}

Cox v. Louisiana,[96] a 1964 case dealing with civil rights demonstrations, relies heavily on *Edwards*. The Court refused to commit itself specifically on whether it was using the danger test, but, in fact, it considered precisely those elements and dealt with them in precisely the same way as would a Court specifically using the test.

There is also one important piece of negative evidence for the continued survival of the rule. Its opponents early stumbled on the notion that some types of speech, such as abusive swearing (fighting words), were excluded from First Amendment protection altogether, and thus naturally did not fall under the danger rule. Excluding this form of speech was a neat way of avoiding application of the danger rule. This technique was followed in the *Beauharnais* case, when a so-called group libel law was given the same exception to First Amendment limitations that traditional libel laws have generally enjoyed. The Court has treated obscenity law in exactly the same way: obscene material is not protected by the First Amendment and, therefore, is not subject to the clear-and-present-danger rule. Rigorous standards, however, are applied to insure that non-obscene material is not deprived of its First Amendment protection under the guise of obscenity control. Actually, technical exclusion of obscenity from First Amendment protection, plus the elaborate defenses against mis-classification, add up in the end to giving allegedly obscene materials every benefit of the First Amendment except the clear-and-present-danger rule. The continued use of the exclusion device is a sort of backhand admission that if certain types of speech were not excluded, they would still be covered by the danger test. If the test had lost all vitality, the Court would not have to engage in all the logical nonsense necessary to avoid it through the exclusion rule.

Moreover, neither the rule nor the rationale that lies behind it has ever been successfully refuted in the opinions, for the *Dennis* opinion simply does not hold up on any count. The fact situation there and the Court's treatment of it did not show that there were unanticipated developments in politics that made Holmes' and Brandeis' concepts obsolete. On the contrary, the fact situation showed conclusively that the market place rationale and the clear-and-present-danger test were fully applicable to the problem of Communist subversion. Had they been applied, the Court would have been saved its long excursion into a never-never land that had no relation to the real circumstances of the prosecution. The real trouble with the clear-and-present-danger rule exposed in *Dennis* was that the rule would have forced the Justices to protect the First Amendment against flagrant violation when they didn't want to protect it. Indeed, it is perfectly clear that in *Dennis*, Hand and {71}

Frankfurter sought to scuttle the rule, and its market place and preferred position rationales, not because they failed to make sense in terms of the philosophy of freedom of speech, but precisely because they did make sense, and Hand and Frankfurter wanted the Court to have very little to do with freedom of speech. Hand's circuit opinion, so carefully followed by Justice Vinson, talks a great deal about the relation of clear-and-present-danger to a coherent theory of the First Amendment. His decision, however, is actually determined not by the view that clear-and-present-danger is incompatible with a proper interpretation of the First Amendment, but by the belief that the Supreme Court is incompatible with the First Amendment. These opinions are not honest appraisals of whether clear-and-present-danger is a workable doctrine for relating the First Amendment to statutes prohibiting speech; they are smoke screens behind which judges hide their refusal to relate the First Amendment to statutes prohibiting speech. In short, they are not refutations of the clear-and-present-danger doctrine at the level of theory of freedom of speech but at the level of the role of the Supreme Court. And at that level, the arguments of the modest are based on a fundamentally false vision of American government and the Court's place in that government.

Neither has the fundamental core of the clear-and-present-danger rule—that is, the traditional distinction between thought and action—been successfully challenged. From its origin in the law of attempts, the clear-and-present-danger rule has been basically designed to indicate that courts may use the criminal law only to punish men for what they do, not what they say or think. To be sure, not everyone accepts this fundamental notion, but no one on the Court at least has yet suggested that the Constitution or the Court will allow men to be sent to jail simply for saying something the government does not like. This distinction between thought and action may yet serve as a stable core around which the freedom of speech guarantees originally embodied in the rule can be rebuilt. It may not contain an absolute philosophical truth, but most of us could agree to it as a rule of political prudence for the immediate future.

In discussing *Yates v. United States* I tried to show that the principle to be found there might be that clear-and-present-danger remained the general rule, but that presentness of organization might be substituted for presentness of danger when subversive organizations were involved. Nevertheless, the danger rule fell into limbo after *Dennis,* but has now been at least tentatively revived in two of its traditional areas—contempt by publication and hostile audience. At the same time, the Court has {72} now indicated that it did, after all, mean that subversive groups were to be treated as a special exception to normal First Amendment rules.[97] Both the revival of clear-and-present-danger doctrine and the acknowledgment of this exception doctrine occurred just when Justice Frankfurter was leaving the Court and the general influence of judicial modesty was declining in legal circles. It could well be that clear-and-present-danger, or at least the core of the doctrine, has now survived the onslaught of the modest and will be with us for some time to come. Nevertheless, we must now turn to that onslaught, and more particularly to its principal doctrinal vehicle, the balancing of interests test.

NOTES to Chapter Two

1 Thomas I. Emerson, "Toward a General Theory of the First Amendment," *Yale Law Journal*, vol. 72 (1963), p. 877.

2 Judith Shklar, *After Utopia* (Princeton, 1957).

3 Daniel Bell, *The End of Ideology* (Glencoe, Ill., 1959).

4 Louis Hartz, *The Liberal Tradition In America* (New York, 1955); Daniel Boorstein, *The Genius of American Politics* (Chicago, 1953).

5 249 U.S. 47, 52 (1919).

6 250 U.S. 616, 624 (1919).

7 *Id.*, p. 627.

8 *Id.*, p. 628.

9 268 U.S. 652 (1925).

10 274 U.S. 357, 372 (1927) (concurring).

11 *Debs v. United States*, 249 U.S. 211, 214-15 (1919).

12 *Abrams v. United States*, 250 U.S. 616, 628 (1919) (emphasis added).

13 *Abrams v. United States*, 250 U.S. 616, 630 (1919); *Gilbert v. Minnesota*, 254 U.S. 325, 334 (1920).

14 Alexander Meiklejohn, "The First Amendment and the Evils That Congress Has a Right to Prevent," *Indiana Law Journal*, vol. 26 (1951), pp. 480-81.

15 249 U.S. 47, 52 (1919).

16 250 U.S. 616, 630 (1919).

17 Richardson, "Freedom of Expression and the Function of the Courts," *Harvard Law Review*, vol. 65 (1951), pp. 16-17.

18 *Whitney v. California*, 274 U.S. 357, 372, 378 (1927) (concurring).

19 *Bridges v. California*, 314 U.S. 252, 263 (1941).

20 *Abrams v. United States*, 250 U.S. 616, 630 (1919).

21 *Whitney v. California*, 274 U.S. 357, 372, 377-78 (1927) (concurring).

22 Edward S. Corwin, "Bowing Out 'Clear and Present Danger,' " *Notre Dame Lawyer*, vol. 27 (1951), pp. 332-34.

23 *Freedom, Virtue and the First Amendment* (Baton Rouge, 1957), pp. 198-228.

24 *Collected Legal Papers* (New York, 1944), p. 258.

25 *Swift and Co. v. United States*, 196 U.S. 375, 396 (1905); *Hyde v. United States*, 225 U.S. 347, 388 (1912) (dissent). Professor Yosal Rogat has recently {73} called my attention to a similar treatment of attempts and clear and present danger in his "The Judge As Spectator," *University of Chicago Law Review*, vol. 31 (1964), p. 213. We are not, however, in agreement on the significance of the relation or the value of the danger rule.

26 *Massachusetts v. Kennedy*, 48 N.E. 770, 771 (1897).

27 *Hyde v. United States*, 225 U.S. 347, 387-88 (1912) (dissent).

28 *Commonwealth v. Peaslee*, 59 N.E. 55 (1901).

29 Oliver Wendell Holmes, Jr., *The Common Law* (Boston, 1881), p. 68.

30 *Schenck v. United States*, 249 U.S. 47, 52 (1919).

31 *Shaeffer v. United States*, 251 U.S. 468, 486 (1920).

32 249 U.S. 182 (1919).

33 *Commonwealth v. Peaslee*, 59 N.E. 55, 56 (1901).

34 Holmes, *The Common Law*, pp. 65, 68.

35 *Commonwealth v. Peaslee*, 59 N.E. 55, 56 (1901).

36 *Hyde v. United States*, 225 U.S. 347, 387-88 (1912) (dissent). See also *Swift and Co. v. United States*, 196 U.S. 375, 396 (1905). Holmes was probably drawing on the leading English precedent, *Rex v. Scofield*, Cald. Magis. Cases 397, 400 (1784).

37 301 U.S. 242 (1937).

38 *Fiske v. Kansas*, 274 U.S. 380 (1927); *Near v. Minnesota*, 283 U.S. 697 (1931); *Grosjean v. American Press Co.*, 297 U.S. 233 (1936); *Lovell v. Griffin*, 303 U.S. 444 (1938); *Stromberg v. California*, 283 U.S. 359 (1931); *Dejonge v. Oregon*, 299 U.S. 353 (1937); *Hague v. C.I.O.*, 307 U.S. 396 (1939); *Schneider v. Irvington*, 308 U.S. 147 (1939); see also 295 U.S. 441, 448 (1935).

39 For a box score on the period 1943-49, see Mendelson, "Clear and Present Danger—From Schenck to Dennis," *Columbia Law Review*, vol. 52 (1952), p. 314.

40 *West Virginia Board of Education v. Barnette*, 319 U.S. 624 (1943).

41 *Taylor v. Mississippi*, 319 U.S. 583 (1943).

42 310 U.S. 88 (1940).

43 301 U.S. 242 (1937).

44 310 U.S. 106 (1940).

45 330 U.S. 75 (1947).

46 *Thomas v. Collins*, 323 U.S. 516, 530 (1945); *Pennekamp v. Florida*, 328 U.S. 331, 334 (1946); *Bridges v. California*, 314 U.S. 252 (1941); *West Virginia Board of Education v. Barnette* ("Second Flag Salute Case"), 319 U.S. 624, 639 (1943); *Craig v. Harney*, 331 U.S. 367 (1947); *Schneiderman v. United States*, 320 U.S. 118 (1943); *Giboney v. Empire Storage Co.*, 336 U.S. 490 (1949).

47 *United States v. Carolene Products Co.*, 304 U.S. 144 (1938). See especially *Jones v. Opelika*, 316 U.S. 584, 600 (dissent).

48 323 U.S. 516, 529-30 (1945).

49 319 U.S. 583 (1943).

50 314 U.S. 252 (1941).

51 322 U.S. 680 (1944).

52 *Schneider v. State*, 308 U.S. 147, 162 (1939).

53 See *Thornhill v. Alabama*, 310 U.S. 88 (1940); *Cox v. New Hampshire*, 312 U.S. 569 (1947); *Saia v. New York*, 334 U.S. 558 (1948); *Cole v. Arkansas*, 338 U.S. 345 (1949).

54 The principal case is *Chaplinsky v. New Hampshire*, 315 U.S. 568 (1942). See also *Cantwell v. Connecticut*, 310 U.S. 296, 309, 310 (1940); *Douglas v. Jeannette*, 319 U.S. 157, 180 (1943) (concurrence). {74}

55 *Miversville School District v. Gobitis*, 310 U.S. 586 (1940).

56 336 U.S. 77 (1949).

57 314 U.S. 252, 279 (1941).

58 *Id.* at 283.

59 *West Virginia Board of Education v. Barnette*, 319 U.S. 624, 663 (1943).

60 *Bridges v. Wixon*, 326 U.S. 135 (1945) (concurring in Stone's dissent).

61 328 U.S. 331, 352-53 (1946).

62 331 U.S. 367, 391 (1947).

63 *Pennekamp v. Florida*, 328 U.S. 331, 334, 353 (1946); Second Flag Salute Case, 319 U.S. 624, 663 (1943).

64 "This is a clash of rights, not the clash of wrongs. . . . For resolving such clash we have no calculus. . . . We are not the primary resolver of the clash . . . , we [should not] exercise our judicial power unduly and as though we ourselves were legislators by holding with too tight a rein the organs of popular government. . . . And since men equally devoted to the vital importance of freedom of speech may fairly differ in an estimate of the danger in a particular case, the field in which a State may exercise its judgment is, necessarily, a wide one." Letter from Frankfurter to Stone, May 27, 1940, given in full in Alpheus T. Mason, *Security Through Freedom* (Ithaca, 1955), pp. 217-20.

65 *Minersville School District v. Gobitis*, 310 U.S. 586, 595 (1940).

66 *Chaplinsky v. New Hampshire*, 315 U.S. 568, 572 (1942). Cf. *Winters v. New York*, 333 U.S. 507, 510 (1947). The Court may have taken its cue here from Professor Chafee. See *Freedom of Speech* (New York, 1920, 1941), pp. 149-50.

67 337 U.S. 1 (1949).

68 340 U.S. 315 (1951).

69 339 U.S. 382 (1950).

70 *Id.* at 397.

71 341 U.S. 494 (1951).

72 *Id.* at 512.

73 *United States v. Dennis*, 183 F.2d 201, 212 (2d Cir. 1950).

74 341 U.S. 494, 509 (1951).

75 *Commonwealth v. Kennedy*, 48 N.E. 770, 771 (1897). The crime was attempt to poison. See also *The Common Law*, pp. 68-71.

76 *Dennis v. United States*, 341 U.S. 494, 504, 525 (1951).

77 *Id.* at 545.

78 *Chaplinsky v. New Hampshire*, 315 U.S. 568 (1942); *Beauharnais v. Illinois*, 343 U.S. 250, 267 (1952); *Roth v. United States*, 354 U.S. 476 (1957).

79 Walter Berns, *Freedom, Virtue and the First Amendment* (Baton Rouge, 1957), p. 206.

80 Since the Supreme Court accepted the lower court's construction of the Smith Act, requiring not simply advocacy of overthrow but advocacy of a rule or principle of action designed to bring about overthrow as speedily as circumstances would permit, and assumed that the evidence supported the findings in the lower court that the individuals charged had personally undertaken such advocacy, and professed to find a clear and probable danger, *Dennis* does not constitute a conviction for belief. (The judges' language was frequently that of intent, but we have already noted the rather confusing tendency to deal with clear-and-present-danger in intent terms.)

81 See *Dennis v. United States*, 341 U.S. 494, 504, 581 (1951) (dissent). {75}

82 *Yates v. United States*, 354 U.S. 298 (1957).

83 *Id.* at 321-22.

84 343 U.S. 250 (1952).

85 367 U.S. 203 (1961).

86 ". . . the membership clause . . . does not cut deeper into the freedom of association than is necessary to deal with 'the substantive evils that Congress has a right to prevent'" (citing *Schenck v. United States*). 367 U.S. 203, 229 (1961).

87 350 U.S. 422 (1956).

88 370 U.S. 375 (1962).

89 360 U.S.684 (1959).

90 *Id.* at 689.

91 372 U.S. 229 (1963).

92 *Id.* at 236.

93 *Id.* at 237.

94 *Id.* at 237-38.

95 362 U.S. 199 (1960).

96 85 S. Ct. 453 (1965).

97 *Gibson v. Florida Legislative Investigating Comm.*, 372 U.S. 539 (1963); *Bates v. Little Rock*, 361 U.S. 516 (1960).

Chapter Three

BALANCING OF INTERESTS

Balancing: A Tactical History

THIS CHAPTER WILL be devoted to the growth of the balancing standard as a substitute for the clear-and-present-danger rule and to the current debate between balancers and "absolutists." I have chosen to present the evolution of the balancing doctrine in roughly chronological fashion and in parallel to the development of the clear-and-present-danger rule sketched in the last chapter. The polemic setting in which the balancing doctrine arose in Supreme Court opinions, and its development, not as an independent doctrine, but as a weapon for attacking clear-and-present-danger, are the keys to understanding its logic and function in the great debate over the Supreme Court and the First Amendment.

The argument of those who favor this balancing approach is roughly as follows. Speech cases do not involve simply the rights of the offending speaker. Typically they present a clash of several rights, or a conflict between individual rights and necessary functions of government. For instance, the Jehovah's Witnesses cases concern not only the right of the Witnesses to speak, but also the rights of other citizens to the privacy of their homes or the peaceful enjoyment of public parks and thoroughfares. And the Communist cases are not simply a matter of limiting the speech of Mr. Dennis et al., but also of the right, indeed the duty, of the government to defend the nation against Soviet aggression. The clear-and-present-danger formula forces the Court to focus on the offending speech, and, as a result, the Justices tend to discount the equally important rights and duties on which that speech may infringe. Thus, the formula leads to posing constitutional questions with a false simplicity and favors speech, particularly of the activist or proselytizing variety, over other constitutionally protected interests. To arrive at realistic constitutional judgments in free speech cases the courts should, therefore, abandon the false emphasis of the clear-and-present-danger rule and impartially assess all the competing claims presented in a given case. Only when the damage to free speech outweighs the advantages to society and the protection to other individual rights afforded by the statute at issue, should it be held unconstitutional. {77}

It would, however, be an oversimplification to view the clear-and-present-danger and balancing formulas purely as rivals. They have, since the inception of the clear-and-present-danger standard, been closely intertwined.[1] To be sure, whether a danger was "clear" or "present" might be determined by a relatively simple examination of the immediate facts of the case, but whether the evil was "serious" and "substantive," or indeed even an evil, requires the broadest assessment of social interests. Certainly when Justice Brandeis announced that "The fact that speech likely to result in some violence or destruction of property is not enough to justify its suppression,"[2] he is, in fact, weighing the relative importance to society of the various interests which the law seeks to protect.

The balancing technique frequently appears in the cases in which the Roosevelt Court reintroduced the clear-and-present-danger test and subscribed to the preferred position doctrine. For instance, in 1939 Justice Roberts, speaking for a nearly unanimous Court, struck down a regulation of speech on the basis of the Court's duty "to weigh the circumstances and to appraise the substantiality of the reasons advanced in support of the regulation." Here the balancing formula was used in support of the preferred position doctrine, for it followed the declaration that "Mere legislative preferences . . . may well support regulation directed at other personal activities, but be insufficient to justify such as diminishes the exercise of rights so vital to the maintenance of democratic institutions."[3]

Throughout the heyday of the clear-and-present-danger and preferred position doctrines, the language of balancing, weighing, or accommodating interests was employed as an integral part of the libertarian position. The libertarians found balancing quite in harmony with preferred position since they meant that, when balancing interests, speech was to be given an especially heavy weight because of its central function in the preservation of the democratic process. Balancing and clear-and-present-danger were also looked upon as compatible. If there were no clear and present danger of a substantive evil, then the state's interest in regulation could not be sufficiently strong to outweigh the interest in speech.[4] In short, the proponents of clear-and-present-danger and preferred position were perfectly willing to balance interests as long as it was understood in advance that freedom of speech was an especially important interest, and that the state's interest in suppression only became weighty enough to justify suppression when the speech clearly and immediately threatened actual damage to other fundamental interests of society. This might be called balancing *within* the clear-and-present-danger {78} and preferred position approaches. While the combination of balancing with clear-and-present-danger and preferred position usually meant a clear victory for the speech interest, occasionally even some of the libertarians found the weight to fall on the other side.[5]

The opponents of the libertarians not unnaturally attempted to turn the Court toward balancing *instead of* clear-and-present-danger and preferred position. Two early cases involving door to door canvassers use balancing language without reference to preferred position and clear-and-present-danger,[6] but both deal in effect with time, place, and manner ordinances where the rule of reasonableness, rather than clear-and-present-danger, has generally been employed. *Chaplinsky v. New Hampshire*[7] in 1942 more clearly shows an early use of balancing as an anti-clear-and-present-danger device. Finding that the "fighting words" Chaplinsky used were of such slight social value as to be outweighed by the social interest in order and morality, the Court excluded them altogether from First Amendment—and thus from danger rule—protection. Finally, in *United Public Workers v. Mitchell*[8] and *Kovacs v. Cooper*,[9] balancing language was used to decide against the speech interest and seemed to be introduced as a general doctrinal alternative to clear-and-present-danger. The latter, however, was a time, place, and manner case, so it can hardly be used as evidence of the replacement of clear-and-present-danger by balancing since clear-and-present-danger had never fully replaced the rule of reason in this area.

By the end of the decade of the forties then, balancing language had occasionally been used in the speech cases, but almost exclusively as an adjunct to, and in harmony with, the preferred position and clear-and-present-danger rules. With the single exception of *United Public Workers v. Mitchell*, which involved regulating the political activities of civil servants, balancing had been used independently of clear-and-present-danger only in connection with time, place, and manner regulations where it reflected the continued use of the reasonableness standard, rather than a replacement of clear-and-present-danger and preferred position.

In 1951, however, a cluster of cases involving speech in public places provided Justice Frankfurter with an opportunity to proclaim balancing as the new champion which could drive clear-and-present-danger and preferred position, so offensive to his judicial modesty, from the field. In a single concurring opinion dealing with three cases, and labeled *Kunz v. New York*,[10] he pointed out that "the courts have for years grappled with claims of the right to disseminate ideas in public places as against claims of an effective power in government to keep the peace {79} and to protect other interests of a civilized community," and that "adjustment of the inevitable conflict . . . is a problem as persistent as it is perplexing."[11] After a survey of the cases, Justice Frankfurter finds balancing elements in eighteen. He concludes that "While the Court has emphasized the importance of 'free speech,' it has recognized that 'free speech' is not in itself a touchstone. The Constitution is not unmindful of other important interests, such as public order, if free expression of ideas is not found to be the overbalancing considerations."[12] Behind the calculated ambiguity of this final sentence, of course, lies Frankfurter's distaste for and wry acknowledgment of the frequent close coupling of preferred position with the balancing doctrine.

But most of the cases which he examines do not specifically use balancing language, and, in fact, Frankfurter seems to be reading his own sentiments into them. Indeed, he is undoubtedly aware of the lack of support for his thesis in the actual decisions, since he feels compelled to make the excuse that "More important than the phrasing of the opinions are the questions on which the decisions appear to have turned."[13] What his analysis seems to come down to is that there are a large number of cases in which Justice Frankfurter would have liked to use a balancing formula even if the Court didn't.

The very opinion in which he presents his survey illustrates the point, for it uses balancing as a basis for concurring in two cases where the majority relied on prior restraint and in one where all the Justices except Frankfurter found the clear-and-present-danger issue crucial. And those parts of his own opinion dealing with the specific cases at issue rest on prior restraint, vagueness, and incitement to riot findings, without systematic presentation of the relative weights to be assigned the interests involved. In short, balancing never specifically enters any of the three cases either in the majority or concurring opinions. It actually appears only in Justice Frankfurter's general essay attached to his opinion. It can only be concluded that Justice Frankfurter in his "cruise of the timber" has found no very clear trail.

Nor did Justice Frankfurter do much brush clearing the following year in his *Beauharnais* opinion, where he excluded group libel from First Amendment protection because it was of such slight social value as to be clearly outweighed by the social interest in order and morality.[14] We can be sure that Frankfurter dislikes the clear-and-present-danger test and finds various balancing techniques convenient for avoiding it, but very little light is shed on the balancing process itself.

Nevertheless in *American Communications Association v. Douds*[15] in 1950 the modest wing of the Court did firmly establish balancing as a {80} rival to clear-and-present-danger. In an opinion which is practically a catalogue of means to avoid the clear-and-present-danger test, balancing plays a prominent part. "When the effect of a statute or ordinance upon the exercise of First Amendment freedoms is relatively small and the public interest to be protected is substantial, it is obvious that a rigid test requiring a showing of imminent danger to the security of the nation is an absurdity."[16] This seems plainly enough a substitution of balancing for clear-and-present-danger, but the Chief Justice seems reluctant to take such a clear-cut position. He argues that "not the relative certainty that evil conduct will result from speech in the immediate future, but the extent and gravity of the substantive evil must be measured by the 'test' laid down in the *Schenck* case."[17] This is, of course, to turn the Holmes-Brandeis rationale on its head. Originally clear-and- present-danger was the general rule and the balancing process was used as a subordinate part of that rule to determine whether the evil was sufficiently serious. Now the balancing formula is the general rule and the clear-and-present-danger test is used as a subordinate part of that test to determine whether the evil is sufficiently serious. When it is remembered that it is not some other civil right but commerce regulation which weighs more heavily than freedom of speech and belief in this instance, the potential conflict between the clear-and-present-danger and preferred position doctrines and the balancing technique is even more striking.

Since *Douds* served in many ways as a dress rehearsal for *Dennis v. United States*,[18] it is hardly surprising that balancing shows up again in the latter case as a device for avoiding the clear-and-present-danger rule. Chief Justice Vinson picked up Judge Hand's suggestion that the case involved "a comparison between interests which are to be appraised qualitatively"[19] and strengthened it to read "the societal value of free speech must on occasion, be subordinated to other values and considerations."[20] But more important, the Court adopted Judge Hand's substitute for the clear-and-present-danger rule: "Whether the gravity of the 'evil,' discounted by its improbability, justifies such invasion of free speech as is necessary to avoid the danger." It is, as usual, rather difficult to determine just what is being balanced in this formula. Professor Corwin finds it a weighing of "the substantive good protected by a statute against the 'clear and present danger' requirement."[21] Whether this interpretation or some other is chosen, it is clear that the message of *Dennis* is that Congress may pass laws abridging freedom of speech when the interests it seeks to protect outweigh the interest in free speech.

Perhaps the cause of the confusion lies in the purpose for which the balancing standard was introduced. We have already noted that Justice {81} Holmes' early clear-and-present-danger opinions[22] represented a movement from the general to the particular. The relatively precise demands of the clear-and-present-danger rule forced the Court to something more than the bad tendency test's vague laments over the security of the nation. Justice Frankfurter's concurrence puts his finger on the advantage offered by the balancing standard to those Justices who wished to uphold the *Dennis* convictions. "The demands of free speech in a democratic society as well as the interest in national security are better served by candid and informed weighing of the competing interests, within the confines of the judicial process, than by announcing dogmas too inflexible for the non-Euclidian problems to be solved."[23] In other words, the balancing formula allowed the Court to avoid the burdens placed upon it by the clear-and-present-danger rule, and to resort to a vague, weighing-of-interests rhetoric which, particularly in view of the extremely great weight which may be assigned to national security, allowed it a rationale for upholding any conviction not completely inconsistent with First Amendment demands.

It was, of course, *Dennis* which drove the clear-and-present-danger rule into limbo, with the balancing doctrine tending to replace it, particularly in cases involving subversives. The decision in *Barenblatt v. United States*[24] in 1959 is the high point of this development, and its balancing away of the First Amendment rights of alleged subversives was thereafter cited as a ritualistic incantation whenever leftists proffered First Amendment claims.[25] It was in the course of these opinions, in which the balance between national security and the individual's interest in a particular bit of speech nearly always sent the subversive to jail, that Justices Black and Douglas first attacked balancing as an improper substitute for clear-and-present-danger, and then propounded—as a counter to balancing—various doctrines of the "absolute" inviolability of the First Amendment.[26]

Balancing techniques were also used to add another form of speech, obscenity, to the others excluded from First Amendment protection altogether.[27] Here, as in *Beauharnais*, the form of speech is said to bear so little weight of social interest that its infringement is not balanced against First Amendment protections, but balanced right out of the First Amendment altogether. In the time, place, and manner areas, balancing continued its earlier role.[28]

For a time it seemed that balancing would become the unchallenged master formula for First Amendment cases. In the 1960 term balancing language was used in two cases[29] to strip alleged or admitted Communists of their First Amendment protections, and these decisions were {82} linked to a third which upheld the membership provisions of the Smith Act against First Amendment claims.[30] At the same time as supposed subversives were having their speech rights balanced away, however, another line of balancing opinions was developing. Several southern states had responded to the activities of the NAACP by seeking to force them to reveal their membership lists. In *N.A.A.C.P. v. Alabama*[31] and *Bates v. Little Rock*,[32] the Court used balancing language to protect the NAACP. Neither, however, is quite a balancing of interests case. Alabama had used its interest in regulating foreign corporations as a pretext for exposure. Little Rock had invoked its interest in taxation. In both cases the Court, after saying it was prepared to balance First Amendment claims against such interests, found that the actual regulations involved bore no reasonable relation to the interest claimed by the state. Thus the Court did not actually do any fine balancing of individual versus governmental interests. It simply found that there was nothing to put on the government side of the scale, so that the interests of the NAACP obviously outweighed those of the government.

Then in *Gibson v. Florida*,[33] in which the Court protected the NAACP from the same kind of exposure, but this time by an investigating committee, and in *N.A.A.C.P. v. Button*,[34] which protected the litigational activities of the organization from state interference, a new balancing interpretation came to maturity. Relying heavily on *N.A.A.C.P. v. Alabama* and *Bates*, the Court held that in order to win the balance the state must have "a subordinating interest which is compelling," for "only a compelling state interest in the regulation of a subject within the State's constitutional power to regulate can justify limiting First Amendment freedoms."[35] In neither *Gibson* nor *Button* could the Court find an "overriding and compelling state interest."[36]

The Court was somewhat embarrassed in the *N.A.A.C.P. v. Alabama* and *Bates* opinions by the precedential impact of an earlier case in which it had upheld a New York statute aimed at the KKK that had required the public filing of membership lists.[37] The majority rather feebly distinguished that case, but was not willing to overrule it. Subsequent to *Bates* the Court approved the exposure provisions of national statutes directed against the Communist Party. At the time it was widely felt that the Court was using the wonderfully arbitrary capacities of the balancing technique to bestow First Amendment rights on those organizations it liked and to withhold them from those it didn't.

Since *Button* and *Gibson* also concern the NAACP, these later cases may also be viewed as simply part of a Court campaign to protect the NAACP in its southern struggle. However, the language of "compelling interests" {83} and the fact that *Gibson* announces that not only the NAACP but all "groups which themselves are neither engaged in subversive or other illegal or improper activities, nor demonstrated to have any substantial connections with such activities are to be protected in their rights of free and private association" suggest otherwise. The emphasis on a need for overriding and compelling state interests before the balance will fall in its favor suggests something like a return to the old balancing-cum-preferred position technique that coexisted with the clear-and-present-danger rule in the early forties. For how much difference is there between saying that speech interests will be given special weight and saying that unless the state's interests are especially weighty they cannot overbalance speech? Moreover *Gibson*, while vague, comes very close to saying that any organization that is not allegedly subversive can successfully assert First Amendment rights to private association against the legislative committee's interest in discovering its membership and affairs. It is significant that in all these cases about the only overriding state interest the Court can envision is the fight against Communism. It may then be that the *N.A.A.C.P. v. Alabama-Bates-Gibson-Button* line, combined with the *Barenblatt-Subversive Activities Control Board* line, represent not a special exemption for the NAACP, or even an arbitrary choice of which organizations the Court will protect, but a return to the Court's older defense of speech, but with a special exception for allegedly Communist groups. In short, the NAACP cases may not mean that the NAACP gets more protection than other groups but only that the Communists get less.

It is significant that *Gibson* and *Button* occurred at about the same time that the Court was reintroducing the clear-and-present-danger rule in *Wood v. Georgia*. Just as I have argued that *Yates* preserves the heart of the danger rule but excepts the Communist Party from its complete protection, so *Gibson* and *Button* may be the first sign that the Court is reviving preferred position but excepting Communist groups from its protection. In any event, balancing of the Frankfurter variety has not turned out to be the dominant general formula for free speech cases that it once appeared to be becoming.

Balancing: What Is It?

It would be excessively polite to say that the techniques of balancing employed in the balancing cases were confused. Rather, they were deliberately misleading. The balancing of interests approach is basically derived from Roscoe Pound's theories of social engineering. Pound has insisted that his structure of public, social, and individual interests are all, {84} in fact, individual interests looked at from different points of view for purposes of clarity. Therefore, in order to make the system work properly, it is essential that when interests are balanced, all claims must be translated into the same level and carefully labeled. Thus, a social interest may not be balanced against an individual interest, but only against another social interest.[38] The Supreme Court has so consistently ignored this philosophical and common sense necessity that all of its "balancing" is deprived of intellectual validity.

For instance in *Barenblatt*, which concerned the refusal of a witness before a Congressional committee to answer questions concerning his political activities, the general interest of society in a fully informed lawmaking body was not balanced against the general interest of society in maintaining the privacy of association, nor was Congress' particular need to know the answer to the particular question asked balanced against the particular interest of the citizen in maintaining the privacy of the particular piece of political activity involved. Instead, the whole interest in national security goes on one side of the scale and the particular interest of the particular individual in not answering the particular question goes on the other. Similarly, the decisions in *Dennis*, both at the Circuit and Supreme Court levels, in discounting probability by danger do not deal with the probability that the particular defendants by their particular speeches will cause any particular danger to this particular country. Instead, the decisions speak in the broadest generalities of the dangers of international Communism and balances them against the specific encroachments on the individual contained in the Smith Act. When the fall of Czechoslovakia is balanced against Mr. Dennis' interest in teaching the convolutions of Marxism-Leninism, the issue is never in doubt.

This argument occasionally verges on the most dangerous of all possible lines of reasoning. Particularly if the discounting formulas used in *Douds* and *Dennis* are employed, the weight given national security may be so great as to wreck the scales entirely, for it is always tempting to argue in defense of any repression that the preservation of our state is the fundamental prerequisite for all our liberties. The balance is then struck between the continuation of all our liberties and the "minor" or "temporary" invasion of just one of them. Comment on the potential results of such rationales hardly seems necessary.

Still another variant of this approach is balancing plus exclusion. In the instances of group libel and obscenity, we first weigh the quality (content) of the speech. If it is very light weight—if there is almost no social interest in it—it is excluded from First Amendment protection {85} altogether. This preliminary weighing cum exclusion means that certain speech, which is considered too light, loses without even getting on the First Amendment scale—that is, without any requirement that any weight at all be found for the other side. This might not seem too important if only obscenity were involved. But there have also been suggestions that the speech of Communists, for instance, is very low on our scale of values. When the Court says—as it frequently does—that subversive speech is not protected by the First Amendment, we can logically read the Court as saying: we have in the past found on balance that the need for suppressing subversion outweighed the resulting violations of the First Amendment. But it might also mean that subversive speech in general is so "light" a category that it is not entitled to First Amendment protection. There is a considerable difference between saying that X is protected by the First Amendment, but its protection can on occasion be invaded if, on balance, circumstances warrant, and saying X is not entitled to First Amendment protection at all because on balance it is a kind of speech undeserving of protection. This prebalancing with exclusion is the logical extremity of anti-libertarian balancing. By asserting the general social disinterest in a general category of speech, the particular speech to be punished loses automatically if shoved into that category. And it loses without the need of putting anything in particular or general on the pro-infringement side of the scale.

Not that all the scale tampering is on one side. When balancing is combined with preferred position, as it originally was, the whole weight of the entire national interest in freedom of speech tends to be brought down against the single, particular, and often local interest embodied in the offending statute. Justice Warren in *Watkins v. United States*,[39] dealing with the same problem of recalcitrant witnesses raised in *Barenblatt*, attempted to strike a balance between the need for the "particular interrogation and the right of citizens to carry on their affairs free from unnecessary government interference."[40] The Chief Justice did not balance the need for the particular interrogation against the actual damage to a particular exercise of a specific right of a particular person. He in fact balanced a particular, and therefore rather insignificant, governmental demand against the most general, and therefore most weighty, interests he could delineate. In a companion case[41] Justice Frankfurter adopted similar tactics in balancing the state's need to ask a particular person certain specific questions against broadly conceived interests in academic freedom and free political activity.

Unfortunately, about the only clear things about balancing are the techniques for putting the judicial thumb on the scale. Although courts {86} and commentators speak much of balancing, clarity about its meaning does not come from the frequent repetition of the term. Does "balancing" or "weighing of interests" mean that the Court will simply determine which group or interest is politically the most powerful and award it the decision? Justice Holmes seemed to have been close to this view.[42] But the balancing process is sometimes spoken of as occurring between "social," "society's," or the "community's" interests, and even as being a "qualitative" balance. These expressions certainly imply that something other than a simple weighing of group political strengths is involved. They imply some value or goal or set of goals, i.e., "society's" goals, by which various individual or group claims can be measured. But no court has stated what actual criteria are to be employed.

Nor does balancing seem to imply to all its supporters an examination of various group interests in a multi-group society, for the balance is frequently formulated as that between the interest of the state and that of the individual. If political power were the only criterion involved in this sort of process, the results would always be a foregone conclusion. Obviously something different is intended, for frequently it is the individual's right, not his power, which is thrown into the scales. The point is, however, that if it is not relative political power that provides the criterion for balancing, just what does?

A review of the Supreme Court's balancing cases does not give us a very clear picture of what balancing is, but I think it does give us a quite clear picture of what balancing is for. That wing of the Court dissatisfied with the judicial activism implied by the clear-and-present-danger rule engaged in a frantic search for some means of displacing the rule. They found that the notion of balancing, which had originally been used as part of the clear-and-present-danger and preferred position combination, could be developed as an alternative general standard. Such a standard would destroy all the definite qualities of the earlier doctrines that had spurred the Court into protecting the First Amendment. It did so by creating a criterion of constitutionality so vague and so permissive that the Court would not feel any compulsion to intervene. When balancing seemed to replace clear-and-present-danger in the period beginning with *Douds* and *Dennis*, the now depleted clear-and-present-danger forces gradually went over to the position that absolutely no infringement on freedom of speech was ever permissible, in an effort to counter the notion that any infringement on speech might on balance be allowable. The history of the development of both the balancing and absolutist positions very strongly indicates that both doctrines were invented for purely tactical use, and that both hinge on role of the Court {87} not freedom of speech problems. Any assessment of the current debate between absolutists and balancers, or balancers and non-balancers, which does not keep clearly in mind the polemical origins of the doctrines is likely to make the very grave error of taking them seriously instead of viewing them in their true light as the superficial ploys of the deeper struggle between activist and modest tendencies on the Court.

Balancers v. Absolutists

Indeed, the whole debate over the jurisprudential acceptability of balancing of interests versus absolute rights is little more than a facade behind which role of the Court problems lurk.[43] I tried to show earlier that the judicially modest remain uneasily confronted by an ultimate dilemma. On the one hand, their political philosophy demands that they give up judicial review as undemocratic. On the other, they cannot quite bring themselves to the outright and total rejection of this traditionally and popularly sanctioned institution. It is doubtful that Justice Black has so far forgotten the history of legal philosophy as to really insist that the concept of an absolute right to freedom of speech, unlimited even by notions of reciprocity, is viable. His trumpeting of absolutes is, in fact, designed to force the modest on to one of the horns of their dilemma. If the First Amendment has any definite content, then the modest must either acknowledge that they are abandoning review or enforce that content when Congress does make a law abridging freedom of speech.

This tactical function of the call for absolutes can be seen most clearly in examining the usefulness of "balancing" to the modest. In order to live with their dilemma, the modest must invent a doctrinal stance which will allow them to maintain lip service to judicial review without risking any clash with our gloriously democratic Congress. Balancing fits the bill perfectly.[44] In saying that First Amendment rights may be infringed only when other social interests outweigh the interests in freedom of speech, the modest are continuing to say that the First Amendment does exist as a limitation on Congress, and that the Court is still applying First Amendment standards to Congressional legislation. Thus judicial review is saved. But by using such a vague and (in the politest terminology I can muster) "flexible" First Amendment standard, the modest insure that in nearly every given case, they can approve of Congress' actions.

However, when the going gets rough, when even with a balancing standard to dull their sensitivities to the First Amendment, the modest find themselves confronted by a Congressional statute that cannot be {88} weighed into legitimacy even by juggling the scales, the final falsity of balancing appears. For the very democratic philosophy upon which modesty rests requires that the primary balancing of competing social interests be done in the democratic, legislative chamber, not in the autocratic courtroom. Thus, when any crucial question of balancing arises the modest are allowed, indeed compelled, to yield to legislative judgment. This ultimate surrender has been a constant theme of Justice Frankfurter and his supporters.

> We are not exercising any independent judgment; we are sitting in judgment upon the judgment of the legislature. . . . We are not the primary resolver of the clash [of rights].[45]

> . . . the demands of free speech in a democratic society as well as the interest in national security are better served by candid and informed weighing of the competing interests, within the confines of the judicial process than by announcing dogmas. . . . Primary responsibility for adjusting the interests which compete in the situation before us of necessity belongs to the Congress. . . . How best to reconcile competing interests is the business of legislatures, and the balance they strike is a judgment not to be displaced by ours, but to be respected unless outside the pale of fair judgment. Free speech cases are not an exception to the principle that we are not legislators. . . . It is not for us to decide how we would adjust the

clash of interests which this case presents were the primary responsibility for reconciling it ours.[46]

Against the impediments which particular governmental regulation causes to entire freedom of individual action, there must be
weighed the value to the public of the ends which the regulation
may achieve. . . . Congress itself has expressed . . . both what those
interests are and what, in its view, threatens them. . . . It is not for
the courts to reexamine the validity of these legislative findings
and reject them. . . . We certainly cannot dismiss them as un-
founded or irrational imaginings. . . . The legislative judgment as
to how that threat may best be met consistently with the safe-
guarding of personal freedom is not to be set aside merely because
the judgment of judges would, in the first instance, have chosen
other methods.[47]

The choice of balancing as the Court's First Amendment doctrine not
only serves to preserve the fiction of independent decision while in fact
yielding to Congress, but, where ultimate differences of decision might
appear between Court and Congress, predetermines their outcome by
choosing a decisional method which overwhelmingly favors Congress
over Court. It is as if the International Fencing Champion called out a
{89} Chess Grand Master for one winner take all contest and said, "I
challenge you—to a game of chess."

If we avoid the trap of talking about balancing in general philosophical terms and begin looking at how it actually operates in the hands of its
judicial proponents, we find that balancing is actually nothing more than
the old Holmesian rule of reasonableness, for whenever a potential conflict arises between the balance the legislature has struck and the balance
the Court might strike, great deference, verging on total submission,
must be paid to the legislative body. In the end, every legislative balance
is constitutional except those at which no reasonable man could have
arrived. It must be stressed that both Holmes' rule of reason and the
balancing of the modest, which is simply the same rule in new language,
do not require that legislation must be reasonable to be constitutional.
They require only that someone, not insane, could find some reason to
support the legislation. Since the legislature is the primary balancer, any
balance they achieve, so long as it is not totally unjustifiable, is constitutional. This Holmesian reasonableness test goes far beyond the reasonableness test used by the Court in dealing with time, place, and manner
regulations, for there the Court has traditionally struck its own independent balance, and it has been upon that balance that the ordinance has
stood or fallen.

Having reached the ultimate tie between balancing and judicial sur-render, the strikingly tactical role of the balancing doctrine is again re-vealed. The preferred position doctrine had been designed to bridge the gap between Holmes' judicial deference, embodied in his extreme version of the rule of reason, and his special activism in the First Amendment area, embodied in the clear and present danger rule. Frankfurter himself had openly acknowledged this dualism in Holmes,[48] and had been trying for years to rid the Holmesian legacy of its libertarian elements by direct-ly attacking the preferred position doctrine and thus, to use a Marxian phrase, aggravating the contradictions. Balancing in his hands is simply another way of totally excluding the libertarian elements and reempha-sizing Holmesian self-restraint as the only element in Holmes' thought worth keeping and the only way of dealing with any and all constitutional problems.

In this light too, the rare instances in which Frankfurter uses balanc-ing to find some government action unconstitutional fit neatly into the old Holmesian restraint, for Holmes' rule of reason was also designed to allow the modest to sit snugly between the horns of their dilemma. No clash with the legislature need ever occur, for what legislative act could {90} not be provided with some facade of reasonableness? On the other hand, the Court need never formally and completely give up judicial re-view, it could be maintained lurking in the background—very far in the background—to take care of that rare instance in which the legislature was seized by some aberration that no reasonable man could defend. Thus, in *Sweezy v. New Hampshire*[49] Frankfurter was dealing with a state legislature, which enjoys a somewhat lower status in the canons of self-restraint than Congress, and, more important, with the results of administrative applications of legislative directives that Frankfurter could claim were not properly anticipated by the legislature. Thus Frankfurter could avoid direct confrontation with actual legislative action by arguing, in effect, that the actions led to results that no reasonable man, including the legislators, would have desired if they could have been anticipated. Moreover, the decision is so framed that the legislature can still achieve its restrictive goals through slight alterations in administrative method. Review is thus preserved, even in the context of balancing, but only for those rare instances of almost unconscious legislative irrationality and only where no direct confrontation will occur between Court and legisla-ture over permissible goals.

The opposition to the balancers also has its eye mainly on role of the Court problems, for the opposition does not object to balancing per se, but only to what it describes as "ad hoc" balancing.[50] In general the ar-gument runs that freedom of speech is not absolute in the sense that all speech enjoys absolute immunity from government regulation. Some speech enjoys First Amendment protection. Other speech does not. But those kinds of speech that do fall under First Amendment protection are absolutely protected so that they may not be abridged out of consideration for countervailing social considerations. The problem then is to determine what categories of speech are. protected by the First Amendment and, therefore, absolutely protected. It is in this process of defining or delimiting the scope of the First Amendment that balancing—that is, the harmonizing of freedom of speech with other individual and social interests—should take place. For instance, pure political discourse surely falls within the scope of the First Amendment but, on balance, the Court may decide that speech creating a clear and present danger of a substantive evil, etc., does not.

The rejection of ad hoc balancing—balancing in the context of each individual case—in favor of balancing at the stage of defining the scope of the First Amendment has several tactical advantages for the opponents of balancing cum modesty. First, such a process would force the Court into declaring in advance that certain varieties of speech fall within the {91} protection of the First Amendment. A Court that admitted in one case that a certain kind of speech was included in freedom of speech would then be directly confronted with its earlier decision in later cases dealing with the same kind of speech. If balancing can occur only in deciding whether a given kind of speech is protected in general, then the Justices would lose the ability to change the weights on the scale in each particular case in order to defer to Congress in each case no matter what the Court's general declarations in previous cases.

More important, the demand for balancing at the "defining" stage rather than the balancing of particular factors in each case is an attempt to break out of the intellectually fraudulent way the Court has generally played the balancing game by forcing the Court to always balance the general against the general. If we are trying to "define" what forms of speech are included in freedom of speech, not for this case and this case only, but as a general constitutional principle, then obviously we must weigh the broadest and most general social interests in freedom of speech against other general social interests. The Court will not be permitted to balance the particular interest of one particular individual in one particular speech against the quest for national security, the American Way of Life, and two sports cars in every garage.

Of course, this general interest v. general interest balancing would almost inevitably lead right back to the clear-and-present-danger rule and other libertarian doctrines. Expressed as general interests, free speech and the First Amendment still have such psychological impact that few judges would be willing to balance them away in favor of supposedly greater goods, except where the speech was so closely brigaded with action as to constitute actual incitement to crime. Ad hoc balancing has proven so satisfactory to anti-libertarians precisely because they could portray each individual infringement on speech not as a subordination of the general principle of freedom of speech to some other principle, but as a tiny, little, temporary interruption of the speech of a few people to avoid a tremendous blow to the interests of mother, country, and apple pie. It is precisely because they have not had to openly say "The First Amendment means Congress shall make no law abridging freedom of speech except when it thinks such a law would be good for us," that they have been able to make the Amendment mean exactly that in case by case practice. The call for absolutes, or balancing at the stage of defining, is designed to force the modest into the open and onto ground where they could hardly win a victory.

Finally, the call for defining the scope of the First Amendment, and for providing complete protection within that scope rather than balancing {92} in every case, is obviously designed to destroy the most crucial ploy of the modest balancers who define the decisional process in such a way as to insure the primacy of Congress. If the Court must finally balance social interests in every case, then the Court must finally defer to Congress in every case since legislatures are the primary balancers of interests in our political system. If the Court is defining the scope of a Constitutional provision and seeking to harmonize it with other constitutional provisions, then it is doing a task in which it is traditionally competent and in which it is supposedly the final authority. Professor Charles Fried presents an interesting variant of this argument when, relying on one of the guardians of modesty, Learned Hand, he says that the task of the Supreme Court is to maintain for every part of the political system the role assigned it by the Constitution. The First Amendment constitutionally assigns the role of deciding what to say and not to say to the individual. In defining the scope of the First Amendment, the Supreme Court is, therefore, not encroaching on Congress, but playing its own constitutionally assigned role of patrolling the boundaries established by the Constitution between the various segments of our policy.[51]

These arguments are, of course, simply restatements of the old "The Constitution is law and the Court has a right to interpret law" ploy. And they are made in response to the other old ploy, "The Constitution is policy and the Congress must make policy," for the modest position on the need for balancing and the primacy of Congress in balancing is nothing more than this.

The same translation of the old argument over modesty occurs when the balancers say that the First Amendment has no fixed meaning and the absolutists claim that "Congress shall make no law" must mean what it says, or put another way, that the First Amendment has already done our balancing for us and found that speech outweighs everything else. Professor Mendelson has noted that the anti-balancers repeatedly emphasize "Congress shall make no law," which has a very simple and open meaning, while neglecting "abridging freedom of speech,"[52] for "abridging" and particularly "freedom" have no such simple and open meaning. The founders did not say abridging speech but abridging freedom of speech, and freedom, alas, is a tricky word. It leads us quickly to that morass which opens when we seek to distinguish liberty from license, and "true" freedom from slavery to the passions or abuse of freedom. Whenever freedom pops up in the course of Western philosophy true freedom is not far behind. And true freedom almost always ends up meaning doing what is good for us, not doing what we want to do. {93} This in turn usually means not doing things that somebody else, sometimes labeled God and sometimes the general will, tells us not to do.

The founding fathers were snugly settled in this tradition, and when they said freedom of speech they could not possibly have meant that all individuals had the unlimited right to say absolutely anything they pleased whenever they pleased. The literal words of the First Amendment do not, as the absolutists sometimes suggest, solve the old philosophical debate by plumping for a definition of freedom of speech as the total liberty of every individual speaker from outside limitation. Indeed, the First Amendment does not define freedom at all and, in failing to do so, simply incorporates the old debate over the meaning of freedom into the Constitution itself. In the light of that old debate, which is still at the unresolved core of political philosophy, or the absence of political philosophy, the First Amendment does not deliver the absolutely clear condemnation of government limitations on speech that a casual reading might suggest.

Indeed, Professor Levy tells us, after rigorous examination of the historical evidence, that all the founders wished to do concretely was to incorporate Blackstone's notions of freedom of speech into the Constitution.[53] For Blackstone freedom of speech meant freedom from prior restraint—that is, freedom from censorship before publication—but certainly not the abolition of subsequent punishment through the laws condemning libelous or seditious utterances.

In the end, however, Levy's researches are not going to solve our problems for us. First of all, the founders' intentions are not sufficiently uniform. Indeed, it would be surprising if they were, considering the ambiguous tradition out of which they arose. Moreover, if their intentions are not perfectly clear, the intentions of the original ratifiers are even less clear. No simple, clear command can be drawn from the history of the First Amendment. Secondly, even if the historical evidence were clearer than it is, it is irrelevant. As with all other constitutional provisions, it is not the founders' intentions but our intentions that count. It is, I think, a universally accepted truism that the glory of our Constitution is that it is a generally worded, and thus highly flexible, document that allows—indeed requires—new interpretations to fit new situations. To say that the First Amendment contains no absolutely clear historical command, or that the command it contains has since been altered or even misunderstood, is simply to say that the First Amendment is like any other provision of the Constitution. It too requires that we decide what we want it to mean. The real question is, should the Supreme {94} Court be the agency of government that decides what we want it to mean?

It is at this point that the debate between balancers and absolutists returns to the old debate over modesty. Professor Mendelson keeps insisting that the words of the First Amendment and the history of its adoption do not give us a clear command to absolutely protect freedom of speech and are, in fact, extremely vague—almost meaningless. This is important to Professor Mendelson because of his hesitancy to allow the Supreme Court to do anything. If the First Amendment did contain a clear command from the founders, then the founders could be blamed, so to speak, for Supreme Court enforcement of the Amendment. It would not be the Court but the founding fathers who commanded Congress to make no law. If the Amendment is initially vague, then in the course of its enforcement the Supreme Court will become responsible for saying what it means now. It is precisely this kind of policy-making responsibility for the Supreme Court that is repellent to the modest for reasons which have nothing to do with the First Amendment, but which hinge on the reasoning outlined in the first chapter of this book.

On the other hand, no matter how often we rake over the historical evidence to show that the First Amendment does not exactly mean what it superficially seems to say, it cannot be denied that the First Amendment is there. The modest, to be sure, wish it were not there. It will be remembered that Learned Hand, for reasons that had nothing to do with freedom of speech and everything to do with his general philosophy of judicial modesty, sought to read the whole Bill of Rights out of the Constitution as far as Supreme Court enforcement is concerned. Nevertheless, for those not in the thralls of modesty, the fact that the Amendment is there is sufficient justification for Supreme Court intervention, and the fact of its vagueness simply gives the Court a wide range of discretion in creating its meaning.

Unfortunately the anti-balancers, particularly those on the Court, have frequently responded to the historical arguments of the balancers by counter historical arguments of their own designed to show that the framers were absolutist libertarians, rather than by going to the heart of the debate over modesty that the historical arguments disguise. The result is that the two sides endlessly quote Jefferson and Madison at one another

—or rather, quote Jefferson and Madison at themselves, for the two great Virginians each wrote on both sides of the question. All this only shows what we noted earlier: that the philosophic tradition of freedom contains a series of paradoxes, and that the founders were aware of these paradoxes. Stripped of all the scholarly camouflage, in the final {95} analysis one side is arguing that the First Amendment is not mathematically clear and, therefore, the Supreme Court would have to create a meaning for it—that is, make policy—in enforcing it—something the Supreme Court should not do. The other side is arguing that the First Amendment is a part of the Constitution and like other parts of the Constitution is thus a general authorization to the Supreme Court to participate in policy-making in the course of judicial review. The clash then is not really about history or about what "no law abridging the freedom of speech" did, does, or should mean, but about policy-making by the Supreme Court—in short, the same old debate outlined in chapter one. The modest, because they are modest, emphasize the vagueness and incompleteness of the First Amendment as an excuse for Supreme Court avoidance of policy-making in the speech field. The immodest emphasize the existence of the First as an authorization for continued Supreme Court policy-making. In the end, whether one seizes on the imperative of "Congress shall make no law" or on the ambiguity of "abridging the freedom of speech" depends on attitudes toward the political role of the Supreme Court here and now, not on the logical grammar of statutory construction or on the historical grammar of the founders' intentions.

In general then, the debate over balancing is simply the old debate between judicial modesty and judicial activism, disguised in language that does little more than make the points at issue somewhat more obscure than they initially were. For this reason the balancing arguments of the modest are, for the most part, not worthy of serious independent consideration. I hope I have been able to show in the first chapter of this book that judicial modesty is a politically unrealistic position and that the dilemma of the modest—their uneasy vacillation between judicial review and judicial surrender—can be resolved by looking at the real Court in the context of real government and real politics. Once its base in judicial modesty is undermined, balancing, at least of the Frankfurter variety, falls of its own weight.

Balancing Minus Modesty

If balancing were legitimately proposed as a technique of independent judicial judgment rather than as a camouflage for judicial surrender, it might be found to have certain merits. Indeed, the anti-balancers and absolutists have sometimes come close to speaking in these terms. It would, therefore, seem worthwhile to examine balancing as a potential First Amendment doctrine for the Supreme Court, free of the freight of judicial modesty that usually accompanies such consideration. {96} Assuming that the Supreme Court is not incapacitated from making First Amendment decisions—assuming, in other words, that it is capable of independent political judgments in its sphere just as other government agencies are in theirs—is the balancing doctrine a useful tool for arriving at and justifying such decisions?

From the outset we run into certain special difficulties in using balancing in connection with the First Amendment. One of the most striking features of the balancing doctrine is that it lacks jurisprudential coherence and tends to degenerate into a rhetorical trick unless the interests on both sides of the scale are categorized at the same level of generality. We have seen that the modest have tended to inflate the antispeech interest, for instance national security, to its most general level while reducing speech to the particular interests of a single speaker. Conversely, the libertarians constantly tend to define the speech interest in the most universal terms. However, if we wish to give any substance to the First Amendment through judicial enforcement, this latter form of juggling the scales seems unavoidable. Every restriction upon or punishment of utterance not only hampers the particular person affected but also acts to intimidate other potential speakers as well. Of course, all prosecutions act as intimidations, but, while a prosecution for murder only serves to prevent other persons from performing a single, narrow classification of acts readily separable from other forms of action, speech tends to be a seamless web. Furthermore, the before-the-fact nature of much speech regulation, combined with the vagueness of criteria for controlling speech, allows a degree of hidden discrimination against persons or groups which is more difficult to perpetrate, or at least more easy to expose in other areas of law. Thus, those cases which do arise tend to be fleeting glimpses of a larger problem than the particular rights of the individual involved. The *Thornhill* rule, which allows one person to plead the rights of another when speech is involved, is the judicial recognition of this reality.

In short, those concerned with freedom of speech have tended to emphasize the paradox that, while any government action against any speech may intimidate all speakers, most individual speeches do not intimidate all government actions. The speaker who denounces the draft may be interfering with the government's interest in national security but is certainly not obstructing its urban renewal program. The government which arrests the anti-draft speaker, tends to coerce everyone who wishes to voice any kind of unpopular sentiment. Thus, it seems realistically necessary to generalize the interest in speech and to particularize the interest in repression. Does the government's interest {97} in preventing speech against the draft outweigh society's interest in being able to express and hear unpopular views? Nevertheless the answer to this question leads straight back to the general-particular game which undercuts the intellectual vitality of the balancing technique. The traditional doctrines of prior restraint, vagueness, preferred position, and clear-and-present-danger seem to be a better way of expressing the actual considerations at play than does this unbalanced balancing.

Indeed, the mixture of general and particular may be inevitable not only in the speech cases but in balancing as a whole. A court which continuously attempted to balance at the most particular level would become an unbearable busybody, far exceeding any acceptable concept of the judicial role, even those totally unburdened by the traditional notions of judicial modesty. Congressional investigations, which have been a principal arena for First Amendment balancing, illustrate this point. The problem in *Barenblatt* and its progeny was that the entire interest in national security was balanced against a particular individual's interest in remaining silent about a particular political activity. Ideally the balance might have been between the particular interest of Congress in acquiring the particular answer against the actual damage to the enjoyment of freedom of speech by Barenblatt and others that would have resulted from forcing him to answer. But such a procedure would require the Court to examine in the minutest detail the entire course of the investigation. For instance, if the committee already had the information that it requested from Barenblatt, its interest in his answer would be correspondingly reduced. If the committee had confirmation of the initial information from a second and reliable source, its interest would be still further reduced. If the information requested was extraneous to the pattern of testimony being developed by the investigation, the committee's interest would sink lower yet. Nevertheless, the Court can hardly be expected, or allowed, to undertake the kind of roving and detailed censorial supervision over Congressional committees or other government agencies that would be required in order to obtain this sort of detailed information.

The other great difficulty of balancing at the most particular level is that it even further exaggerates the lack of continuity and predictability that is characteristic of all ad hoc balancing. Again using the Congressional investigation example, even if the Court arrived at a particularistic balance in the instance of one recalcitrant witness, it would have delivered no message about the First Amendment to future committees or future witnesses. There is, after all, little chance that the particulars of a later interrogation will correspond exactly to those of a former, and {98} without such exact correspondence, neither the committee nor the witness can define their own constitutional positions from an earlier highly particularistic balance.

Moreover, even at the level of greatest sensitivity to freedom of speech, the Court must recognize that its decision in support of a given witness's right of silence will tend to encourage recalcitrance in later witnesses, and thus to hamper later investigations. Therefore, even in the most particularistic balancing, the Court must consider the interest of Congress, not only in the information to be gained from the current witness but in its power to get answers from later witnesses. Thus the particularistic balance tends to drift back from the particular need of Congress for knowledge in a given case to the general interest of Congress in fruitful investigation.

Nor is it possible to cure the difficulties of particularistic balancing by jumping to the opposite extreme and balancing on the most general level, for on that level you may simply run into what Professor Friedman[54] calls the antinomies of law. You cannot balance freedom in general versus security in general, or at least you cannot arrive at any result from such a balancing. If we view the Congressional investigating committee versus the recalcitrant witness as the interest in security versus the interest in freedom, we have not taken the first step toward balancing, but have admitted that we have reached an impasse, for no one can assign a greater weight to one of these than to the other.

Thus, for balancing to work at all as a formula for judicial decision, it would seem that the balancing must be done at some level between the completely general and the completely particular. However, even at this level it seems impossible to avoid the broadest social considerations whenever the balancing formula is employed. For when balancing is conceived of as taking place on the level of the particular claims of various actual social groups, relative weights can be assigned them only in the context of the universe of social claims. There can be no choice between the claim to free speech of the magazine solicitor and the claim to privacy of the householder in vacuo. There has been no indication in the reports that all claims are considered equal. The choice inevitably depends on the judge's notion of the relative value to society as a whole of the various claims, as well as on the degree of damage to each.

If the balance is between legal rather than social claims, the same results follow. Since legal claims need to be balanced only when both have some recognition in law, the decision between them would have to be made on a "nonlegal" basis. Similarly, if "values" are the things to be balanced, the results will depend on some standard against which competing values can be ranked. {99}

Thus the mixture of general and specific considerations in the balancing cases seems inevitable and, on the whole, advisable. But the result of the mixture is further uncertainty in an already uncertain process. The past cases indicate that judges will pick and choose among particular and general considerations, loading the scale on one side or the other to suit their convenience.

The Court as Social Engineer

There can be little doubt that the enormously influential writings of Roscoe Pound, which were built around concepts of balancing interests and social engineering, have been largely responsible for the popularity of balancing with the Supreme Court. Pound has surely been the leading figure in modern American jurisprudence. It must be remembered, however, that for Pound the balancing of interests is the task of the whole system of American government, not of the Supreme Court alone. Once the Court is seen as an integral part of the national government's political structure, it becomes obvious that it cannot be expected to do the job of the whole in which it is only one of the parts. And having recognized the clientele or representational function of the various segments of the government, it seems clear that the way in which the Court could assure a true balancing of values is by representing those values which are unlikely to find champions elsewhere in government.

Of course, like most political questions, this is one of degree. Most government agencies represent their clientele within some over-all concept of the public interest, so that they tend to mitigate extreme group claims and generally exercise sufficient restraint to keep the machinery moving on a roughly equitable basis. To this extent the Court too must balance its clientele's against the public's interests. It need not push every extreme claim offered by every potential group. Nevertheless, the main point is that if the Court attempts a complete and impartial balancing of all claims, it is likely to under-represent its own clientele. While the Court remains within a political process where all other agencies push particular claims, such under-representation means that the final product of the political calculus will be especially unfavorable to the groups depending on the judiciary. In other words, too much balancing by the Supreme Court is likely to upset the balance of the political process as a whole.

Paradoxically enough, while the modest were adopting balancing as a device for crippling the Court in the First Amendment area, the notion that the Court could act as singlehanded balancer was plausible at all {100} only because of our traditional tendency to think of the Court as some sort of Olympian body set above and beyond politics and government and hurling its thunderbolts of judicial review. Once Pound's concepts are seen in the light of the real political world in which the Court operates, it becomes quite clear that anyone who insists that the Court act as a general social engineer of our society is proposing a task so impossibly great that his suggestion can be nothing more than the preliminary to a call for judicial abdication.

Pound's "social engineering" phrase has always had an unfortunate kind of technocratic ring about it. It suggests the cold, rational, and independent manipulation of society by a possessor of the pure knowledge and the pure power to shape his material as he pleases. In short, the phrase imports all the apoliticism of its Benthamite origins. "Politician" would have been a better term than social engineer. For politician suggests the delicate interplay between reflecting and defining or coalescing interests, between shaping events and being shaped by them that is the actual lot of those seeking to balance the interests in our society. To the extent that the Supreme Court wants to take on Pound's assignment, it too will have to act as politician—that is, submit itself to the process of politics, not seek to become a substitute for it. The Supreme Court is even less in a position to act as an omnipotent Benthamite social engineer than many of its rival political agencies. Therefore, to the extent that balancing is the task of the legal system, it behooves the Court to discover precisely what actions on its part will contribute to balance in the political system as a whole as it actually operates now with all its faults and imbalances. More often than not such action will consist not of coolly and impartially balancing all the interests before it, but of vigorously championing those interests that seem to be getting insufficient weight in the rest of the political process. Because the Court has a less fixed constituency than, for instance, the junior Senator from Nevada or the Department of Agriculture or the Interstate Commerce Commission, it is in a better position than most governmental actors to swing its weight to the points on the scale that need it most.

The great mistake of the balancers, or rather their deliberate tactic, has been to apply Poundian phrases like balancing of interests to the Supreme Court without applying the Poundian content behind those phrases. A true jurisprudence of interests does not require the Court to balance the interests in each individual case and only in some overly narrow bailiwick, but to act in such a way as to contribute to the most efficient balancing of interests by that multi-headed social engineer we call the political process. {101}

In spite of the risks of misdirection, applying the notion of balancing to the work of the Supreme Court, and more particularly its First Amendment work, is useful in some ways. In the first place, as an empirical description of how the Justices decide cases, balancing is obviously on the right track. The cases that reach the Supreme Court are, by process of elimination in the lower courts, those for which no simple "legal" answer is available. Most are likely to involve the clash of competing social claims, all of which the Justice must consider. We have seen that the clear-and-present-danger rule, for instance, was designed to strike a balance between freedom of speech and national security which would preserve both by allowing a speaker to continue speaking up to the point his speech became an actual, immediate threat to national security. When a religious sect wishes to blare forth its soul searing and ear curling message through loud speakers in a public park on the day of rest, or a newspaper wishes to warn a judge that failing to convict the rascals will bring the public wrath down on his head, surely the Justices must consider the citizen seeking peace and quiet and the defendant seeking a fair trial as well as the speaker seeking to broadcast the word of righteousness. In some metaphysical way there may be absolute rights in the sense of a final reserve of human personality and moral autonomy that no one may rightfully violate. But more immediately, the rights of each must surely be viewed as circumscribed by the rights of others, so that a right is operationally little more than a claim that the actions of each be circumscribed no more and no less than is necessary to allow maximum scope for the actions of others. It would be possible to trot out the whole modern utilitarian jurisprudence of rights and duties, or claims and privileges to support this point,[55] but it hardly seems necessary, so universally is it recognized—even among the most absolutist libertarians—that rights are reciprocal. If the heckler actually had an absolute and unlimited right to exercise his freedom of speech against the speaker, the First Amendment would in fact read, "Congress shall make no law forbidding he who can shout the loudest from being heard." Thus courts, and particularly the Supreme Court, must be prepared to adjust and delimit rival rights lest all rights become meaningless.

The anti-balancers sometimes seek to avoid this unpalatable truth by arguing that the First Amendment has already done our balancing for us by deciding that the rights of free speech shall have priority over conflicting claims. As we have seen, neither the literal wording of the Amendment nor the intentions of the framers are sufficiently clear to support such a proposition. The First Amendment can mean that at {102} least some kinds of speech are so important to our society that they will always be favored over any and all other social interests. But the Amendment will mean that because we make it mean that. Absolute protection for speech may be the result that our balancing of claims dictates, but it will be *our* balancing. We cannot avoid the responsibility for striking that balance by claiming that the founders did it, because they did not.

At its most extreme, ad hoc balancing as a concomitant of modesty silently repeals the First Amendment by allowing any invasion of freedom of speech that the legislature feels is justified. But in combatting this tactic, it seems unwise to go to the opposite extreme of insisting that the First Amendment absolutely forbids any infringement on the right of speech without any consideration of other rights when neither the history of the Amendment, common sense, nor the canons of jurisprudence will support such a position. It is the responsibility of those who must bring the constitutional provision to life to decide just where between the extremes of hollow, moral admonition and reckless, absolute prohibition the First Amendment falls.

Even if we assume the most absolute meaning for the First Amendment, the need for some sort of balancing at some stage in the process of making First Amendment decisions is vividly illustrated when speech comes into conflict with other rights protected by the Constitution. We have seen this in the fair trial cases. The Fifth and Fourteenth Amendments guarantee the citizen due process of law in language no less demanding than that in which the First Amendment guarantees free speech. If a newspaper in the course of a trial uses its First Amendment freedoms to attempt to intimidate judge and jurors, there is obviously a conflict between two equally protected rights which cannot be solved by trumpeting about the glories of free speech.

The Failure of Balancing

The fair trial cases, however, also show that the problem of conflicting rights can be handled without resorting to official adoption of the ad hoc balancing approach. Both commentators and Justices can be fully aware of the subtleties of social adjustment required in adjudication of First Amendment claims, even while shaping rules for more vigorous judicial protection of those claims than ad hoc balancing provides. While admitting that, in fact, an element of balancing always enters into First Amendment decisions, it seems to me undesirable for several reasons to maintain the balancing formula of the fifties as the official and general doctrine of the Court. {103}

First of all, it will be almost impossible at this late date to rid the formula of the elements of judicial surrender with which it has long been associated. The very phrase, balancing of interests, has such a legislative ring about it that it undermines judicial self-confidence unduly. Secondly, the ad hoc quality of Frankfurterian balancing did in the past, does in the present, and in all likelihood will in the future, not only present a picture of an arbitrary Court dealing out drum head justice case by case, but, also of one that constantly tampers with the weights in the process of balancing. In terms of the Court's public image, it would be better to formulate a few general constitutional rules which would be summary statements of the Court's views on where the balance should currently be struck between speech and other rights. Clear-and-present-danger, preferred position, and the prohibitions against prior restraint and vagueness are precisely such statements. All four of these doctrines were consciously and specifically designed to fit freedom of speech into the context of overall social needs.

More important, rules transcending the ad hoc would give somewhat clearer directions to lower courts and prosecutors, and possess more of the qualities of stability and predictability than the balancing technique. To be sure, balancing has in the past given a high degree of predictability, but that is because it was used fraudulently. Lower courts, after carefully studying a half dozen of the Supreme Court's balancing opinions, got a clear message to balance in such a way that the alleged subversive always loses, Congress always wins, and the First Amendment is conveniently sidetracked. But if ad hoc balancing were to be used without its customary freight of modesty and the accompanying consistently false loadings of the scale against freedom of speech, it would become such a subtle method, so dependent on the exact nuances of the facts of a given case and on the rather ethereal guesses of the Justices about just what the results would be to whom and when, that it would seem impossible to use a Supreme Court decision in one case as a guide to lower courts in deciding the next.

Furthermore, the role of the Supreme Court in the area of the First Amendment has been at its best as a sensitizer of the American public to freedom of speech. A balancing formula, even when used without excessive self-restraint and with as fair a distribution of the weights as possible, cannot serve as an adequate slogan for maintaining the public consciousness of the value of free speech. The market place rationale and the clear-and-present-danger rule were ringing symbols that had considerable impact on the minds of citizens and legislators tempted to try just a little book burning for the sake of some greater good. The {104} repeated use of these principles by the Supreme Court pounded them into our political vocabulary and thus into our political ways of thought, so that they could work as self-activating safeguards against the temptation to solve our problems by restricting somebody else's freedom. The balancing formula does not have any such dramatic impact; quite the contrary, it introduces so many ifs, ands, and buts that it is useless as a safeguard for anything. Indeed, its principal impact is to provide a cheap and rapid rationale for anyone who wishes to destroy our liberties in the name of some glorious cause, for freedom of speech can, on balance, be subordinated to anything that is given a weighty enough label.

This leads us to the final and decisive reason for abandoning balancing as the general institutional formula for the Supreme Court in freedom of speech cases. If, as I have argued earlier, it is not the job of the Court but of the political system as a whole to balance the interests of society, a general balancing formula in the First Amendment area is surely going to under-represent the claims of free speech in the political process as a whole. The Court needs constitutional rules that will symbolize and effectuate its role of vigorously representing those groups that are not vigorously represented elsewhere in the government. The balancing formula, with all its Poundian implications of omnipotent neutrality, will not suit the Court's job as one political actor among many in the complex business of group representation. The Court must be conscious of the fact that various rights must be accommodated to one another within our society, but it must also be conscious and make others conscious that its role is neither the initial nor the final balancing of all social interests, but some marginal contribution to the process of balancing achieved through judicious and discriminating political action. The balancing formula tends to obscure this role while other constitutional doctrines tend to bring it to the fore. In this sense, activist doctrines such as clear-and-present-danger and preferred position acknowledged the actual and necessary play of interests in American government and politics more fully than the balancing formula has ever done.

Conclusion

Both in its polemic origins and in its current rationale, the balancing of interests doctrine is little more than the old judicial modesty, slightly disguised by new terminology, but with the same fundamental inability to solve the dilemma of judicial review created for the modest by their own unrealistic political vision. The opponents of balancing, absolutists if you like, have fallen in with this game and continue the old debate {105} over modesty in the new language of balancing and anti-balancing. However, they have so far done little more than seize upon each of the balancing ploys that disguise the modest's dilemma and reshape or reject it in such a way as to sharply reconfront us with that dilemma.

No one has argued so far that all speech of all sorts under all conditions must be absolutely free of government regulation. Everyone is a "balancer," if by that we mean that speech cannot be dealt with totally in vacuo, but must be placed in its social and political contexts when deciding the scope of First Amendment protections. However, the adjustment of First Amendment to other rights can be achieved through the construction of a great many formulas other than balancing of the Frankfurter sort. Indeed, once unrealistic qualms about judicial enforcement of the First Amendment are put aside, the balancing formula does not provide either an adequate constitutional rhetoric for clothing the Court's actions or a particularly useful guide to such action. Balancing is so deeply infected by its modest origins that, while it may still occasionally be useful in particular instances, it cannot be maintained as a general formula for a Court bent on fulfilling its First Amendment responsibilities. Such a formula is, to my mind, available, but it is the preferred position, not the balancing, doctrine. Consequently, we must return for another look at preferred position and the clear-and-present-danger rule historically associated with it.

NOTES to Chapter Three

1 Two of the figures most closely associated with the clear-and-present-danger standard have been ardent protagonists of the balancing approach. See Oliver Wendell Holmes, "The Path of the Law," *Harvard Law Review,* vol. 10 (1896-97), pp. 457, 467; Holmes, *Collected Legal Papers* (New York, 1920), p. 184; Chafee, *Free Speech,* 1948 ed., pp. 31-33.

2 *Whitney v. California,* 274 U.S. 357, 378 (1927) (concurring).

3 *Schneider v. United States,* 308 U.S. 147, 161 (1939).

4 *Cantwell v. Connecticut,* 310 U.S. 296 (1940); *Bridges v. California,* 314 U.S. 252 (1941); *Thomas v. Collins,* 326 U.S. 516 (1945); *West Virginia Board of Education v. Barnette,* 319 U.S. 624 (1943); *Minersville School District v. Gobitis,* 310 U.S. 586, 603 (1940) (dissent); see also the letter from Stone to Frankfurter quoted in Mason, "The Core of Free Government, 1938-40; Mr. Justice Stone and 'Preferred Freedoms,' " *Yale Law Journal,* vol. 65 (1956), p. 615; *Martin v. Struthers,* 319 U.S. 141, 150-51 (1943) (concurrence); *Pennekamp v. Florida,* 328 U.S. 331, 336, 346-47 (1946); *Marsh v. Alabama,* 326 U.S. 501 (1946); *Saia v. New York,* 334 U.S. 558 (1948).

5 *United Public Service Workers v. Mitchell,* 330 U.S. 75 (1947); *Kovacs v. Cooper,* 336 U.S. 77 (1949). {106}

6 *Jones v. Opelika,* 316 U.S. 584 (1942); *Martin v. Struthers,* 319 U.S. 141 (1943).

7 315 U.S. 568 (1942).

8 330 U.S. 75 (1947).

9 336 U.S. 77 (1949).

10 340 U.S. 268 (1951).

11 *Id.* at 275.

12 340 U.S. 268 at 282.

13 *Id.*

14 *Beauharnais v. Illinois,* 343 U.S. 250 (1952).

15 339 U.S. 382 (1950).

16 *Id.* at 397. Similar language is used at pp. 399-400.

17 *Id.* at 397.

18 341 U.S. 494 (1951).

19 *United States v. Dennis*, 183 F.2d 201, 212 (1950).

20 *Dennis v. United States*, 341 U.S. 494, 503 (1951).

21 Edward S. Corwin, "Bowing Out 'Clear and Present Danger,' " *Notre Dame Lawyer*, vol. 27 (1951), p. 358.

22 *Schenck v. United States*, 249 U.S. 47 (1919); *Abrams v. United States*, 250 U.S. 616 (1919).

23 *Dennis v. United States*, 341 U.S. 494, 524-35 (1951). See also p. 542: "a survey of the relevant decisions indicates that the results which we have reached are on the whole those that would ensue from careful weighing of conflicting interest"

24 360 U.S. 109 (1959).

25 See *Braden v. United States*, 365 U.S. 431 (1961).

26 See the citations gathered in Laurent B. Franz, "The First Amendment in the Balance," *Yale Law Journal*, vol. 71 (1962) p. 1424, note 3; also see *Gibson v. Florida Legislative Investigating Committee*, 83 S. Ct. 889 (1963) (concurrences).

27 *Roth v. United States*, 354 U.S. 476 (1957).

28 *Poulos v. New Hampshire*, 345 U.S. 395 (1953); *Breard v. Alexandria*, 341 U.S. 622 (1951); *Staub v. Baxley*, 355 U.S. 313 (1958).

29 *Konigsberg v. State Bar of California*, 366 U.S. 36 (1961); *Communist Party v. Subversive Activities Control Board*, 367 U.S. 98 (1961).

30 *Scales v. United States*, 367 U.S. 263 (1961).

31 357 U.S. 449 (1958).

32 361 U.S. 516 (1960).

33 83 S. Ct. 889 (1963).

34 83 S. Ct. 328 (1963).

35 *Id.* at 341.

36 *Gibson v. Florida*, 83 S. Ct. 889, 894 (1963).

37 *New York ex rel. Bryant v. Zimmerman*, 278 U.S. 63 (1928).

38 Roscoe Pound, "A Survey of Social Interests," *Harvard Law Review*, vol. 59 (1945) p. 2.

39 354 U.S. 178 (1957).

40 *Id.* at 205 (1957).

41 *Sweezy v. New Hampshire*, 354 U.S. 254 (1957).

42 "If in the long run the beliefs expressed in proletarian dictatorship are destined to be accepted by the dominant forces of the community, the only meaning {107} of free speech is that they should be given their chance and have their way." *Gitlow v. New York*, 268 U.S. 652, 673 (1925). Cf. Holmes, *Collected Legal Papers* (New York, 1920), p. 181.

43 The general outlines of this debate may be followed in Charles L. Black, "Mr. Justice Black, the Supreme Court, and the Bill of Rights," *Harpers Magazine* (Feb. 1961), pp. 63-68; Laurent B. Frantz, "The First Amendment in the Balance," *Yale Law Journal*, vol. 71 (1962), pp. 1424-50; Frantz, "Is the First Amendment Law?—A Reply to Professor Mendelson," *California Law Review*, vol. 51 (1963), pp. 729-54; Charles Fried, "Two Concepts of Interests: Some Reflections on the Supreme Court's Balancing Test," *Harvard Law Review*, vol. 76 (1963), pp. 755-78; Wallace Mendelson, *Justices Black and Frankfurter: Conflict in the Court* (Chicago, 1961); Mendelson, "On the Meaning of the First Amendment: Absolutes in the Balance," *California Law Review*, vol. 50 (1962), pp. 821-28; Mendelson, "The First Amendment and the Judicial Process: A Reply to Mr. Franz," *Vanderbilt Law Review*, vol. 17 (1964), pp. 479-483. Footnote references in these articles will give the reader information on much other relevant material, including most of the pronouncements of Justice Black.

44 "Above all, the open balancing technique is calculated to leave 'the sovereign prerogative of choice' to the people—with the least interference that is compatible with our tradition of judicial review. Absent that tradition in utterance cases, the Court might logically accept Learned Hand's view that the first amendment ... is too uncommunicative ... to be treated as law." Mendelson, "On the Meaning of the First Amendment," p. 826.

45 Letter from Frankfurter to Stone concerning the First Flag Salute Case, quoted in Mason, "The Core of Free Government, 1938-1940," pp. 614-15.

46 *Dennis v. United States*, 341 U.S. 494, 550 (concurrence).

47 *Communist Party v. Subversive Activities Control Board*, 367 U.S. 1, 91-97 (1961).

48 *Mr. Justice Holmes and the Supreme Court* (Cambridge, Mass., 1938), p. 51.

49 354 U.S. 234 (1957).

50 I am aware that Justice Black has sometimes stated the "absolutist" position in a more extreme way than that outlined here, but I believe that I am presenting a fair reflection of even his position when his more extreme statements are read in the light of his more cautious ones and of his over-all voting record. See particularly *Tally v. California*, 362 U.S. 60 (1960); *Wood v. Georgia*, 370 U.S. 375 (1962); *Edwards v. South Carolina*, 83 S. Ct. 680 (1963); Black, "The Bill of Rights," *New York University Law Review*, vol. 35 (1960), p. 867.

51 Fried, *op. cit., supra.*

52 "On the Meaning of the First Amendment," *op. cit., supra.*

53 Leonard Levy, *Legacy of Suppression* (Cambridge, Mass., 1960).

54 *Legal Theory* (1953), ch. 30.

55 For a brief summary see Sidney Hook, *The Paradoxes of Freedom* (Berkeley, 1962).

Chapter Four

THE FUTURE OF THE FIRST AMENDMENT

IN THIS CHAPTER I am going to argue that the Supreme Court ought to go back to preferred position and clear-and-present-danger. Going backward in constitutional doctrine is always viewed with a kind of instinctive horror. I am not exactly sure why. In part it is undoubtedly due to a residue of belief in the idea of progress that should have disappeared, but did not quite do so, when our total commitment to the enlightenment philosophy that underlies the idea wavered. In part, going back affronts the notion of a gradually developing and self-purifying common law which is still bred into lawyers along with the notions that legislators—not judges—and statutes—not judicial opinions—are and should be the central font of our law. This common law notion of progress has spilled over into constitutional law, where it takes the form of a constitutional history in which the work of the framers is always successfully adapted to, and properly regulative of, new conditions. Even the unfortunate events of the thirties can now be fitted neatly into that pattern since the Roosevelt Court cured the aberration by new and progressive doctrines—if you choose to call judicial surrender a doctrine.

At least insofar as the First Amendment is concerned, the 1950s will simply not fit into this cheery picture. We all might well return to the dissents of Justices Black and Douglas during this period and read them without the whole freight of sophisticated conventions about what a judge ought and ought not say and do that is normally hauled into our minds by the debate over judicial modesty. For all its inadequate historical and jurisprudential scholarship, their message is a clear and insightful one. They said that without the freedom of each citizen to express his vision of political truth and to seek to convince others of that vision without fear of punishment, the form and substance of our polity was meaningless—in short, that without the freedom to talk politics there is no free politics. They said that this freedom was being attacked by a whole series of direct and subtle, governmental and private, federal and state, legislative and executive punishments and harassments. The dissenting Justices also said that these invasions of freedom of speech were not and could not be confined to those we hate—that in {109} the end they would inevitably reduce the freedoms of many speakers not in league with the Red devil. For it is even easier to cry Communist than to cry wolf, and you can do so successfully far more often. There is always someone who is willing to deprive others of their liberty in the name of some higher good or of some alleged danger.

Finally, Black and Douglas said that all these infringements of speech were inspired by a hysteria—a collapse of our national self-confidence in the face of an alien ideology—that led us to create a phantom land of internal Communist menace that never was and never could be. They argued that the nature and level of domestic Communist activities and the state of our national political health did not require chipping away our basic freedoms and punishing and harassing thousands of our fellow citizens in the name of internal security. And they concluded that the Court, by refusing to invoke the First Amendment, was legitimizing the whole cruel, hysterical, unnecessary, and unrealistic mess that we now retrospectively call McCarthyism.

And they were right. It is no accident, I think, that Justice Black's opinions get anthologized and Justice Frankfurter's get explained. For what Justice Black has to say in praise of free speech and in condemnation of the witch hunting of that period in our history strikes a basic chord of truth that needs no subtle explanation. In fact, if we were to forget that Justice Black was a Justice, if we were presented with his views in vacuo, most of us would immediately agree with him that those "minor and incidental" infringements on civil liberties in the name of protecting us from the Red menace represented a pathological condition in the life of our body politic that ought to be cured and prevented from recurring.

For a time, it was fashionable to praise the lovely legal essays by which Justice Frankfurter approved these painfully unnecessary and unfruitful invasions of our rights, and to condemn the straightforward sermons of Black and Douglas which contained many a home truth but seemed so unlegal. There was a *smug* and condescending rejection of the unlawyer-like truths of the dissenters in favor of the fine honed legalism and complex judicialism of the champion of modesty. The pseudo-sophistication of approving the neat scholastic opinions that nearly always concluded by showing that things we all know to be obnoxiously wrong are constitutionally right has, I hope, largely passed. It must surely be clear by now that Justice Frankfurter and company, no matter what their intentions and legal skills, became official representatives of the worst battering that freedom of speech has received from our government since the Alien and Sedition Acts. {110}

Black and Douglas were correct about the doctrinal vehicle of the fifties as well as the political events. As Justice Black repeatedly pointed out, the balancing doctrine was most useful to those who were willing to stand by and allow our freedom of speech to go by the boards. Because it allowed a flexible weighing in each case without enunciation of any principle to which the Court might have had to stick even when Congress later violated it, and because it constantly repeated that it is constitutionally legitimate for Congress to violate the First Amendment, ad hoc balancing provided a jurisprudential screen behind which judges could always yield gracefully whenever the McCarthy winds blew. Whenever public hysteria against speakers arises, what could be easier than to falsely juggle the weights in order to yield to overwrought sentiment as the Court did in the fifties? By overweighing the danger and minimizing and excusing the damage to free speech, just as the crusading legislature does, the Court can always simply surrender to the hysteria, and in surrendering provide it with a cover of constitutional respectability which feeds its fires.

Far superior for a Court that wishes to remain active in the cause of liberty are other and earlier doctrines, which proclaim that speech can be abridged only under the gravest and most immediately dangerous circumstances, and that the Supreme Court will see that it is not abridged otherwise. And how much more likely is the Court to strike a vein of public support in the defense of speech if it has constantly hammered those doctrines home as fundamental to our Constitution, than if it has constantly told the people that legislatures are entitled to deprive us of any of our liberties whenever they think it is good for us—for that, after all, is what the Frankfurterian balancing of the fifties comes down to.

Thus, the Supreme Court's record of the fifties on First Amendment matters is not a solid step forward on which to build, but a pathological condition to be excised. Once it is excised we are returned to the preferred position and clear-and-present-danger doctrines from which we started. The need for such a return is clearly shown by the tragic position of Frankfurter and Hand themselves. If one rereads Frankfurter's opinion in *Sweezy v. New Hampshire*[1] where, for once, he throws off his modest mask to speak from the heart, or the painful passages in Hand's *Bill of Rights* where he casts longing glances at the preferred position doctrine,[2] it becomes strikingly clear that these champions of modesty were, their roles as judges aside, in complete agreement with Black and Douglas on the need for freedom of speech in American life and the contemporary threats to that freedom. They were only restrained from {111} giving voice and effect to that agreement by their concept of the role of the judge, and that concept was wrong. Once we realize it was wrong, we are again faced with the solution they might have accepted if they had not been wrong in their concept of the judicial role—that is, with the kind of judicial protection of freedom of speech represented by the preferred position and clear-and-present-danger doctrines of the forties.

I have tried to show at some length in chapter one that the modest were indeed wrong in their concept of the judicial role, and I do not wish to belabor the point unduly. In the face of the real situation, there is no valid political reason for the Supreme Court to modestly withdraw before the voice of Congress, as there might be in that fictional world of a majoritarian, unified, sovereign Congress that the modest have created for themselves. In the real world no other agencies—not even those within Congress itself, such as the committees or the party leadership—give up the fight because Congress has spoken. Nor should the Court. Like other governmental agencies, its contribution to American politics must be reckoned on the basis of how vigorously it furthers the interests it chooses to defend. How representative or democratically enlightened its governmental activities are will depend on what interests it chooses to represent. The Supreme Court contributes most to the governmental system in which it operates by vigorously defending against the encroachments of other interests and agencies those interests vital to the well-being of our society that are not sufficiently defended elsewhere. It is on the basis of this sort of political analysis that the preferred position doctrine ultimately rests. For freedom of speech is one of those interests not sufficiently defended elsewhere, on whose behalf the Court is in a political position to act.

Preferred Position Revisited

The preferred position doctrine, then, must be re-examined in the light of the failure of the fifties, and of the false vision of American politics from which that failure sprung. The employment of the doctrine as a protection for minority groups initially disturbed majoritarians because, in the abstract, it seemed to imply that minorities could use the Court to thwart majority will. Once the doctrine is placed within the context of the group aspects of politics, it becomes evident that the Court acts not for a minority against a majority, but for one group against other groups. Indeed, if the Court tends to defend what Truman calls potential groups against organized groups, it is protecting the broader interests. {112}

The notion that the preferred position doctrine serves to withdraw some issues from the democratic process has frequently proved unpalatable. It requires the proponents of preferred position to argue at one and the same time that the Justices must protect the democratic process and that they must not allow all decisions to be made by it. Confusion is, therefore, inevitable when the democratic process yields a limitation on democratic processes as it does, for instance, when legislation restricting speech is passed. We have tried earlier to provide some tentative solutions to this problem. But the difficulty largely disappears, I think, when attacked in the political terms used here. In the actual political process some groups seek to limit speech and use certain agencies of government to reach their goal. Others seek to protect speech and use other government agencies for their purposes. Because the political process is continuous, a victory by the former groups, in the legislature for instance, simply calls forth renewed efforts by the latter groups, and vice versa. When the Court strikes down a law limiting speech, it is not obstructing democracy in the name of preserving the democratic process. It is participating in that process as it exists in the United States, by representing groups who are not sufficiently represented elsewhere. And the Court's action is not final. It is simply another event thrown into the continually turning political hopper.

The larger problem of whether the market place will, in the long run, yield freedom or slavery is more serious, but its importance to the Court has been overinflated by considering the Court apart from the political process as a whole. The Justices are, after all, neither Plato's Legislators nor his Guardians. They are a part, not the whole, of the political process. As such they can neither make the cosmic decisions nor enforce them if they do; the Court cannot institute a wholly controlled market. Even the gradual evolution of the intellectual economy is determined by the political process as a whole. The Court can content itself with making its contribution to that process and, considering the strength of the restrictive forces at work, it need hardly fear that its influence will yield a liberty so extreme that it turns to chaos. For the same reason, the arguments that the First Amendment should not be preferred to other constitutional provisions or that freedom of speech should not be favored over virtue are not very helpful. The preferred position doctrine need not be understood as a universal ranking of values. It is a statement about what interest the Court should represent, given the contemporary political circumstances.

Preferred position, then, refers not to the special importance of certain values to society as a whole, but to the representational role of the {113} Court. It should be remembered that the original formulation of the doctrine in Justice Stone's *Carolene Products* footnote[3] offered just this emphasis on preferred position in terms of the Court's functions. The footnote has been criticized for inconsistency, but it seems to make quite good sense in terms of political if not of legal logic. One paragraph stresses the need to protect minorities, which usually turn out to be the marginal groups representing potential groups. Another notes the special role of the Court in keeping open the democratic process. The specific wording of the First Amendment is the main point of a third. What this all comes down to is that the Court, because of its special position and special constitutional authorization, is the instrument of government uniquely suited to represent the claims of those groups interested in free speech.

In this respect, perhaps, one more word ought to be said about the specific wording of the First Amendment. It is true that neither the plain meaning nor the founders' intentions constitute the amendment as a direct and specific command to the Supreme Court to prevent any and all regulation of speech. But just because the amendment is not entirely clear is no reason to pretend it is not there at all. The singling out of freedom of speech in the Bill of Rights certainly means that the colonial Americans were especially concerned with speech, and that concern has continued in American life. The concrete existence and acceptance of the First Amendment, when combined with the concrete existence and acceptance of judicial review, may not prove in any cosmic sense that the Supreme Court ought to act as a jealous guardian of speech, but they do create public attitudes and expectations which make it politically possible for the Court to take on such a role.

What the public expects a government agency to do, what it considers the legitimate scope of that agency, is an important determinant of what the agency can in fact do. This question of whether the agency is acting according to the rules of the game in taking on a certain area of decision-making is quite apart from, and often more important than, that of whether it made a substantively good or bad decision in a particular instance. The presence in our Constitution of the words "Congress shall make no law abridging the freedom of speech . . . ," no matter what their technical imprecision, insures that a Supreme Court defense of freedom of speech will always appear to most Americans as falling within the legitimate duties of the Justices, even if the particular decision is disliked. In other words, many persons might think the Court had made a bad decision (in striking down some law that shut up the dirty Commies, for example), but few, except those carefully trained in {114} the windings of modesty, would feel that the Court had no right to make such a decision.

Most of us have been taught that the phrases of the Constitution are broadly, rather than narrowly or specifically, worded in order that they might be adapted to meet changing circumstances, and that the Supreme Court has an important role to play in that adaption. If the Court were to interpret the broad wording of the First Amendment to really mean "no law," some might not like the interpretation but few would feel that the Court had shockingly deviated from its traditional duties. In the political calculus of popular expectations the thrust of the First Amendment toward judicial activism in favor of speech cannot be blunted by showing that, like all other constitutional provisions, it does not absolutely command any given interpretation by the Court. Indeed, all the lawyer-like flutter aside, the words "Congress shall make no law abridging the freedom of speech" are surely going to look to most people more like a command that Congress make no law punishing speakers for what they say, than to look like permission to Congress to make any law that it wants punishing speech, as the modest balancers would have it.

All this does not mean that the aura of special importance which surrounds the preferred position doctrine may be seen as an unjustified inflation of a routine political function, for the Court does, after all, have a rather special clientele and a rather special role. Professor Truman notes that the ability of potential groups—that is, of general social and political values, as opposed to special and usually narrowly focused economic interests—to contribute to the political process is largely determined by "the character of the society's means of communication, . . . the adequacy of the information available to them concerning the events."[4] Therefore the Court's concern with free speech, expressed in the preferred position doctrine, not only furthers the interests of the potential group clustered about that value, but also provides the necessary foundation for the effectiveness of all potential groups. The Court's special preoccupation with the continuity and long range evolution of constitutional development, combined with its real political power, make it a peculiarly suitable instrument for interests which lack immediate and specifically organized power but are vital to the general evolution of American government. Here again the modest's dilemma of a Court which is in politics but not wholly so proves to be a peculiarly helpful feature of American government.

Indeed, once the multiple dilemmas of the modest have been dissolved by the application of some political realism, there seems to be no particular reason why even they should not accept the preferred position {115} doctrine. It has always retained some foothold in the Court. Judge Hand comes very close to accepting it.[5] In fact, it seemed implicit in some of his earlier writing, for he had based his faith on a legislature which expressed the common will and then defined the common will in terms of the availability of political means for peaceful change.[6] The seeds of the doctrine may even be found in Thayer, who suggested that judicial lawmaking prevented free discussion.[7] Both Hand and Thayer are, then, concerned with the maintenance of free access to the instrumentalities of political power, and this is the heart of the preferred position doctrine. Professor Freund, who is in good standing with those who oppose "rigid" formulas, has proposed something very like preferred position.[8] The wording of the First Amendment and the continued acceptance of the political philosophy it represents must provide some comfort for those of the modest who object to the importation of outdated economic philosophies into vague constitutional provisions.

FREEDOM OF SPEECH

Implementing Preferred Position: Clear-and-Present-Danger

Theoretically, of course, the preferred position doctrine might be used in conjunction with a number of different constitutional formulas. It has been used in conjunction with balancing, but the two are basically incompatible, except perhaps in very special instances. The balancing technique inevitably demotes speech from its special position to a position as simply one of the many interests to be balanced by the courts. Thus, the clear-and-present-danger rule remains the most suitable vehicle for the preferred position doctrine. By establishing an especially rigorous constitutional rule for speech legislation, it gives practical application to the Court's preference. By emphasizing the distinction between thought and action, reminding the people and their representatives that government rightfully punishes men for what they do, not for what they say, it serves constantly to re-emphasize a basic American belief which is the final protection for speech in the United States.

This intimate connection between clear-and-present-danger and preferred position can best be seen if we again briefly look at just what the preferred position doctrine is. Preferred position is itself historically and logically derived from the clear-and-present-danger rule, for the danger rule, in effect, puts the burden of constitutional proof on the legislature. Legislation effecting speech was constitutional only if a clear and present danger could be demonstrated. Such a shift in the burden of proof was contrary to Holmes' well known insistence that a presumption of constitutionality should attach to legislative action. The preferred position {116} doctrine, by providing a rationale for refusing that presumption where speech is involved, was in one sense little more than an addendum to the danger rule designed to save Holmes' consistency.

Both doctrines, of course, ultimately spring from the same market place rationale. We have noted the connection between that rationale and the clear-and-present-danger doctrine at some length earlier. The defenders of preferred position took the same ground when they argued that speech regulation was qualitatively different from economic regulation because interests that were adversely affected by economic regulation could resort for remedy to the political process, while those silenced by speech regulation were cut off from the self-curative powers of the democratic process contained in the central institution of democracy, the communication of political ideas and claims. Preferred position and clear-and-present-danger, then, both basically rest on the notion that speech is not just another particular interest to be regulated in the public interest, but is the essential medium through which the public interest is pursued, and thus is entitled to much more rigorous judicial protection than the more routine and narrowly defined and represented interests.

To demonstrate that preferred position shares a common basis with, and was indeed historically derived from, clear-and-present-danger does not, of course, prove that preferred position cannot stand alone or operate in conjunction with other constitutional rules. But a rather strong natural affinity certainly exists between the two doctrines. That there is something more than an affinity becomes clear when we try to pin down exactly what the preferred position doctrine means. First of all, and most precisely, preferred position, besides the simple repetition in opinions of the rhetorical statement that speech is particularly important, means that the Court will not entertain its normal presumption in favor of the constitutionality of a statute when speech is involved. (It must always be emphasized that the doctrine was not carried to the opposite extreme of presuming unconstitutionality.) At the time the doctrine was originated, its supporters undoubtedly believed that such an elimination of presumption would implement their preference for freedom. But the episode of ad hoc balancing teaches a different lesson. Even without the presumption of constitutionality, speech regulation can be repeatedly approved simply by marshaling opposing interests worthy of protection. Where the constitutionality of legislation restricting speech is tested in conjunction with balancing, the presumption aspects of the preferred position doctrine simply mean that speech starts even with other interests, instead of being especially handicapped by the {117} presumption that Congress' regulation of it was correct. Thus, if the only content of preferred position were the elimination of the normal presumption of constitutionality, the doctrine would not necessarily mean that the Court would especially prefer speech, but only that it would not especially disprefer it.

On the other hand, when the presumption aspects of preferred position are used as a device for passing the clear-and-present-danger rule through the screen of Holmesian modesty which would normally prevent its application to legislation, the preferred position doctrine does become an operational preference for freedom. Simply slipping off the armor of presumption otherwise worn by statutes infringing speech does not actually favor speech very much, but slipping it off so that the Justices may then effectively strike with the clear-and-present-danger rule favors it a great deal, for the clear-and-present-danger rule itself states the special preference for freedom. Speech is not to be regulated when it is convenient or reasonable or useful to other interests, but only when a clear and present danger of a serious, substantive evil exists. Thus, while preferred position means only that the normal presumption of constitutionality is eliminated, it is actually the operation of the clear-and-present-danger rule through the preferred position doctrine, not the doctrine itself, that creates a preference for freedom.

FREEDOM OF SPEECH

The preferred position doctrine is something more than the elimination of the presumption of constitutionality when legislation effecting speech is involved. It is also a mood expressed by a rhetoric.[9] It is the repeated expression in the opinions of the forties of a special concern for freedom of speech merited by the crucial role speech plays in the American democracy. Such moods, and their expression, are important educators of public opinion. Moreover, as reflections of the Justices' real concerns, they are undoubtedly the most important safeguards for freedom of speech. No constitutional rule or principle, be it ever so ironclad, is nearly so important for the protection of speech as the acute commitment to freedom of speech among the Justices themselves, expressed and, hopefully, reinforced by the rhetoric of preferred position. In this sense, preferred position must always be the cornerstone of judicial protection of speech against the pressing demands for its limitation that always seem so vital at the time.

Unfortunately, for two interrelated reasons it is not enough for the Justices to make general declarations of their preference for freedom. First, it is never good public relations for the Justices simply to go about saying that we like freedom of speech, we think freedom of speech is important, therefore, we are going to go out of our way to protect freedom {118} of speech. It is far better to have some principle—slogan, if you like—that will appeal to some immutable truth of American life—or as close to an immutable truth as we ever get. It is always better for a judge to defend a principle than to state a preference. Secondly, other judges and lawyers, as well as the public, seem to be greatly comforted by principles. There is no need here to go into all the jurisprudential whys and wherefores of this psychological phenomenon. It must simply be conceded that lower courts and prosecutors are going to be very unhappy if the only guidance they can get from the Supreme Court is that the Justices especially like freedom of speech. Thus, both in terms of gaining public support for a stand in favor of freedom of speech and of impressing that stand adequately on its subordinates, the Supreme Court requires some principle to give substance to its preference for freedom.

I should think that principle is one that we have discussed before: that government can only send men to jail for what they do, not for what they think. Such a principle is surely one that is likely to strike a respondent chord in American tradition. It is also one that can be derived from the whole history of Supreme Court treatment of the speech cases. We have seen that the clear-and-present-danger rule was derived from the law of attempts, and thus specifically designed to embody this principle. Therefore, all of the clear-and-present-danger opinions from the twenties to the present can be offered in its support. The majority in *Gitlow v. New York*,[10] which rejected clear-and-present-danger, agreed that incitement, i.e., speech closely linked to action, must be distinguished from simple teaching, so that all the opinions of the twenties in which the first and fundamental approaches of the Court to the First Amendment were made can be said to have been solidly grounded on the thought-action distinction.

Even those areas where First Amendment protection has been denied illustrate the continued concern with thought versus deed. Thus, the "fighting words" doctrine of *Chaplinsky* deals with speech which is likely to provoke immediate retaliation, and group libel laws were approved against a background of hate group violence. The hostile audience cases seem to have given the Court so much trouble precisely because they represent such a tangled web of abstract belief and physical violence.

The *Dennis*[11] decision, which so much reduced the vitality of the clear-and-present-danger rule does not abandon the belief-action distinction. Indeed, in a perverse way it reinforces it by the judicial manipulations which, in reality, punished the speakers not for speaking but for engaging in world revolution. Even in *Douds*,[12] which comes so close to {119} thought control, the Court claims to be dealing not with speech but action—that is, the possibility of political strikes. And in *Yates v. United States*,[13] one of the last of the key Communist cases, the distinction between abstract teaching and incitement to action not only is the decisive factor in the decision, but is established as the central tenet of First Amendment protections.

In this respect *Scales v. United States*,[14] an important decision of 1961, is particularly revealing. The Court was there confronted with the clause of the Smith Act that made simple membership in the Communist Party illegal. *Scales* came before the Court at a time when it was dominated by that coalition of the modest and anti-libertarian that had made *Dennis*, *Barenblatt*, and all the other assaults on the First Amendment possible. However, even to this coalition the membership clause was so constitutionally distasteful that they avoided deciding the case for several terms. It is typical of the modest, of course, that their belief that outlawing simple membership in a political party was contrary to every standard of American democracy in which they believed led them not to spring forward to declare the statute unconstitutional, but only to stall as long as possible before approving it. For in the end, when brought face to face with a command of Congress, no matter how vicious, their peculiar philosophy left them no choice but to applaud the Congressional dictate by certifying its constitutionality. In the end the modest majority did just that.

The statute, however, was so truly un-American, and a decision that allowed Congress to outlaw a political party carried so much precedential danger for the future, that even the modest sought desperately for some means of undoing the mischief that their own philosophy required them to approve. The Court, therefore, held that the constitutionality of the statute was saved because when the Congress had said membership it had really meant active, knowing membership with specific intent. Of course, Congress had meant nothing of the sort, and the acrobatic display of statutory interpretation necessary to have made it mean all that simply demonstrated again the paradox of modest Justices who cannot bring themselves to challenge Congress, but yet cannot completely escape the feeling that they owe some independent duty to the Constitution.

However, from our point of view here, what is interesting is the method used to gloss over the fundamental contradictions of modesty so strikingly presented in *Scales*. The Court held that, in order to fall under the ban of the statute, membership must have been active in the sense that the defendant must have been engaged in Communist Party activity, {120} not simply have been an enrolled member, must have included personal knowledge that the goal of the Party was overthrow of the government by force and violence as speedily as circumstances permitted, and must have been with specific intent to join in bringing about that overthrow as speedily as circumstances permitted. In other words, driven to the wall by the confrontation between their modesty and an obviously unconstitutional statute, the modest resorted to the traditional distinction between thought and action. Only when membership was participation in actual arrangements and preparations for revolution, not simply identification with the philosophy of Communism, could it be constitutionally outlawed.

Put another way, the standards of proof required by the Court are so strict that anyone who could have been convicted under the membership clause could have been convicted under the conspiracy to advocate clause involved in *Dennis* and *Yates*. The government would have to prove so great a level of actual participation in Party affairs aimed at actual revolution in order to show active, knowing membership with specific intent, that it could just as well use one of the conspiracy prosecutions initially aimed at the leaders of the Party, rather than resort to the membership clause with which it initially hoped to get the rank and file. Without sufficient proof to satisfy *Yates*, the government cannot prove membership of the sort that is required for conviction in *Scales*. Thus, in practice *Scales* almost eliminates the membership clause of the Smith Act and leaves the conspiracy to advocate provisions with the limitations imposed by *Yates*. Those limitations were, if you will remember, that advocacy of doctrine was constitutionally protected and only incitement to criminal action might constitutionally be condemned.

I am not seeking to defend the majority opinions in *Scales*. They are such transparent attempts by the modest to have their cake and eat it too that they are more than slightly ridiculous. My point is that even a modest court, and even the least libertarian of its members, when confronted by an ultimate assault on the political liberties of the First Amendment, resorted to the distinction between thought and action as the fundamental constitutional principle against which legislation was to be tested. Speech or behavior which reflected political belief was constitutionally protected; speech or political behavior which was part and parcel of revolutionary action was not.

Thus, the distinction between thought and action can be derived as the fundamental principle emerging from the whole history of the speech cases,[15] and it is a principle that can give substance to the preferred position doctrine, can make it something more explicit and jurisprudentially {121} satisfactory than the enunciation of a mood. The clear-and-present-danger rule is the tool that Holmes invented for applying precisely this principle to the facts of the actual cases that the Court must decide. It is a method by which the judge can distinguish speech that is simply speech from speech that is so closely linked temporally and causally to action that it is part of action itself and, therefore, constitutionally subject to regulation. Thus, the employment of the clear-and-present-danger rule seems to me the best means of translating the preferred position doctrine into specific constitutional decisions. The distinction between thought and action is the neutral constitutional principle that can be used to express the Court's special political role in the protection of speech that we refer to under the shorthand label of preferred position. The clear-and-present-danger rule is the working method for applying that distinction to the particular cases in which the Court must fulfill that role.

Clear-and-Present-Danger in Defense of Free Speech

One of the curious intellectual phenomena surrounding the clear-and-present-danger doctrine is that while, as we have seen, the opponents of judicial activism dislike it because it would lead to supposedly excessive judicial protection of speech, some of the defenders of freedom of speech oppose it because it allegedly does not offer enough protection. This might suggest, to borrow from an old fairy tale, that clear-and-present-danger was not too hot, and not too cold, but just right. However, the criticisms of such scholars as Professors Meiklejohn and Emerson are worthy of more careful consideration.

Professor Meiklejohn felt that public political speech should be absolutely protected from all abridgment.[16] His logical and historical arguments for proving that this is precisely what the First Amendment actually does mean are open to serious question, but are in fact largely irrelevant. This is what Professor Meiklejohn wanted the Supreme Court to say the First Amendment means, and the words of the Amendment will bear such an interpretation. It is what we want, not what the founders wanted, that counts. Meiklejohn objected to the clear-and-present-danger standard because it admits that some abridgments of even public political speech are constitutional under certain circumstances, and thus breeches his proposed wall of absolute protection. However, since he would have permitted reasonable regulation of time and place of speaking,[17] and argued that words that are part of criminal deeds are criminal, he was not so absolutist as he might seem. Indeed, the {122} clear-and-present-danger rule seems to me to be simply another way of saying what he himself said: "Words which incite men to crime are themselves criminal and must be dealt with as such."[18]

This point becomes clearer when we consider one of the main elements in Professor Emerson's attack on the rule.

> The formula assumes that once expression immediately threatens the attainment of some valid social objective, the expression can be prohibited. To permit the state to cut off expression as soon as it comes close to being effective is essentially to allow only abstract or innocuous expression.[19]

Given the context in which their opinions were written, I do not think the framers or later users of the clear-and-present-danger rule meant threat to the "attainment of some valid social objective" when they wrote "danger of a serious, substantive evil that Congress has a right to prevent." Nor need we. For instance, if we admit that the guarantee of a fair return to farmers is a valid social objective, then a union leader who got up and said, "Let's all go out and vote against any Congressman who has voted in favor of farm subsidies," might well be threatening "the attainment of some valid social objective," but surely no one, least of all Holmes and Brandeis, ever supposed that his speech would be punishable under the clear-and-present-danger doctrine. The doctrine states that freedom of speech is the rule. A statute which forbids all speeches in opposition to federal farm policy would thus be clearly and directly unconstitutional. On the other hand, a statute that forbids speakers to council forcible resistance to federal farm policy might be constitutional under the clear-and-present-danger rule, not because such speech threatened the attainment of the farmers' interests, but because it threatened mayhem on the rural roads. The clear-and-present-danger rule is designed "to cut off expression as soon as it comes close to being effective," but effective at creating criminal action, not effective at gaining its goals within the democratic process. It is the balancing opponents of clear-and-present-danger who would allow expression to be cut off if it sufficiently threatened the attainment of any Congressionally favored interests. The proponents of clear-and-present-danger are only willing to cut off speech when it threatens the most fundamental interest, our interest in having the laws obeyed and in changing them through our legitimate political processes rather than by the direct, physical violation of the law that would make such processes meaningless. If the twentieth century has taught us anything it is that freedom of speech is operationally useless if the other fellow has the gun and is allowed to use it, or if {123} political quarrels are settled on the basis of which a mob can control the streets. It seems to me that the clear-and-present-danger rule thus aims at precisely what Professor Emerson is aiming at: "the maintenance of an effective system of free expression." It insists that every speaker is free to say what he pleases unless and until his speech is so closely connected to illegal action that it becomes part of illegal action. Surely, no matter how absolute a defender of freedom of speech one may be, that defense cannot include protection for speech which is part and parcel of criminal action.

Professor Emerson's argument, however, does reveal one need for clarification in the clear-and-present-danger rule that arises from too often repeating the rule without the premise from which it is derived. What if Congress passed a law declaring that all speech espousing socialism is punishable by three years in jail. In this way speech itself would become criminal action, and a socialist speaker under the clear-and-present-danger rule, as I have just expounded it, would be subject to imprisonment because his speech was not only a clear and present, but also an immediate and direct violation of a criminal statute. But the premise behind the clear-and-present-danger rule is that such a law could never be constitutionally passed by Congress in the first place because the First Amendment forbids making speech itself criminal. It might be well, then, to add an explanatory addendum to the clear-and-present-danger so that it reads: Speech is constitutionally punishable when it constitutes a clear and present danger of a serious substantive evil, other than more speech, that Congress has a right to prevent, for the First Amendment prohibits Congress from forbidding any doctrinal variety of speech itself, no matter how serious and substantive an evil the Congress may believe that speech to be.

Too much preoccupation with the presentness aspect of the clear-and-present-danger rule in recent years has obscured the basic message of the rule, the message that *speech may not be abridged at all* except in those few peculiar instances in which a clear and present danger of criminal action exists. When the Supreme Court finds that a statute directly abridges speech and is thus unconstitutional, it need not mention clear-and-present-danger to follow the basic ideas that lie behind the danger test. In two recent cases the Court has moved directly to the position that the

First Amendment forbids limitations on the substance of speech without bothering about secondary formulas. The first, *New York Times v. Sullivan*,[20] in effect declares that the Alien and Sedition Acts were unconstitutional and that criticism of public officials may not be punished either as seditious or personal libel. In the second, *Lamont v. Postmaster* {124} *General of the United States*,[21] the Supreme Court for the first time in its entire history declared a Congressional statute unconstitutional as violative of the First Amendment. The statute imposed elaborate requirements on the delivery of Communist propaganda mailed into the United States from abroad. The Court found that the statute tended to inhibit the flow of certain ideas, and that the First Amendment forbids the inhibition of ideas which the government for one reason or another deems undesirable.

In yet another case, *Griswold v. Connecticut*,[22] the Court was hardpressed to find reasons for declaring Connecticut's laws forbidding the use of contraceptives unconstitutional, and piled the First Amendment along with many others to support a constitutional right to privacy which would keep the police out of the bedroom. What is interesting for our purposes is that in the First Amendment portions of the opinion the Court argued that ". . . the State may not, consistently with the spirit of the First Amendment, contract the spectrum of available knowledge."[23] Here again the Court is stressing that the First Amendment will not allow the government to regulate the substance of speech. These direct invocations of the First Amendment serve to remind us that the clear-and-present-danger rule is designed to implement an even more general rule forbidding the regulation of the content of speech. To state the implementing device is also to require the general rule.

However, some of the defenders of Holmes' modesty have claimed that the test did not mean this to Holmes. Pointing to the actual circumstances in *Schenck* and *Abrams*, they argue that Holmes meant the rule only as a test of the enforcement of statutes that were not themselves aimed at speech but which might be wrongly administered so as to abridge speech, leaving Congress free to make legislation directly abridging speech if it wished to. Holmes, however, dissented from just such an argument in *Gitlow*. To argue that Holmes is not testing the validity of the statute, but merely demanding that administrators and judges pretend that the statute does not exist except when it meets the clear-and-present-danger requirement, seems a more frantic verbal maneuver than even the preservation of Justice Holmes' modesty deserves. The *Abrams* dissent had, after all, spoken of what speech the United States might or might not "*constitutionally*" punish,[24] and the *Whitney* concurrence had certainly offered clear-and-present-danger as a test under which legislation might be voided. It must finally be admitted that Holmes and Brandeis were not quite the modest maidens that the more recent members of the judicial purity league would have liked them to be. {125}

While sometimes attacked for not giving sufficient protection to speech, probably the basic cause for the doctrinal decline of the danger rule is the widespread feeling that it was inadequate to meet the Communist menace because it gave too much protection to speech. *Dennis v. United States*[25] provides the anchor for this belief and we have already noted that *Dennis* is hardly a fair test of the rule since it was used, or rather abused, there by judges who had ulterior motives for destroying its effectiveness. In their judicial modesty they resented any doctrine that might effectively enlist the Supreme Court in defense of freedom of speech. Aside from issues of modesty, the main argument is, of course, that the clear-and-present-danger rule would allow the Communists to prepare the revolution at leisure, so that by the time there is a clear and present danger of a revolution, it is too late to stop it. Although this position has a certain impact at the purely verbal level, it fails to hold up under even a minimum application of reality. Failure to get beyond the verbal level was, of course, encouraged by the government's evidence in *Dennis* itself which was simply an anthology of the writings of Marxism-Leninism.

As an aside it might be noted that, even at this level, you cannot prove the Communists were advocating overthrow by force and violence since the Marxists themselves have now been quarreling for a hundred years over whether the canon requires violence against all free, Parliamentary regimes. But leaving the academic analysis of Marxist dogma aside, the whole history of Communist take-overs, as well as the writings of the leading Communist revolutionaries from Lenin to Mao, indicate that just talking does not make the revolution. If the clear-and-present-danger rule allows the Communists only to keep talking until the revolution comes, the revolution is never going to make it. In order for Communists to create a revolutionary situation or to gain control of such a situation, they must, according to our experience and their most authoritative revolutionary writers, do far more than advocate. They must perform innumerable acts of organization, planning, and violence which must amount at the very least to seditious conspiracy. If the Communists should ever become so far a victim of left wing deviation as to actually begin laying the real groundwork for revolution, the clear-and-present-danger rule will not prevent their dispatch if they have so much as stored their first gun, excited their first riot, or made their first plan as to where they will lead the mob on the great day. It is only because the government was unwilling or unable to bring forward any evidence of such active preparations at the time of the Smith Act indictments that, in *Dennis*, it had to attempt the totally abstract charge of conspiracy {126} to advocate, and only for this reason that it became necessary to trample on the danger rule to get at the Communists. The clear-and-present-danger rule will prevent you from legally throttling people you disagree with, but it will allow you to put potential revolutionaries in jail a very long time before they could complete the very elaborate, concrete, and long drawn out preparations that would be required to bring about a revolution in modern day America.

The clear-and-present-danger rule has also been subject to considerable criticism for its supposedly mechanical qualities and its vagueness in application. I think most of this criticism originated with Justice Frankfurter and his modest followers. Sooner or later nearly any rule or doctrine which would have constrained the Court to declare any statute unconstitutional was denounced by Justice Frankfurter as a rigid and mechanistic substitute for thought. Such rigid and mechanistic formulas were invariably condemned in favor of a pragmatic, case by case assessment of the practical factors involved. Not surprisingly, the pragmatic, case by case assessment almost invariably found some way of labeling the statute constitutional. The rigidity which bothered Justice Frankfurter about the clear-and-present-danger rule, or for that matter the ban on prior restraint, was that, once declared, such a doctrine would have forced the Court to declare some of the worst subsequent flights of legislative hysterics unconstitutional. Case by case, pragmatic thinking, on the other hand, allows the Court to adjust its own opinions—not social interests—to whatever new legislation comes along. Like so much else in the debate over free speech, the attack on clear-and-present-danger as rigid and mechanistic is best understood in the context of the tactics of the modest to actually abandon judicial review, about which they feel so guilty, without abandoning the façade of review.

It is true that the problems of any given case cannot be solved by a ritual incantation of the phrase clear-and-present-danger, and that the record of the forties does reveal instances in which the rule was invoked by certain Justices as little more than a slogan to cover their preference for the speaker. But the potential for misuse inheres in every legal rule or formula. Indeed, no formula has covered a greater number of unrealistic and mechanical decisions than "pragmatic, case by case balancing of interests." The clear-and-present-danger rule has less potential for artificiality than most constitutional formulas because it constantly reminds the Justice that he is to concern himself with the actual and immediate fact situation of the speech, and its connection with actual conduct, rather than with more ethereal considerations of social interests or philosophic truth. {127}

The clear-and-present-danger rule has also been accused of being vague—of giving insufficient direction to lower courts, prosecutors, and prospective defendants. By and large, looking at the history of the rule, this charge is probably true, but for reasons that have little to do with the merits of the rule itself. The appearance of vagueness in its application is largely the result of decisions like *Feiner, Douds,* and *Dennis,* in which a majority basically hostile to the rule and wishing to reach results opposite to those the rule would have required, nevertheless were so conscious of its precedential impact that they felt compelled to make formal obeisances to it even while acting virtually contrary to both its letter and spirit. Under such circumstances the rule did not, of course, give much direction to lower courts, but those are hardly fair circumstances under which to test it.

More precision in the use of the rule will also result when the fact is frankly recognized, as was not always done in the forties, that clear-and-present-danger does not fit all potential speech cases, and that judges must develop corollaries or substitutes to meet certain situations rather than try to stretch the rule unduly. For instance, we noted earlier that clear-and-present-danger is not sufficient to deal with hostile audience cases because by itself it does not give enough protection to speakers.

Another line of criticism involves the vagueness of the distinction between advocacy and incitement frequently involved in clear-and-present-danger decisions. Courts have for many years attempted to clarify this distinction, but, as Professor Corwin notes in commenting upon Brandeis' concurrence in *Whitney,* the clarification is frequently more verbal than real.[26] However, the criticism itself tends to be largely verbal. The clear-and-present-danger test does not rest on this distinction. Thus both the majority and minority in *Gitlow* attempted to distinguish between advocacy and incitement, and both agreed that mere advocacy could not be punished. And in *Yates* the feeble and confused discussion of this distinction is a smoke screen behind which the Court seeks to take back its *Dennis* decision. It does not really occur as part of the clear-and-present-danger standard, but as a disguise for the damage done by undermining the clear-and-present-danger rule in *Dennis* and the resulting inability to openly return to it in *Yates.*

It is always difficult to capture the complexity of concrete fact situations in abstract words. The terms advocacy and incitement seek to do so in the area of distinguishing thought and speech from action. That is why they are so often used in conjunction with clear-and-present-danger. But the danger rule itself is not an exercise in abstract definition, and can be employed without any reference to "advocacy" and {128} "incitement," which are simply abstract labels for the concrete findings that the danger rule is designed to achieve. It may or may not be convenient to label speech that the danger rule protects "advocacy," and speech that it does not "incitement," but whether the speech is protected or not depends on the application of the rule to the facts, not on the ability to derive satis-factory and mutually exclusive dictionary definitions of the terms. The purpose of the danger rule is not to create precise terms of art but to de-cide whether in actual situations the facts warrant the abridgment of speech. There may at times be a fine line between speech that presents an idea and speech that directs a crime. It is the same fine line that courts are required to draw every day when they are asked to decide whether in a given fact situation the raising of an arm constituted assault or just an excited gesture, a boy scout knife in the pocket meant preparation for a camping trip or possession of burglars' tools, or a billy club over the head was battery or reasonable restraint. Every rule of law is vague in the sense that it can not precisely elaborate what results it should yield in every imaginable fact situation.

Clear-and-Present-Danger and Judicial Capabilities

Solely in terms of ease of application, of course, an absolute test would be the most desirable. Any infringement on speech would then be uncons-titutional and the Justices would be required only to undertake the rather limited task of determining whether any real or potential interference with speech existed. But no one wants this simplicity of application be-cause of its obviously excessive costs in failing to admit that speech rights must, after all, in some way be accommodated to other rights. As soon as this admission is made, however, it commits the Justices to consider complex social circumstances and events beyond the simple question of whether someone did in fact prevent someone else from speaking. Thus, it is always child's play to show that any First Amendment test lying be-tween the extremes of absolute protection for speech and complete lack of protection puts a strain on judicial capabilities. Such strains are an ac-cepted and unavoidable aspect of the Supreme Court's work in many areas other than speech. In anti-trust litigation the Court, for instance, must base its decisions on the most complex and hypothetical calcula-tions derived from a highly imperfect state of economic knowledge. Yet if the anti-trust laws are to mean anything, the Court must decide today whether the purchase of one shoe company by another shoe company now will have a tendency {129} to reduce competition in the shoe indus-try ten years from now. In deciding whether the ICC has been correct in granting a certificate of convenience and necessity to a railroad owned truck line, the Court must decide whether the ICC's action effects the competitive position of railroads and independent truckers in such a way as to best preserve the "natural advantages" of each form of transporta-tion. Examples could be multiplied endlessly. It seems almost indecent to bring up the old stalwart of what constitutes an "unreasonable" search and the whole morass of calculations about the balance of power between the police and the criminal, particularly the organized criminal, that this constitutional problem brings into play.

The question then is always one of degree. Since sociological jurisprudence came into vogue, we have all recognized that the judge must go beyond deciphering the hieroglyphics on the Rosetta stone of digests and indices if he is going to fulfill his social and political responsibilities. The problem is, how far beyond? It seems to me that the clear-and-present-danger test makes fewer demands on the Justices' exploratory capabilities than do most of its rivals. Compared to balancing, it is child's play. There need be no assignment of weights based upon the construction of an ideal society and the calculation of just what balance of interests now will contribute most to such a society in the long run. Nor need the Justices determine exactly what negative impact the pursuit of one interest is having on the pursuit of another, or just exactly how much speech will be lost in order to gain just exactly how much national security.

The danger test requires only the examination of immediate circumstances, rather than the long-range assessment of massive, ill defined social interests required by the balancing formula. It has precisely the same advantage over the old bad tendency test, which required the prediction of events far in the future if it were to be anything more than an excuse for approving whatever interference with speech the legislature desired to make. It is easy enough to go through the motions of declaring that any speech critical of the government must in the long run have a tendency to bring the government into disrepute, and so will eventually lead to evil. But such a role is, in fact, an absolute withdrawal of judicial protection for speech, and we have already noted that absolutes at either end of the protection-non-protection spectrum are technically easy but otherwise undesirable. To determine whether a given instance of current speech will eventually lead to an evil sufficiently grave to warrant restricting the speech now would require a {130} very highly polished crystal ball indeed, and both the bad tendency and balancing doctrines share the necessity of weighing situations in the distant future against immediate ones.

The clear-and-present-danger doctrine generally has the advantage of requiring the judge to deal only with events that have already occurred or were expected to have occurred in the very immediate future if the speech had not been stopped. There is one exception to this proposition. Under the *Thornhill* rule,[27] one person may seek to have a statute declared unconstitutional on its face because of its potential for infringing on other speakers' constitutional rights, even though in the particular instance it did not interfere with his own. Thus, a speaker who was actually and admittedly inciting to riot, but was tried under a statute which forbade "all unsound and violent speech," might successfully ask the Court to declare the statute unconstitutional because it obviously allowed the state to stop any speaker it didn't like, even though in the particular instance it was used against a speaker who personally had no valid claim to First Amendment protection. Under the *Thornhill* rule, then, the Court is in effect asked to predict what unconstitutional uses a statute might be put to in the future.

But the *Thornhill* rule is not an integral part of clear-and-present-danger. It is also used in conjunction with the prohibition of prior restraints, the reasonableness standard for regulation of time, place, and manner of speech, and the rule against vagueness. Under all of these approaches the Court permits itself to inquire not only whether the rights of the defendant have been invaded but whether the statute in question gives so much latitude to administrative officials that they could pick and choose which speakers they wished to punish or forestall and which to leave alone on any basis they saw fit, including their own political prejudices. This level of prediction hardly seems beyond the Court's capabilities, involving as it does not a prediction of what *will* happen, but the typically legal task of anticipating the various potential results that *might* flow from the language of a legal document. This is precisely what the lawyers who draw up contracts and wills do every day. Indeed, the *Thornhill* rule is not really so much a matter of prediction as a method by which the Court requires legislatures to act in a lawyer-like way in shaping the language of statutes so that the range of potential administrative decisions are narrowly and predictably circumscribed.

Even if the clear-and-present-danger rule eliminates long-range prediction, the catch is those events that would have occurred in the immediate future, for whether a clear and present danger exists depends {131} on what you expect to happen next. Taking the easiest problem first, even in the street corner orator situation, the Court, removed a considerable distance in time and place, must seek to discover for itself whether the words used were about to trigger a riot. This requires a considerable knowledge of local conditions and something as ephemeral as the mood of a crowd. One might offhand say that this was too difficult a task for a court. But this is precisely the routine sort of task that courts are expected to undertake. If the First Amendment didn't exist at all the courts would still have to make precisely these calculations in order to determine, under the general evidentiary requirements of criminal law, whether the defendant was in fact guilty of incitement to riot. Just as under the clear-and-present-danger rule, the courts would have to inquire whether the speaker intended to spark a riot. Barring specific proof of intent, which, being proof of a state of mind, is almost impossible to obtain, the courts would, *as a routine part of their criminal law function*, have to determine whether a reasonable man would have had reason to believe that his speech was likely to trigger violence in the circumstances in which the defendant found himself. This is simply a different form of language for precisely the same calculations that the clear-and-present-danger rule requires. Therefore, in this kind of situation the clear-and-present-danger rule imposes no task on the courts that they are not accustomed to in the normal course of applying the criminal law.

What the clear-and-present-danger rule does do is allow the Supreme Court to undertake much of the responsibility for assessing the fact situation that would normally rest finally in the trial court. In the normal course of criminal law these findings of fact would be made primarily by the trial court and be reviewable by the Supreme Court only under the due process clause. In such instances the Supreme Court generally uses the "no evidence" rule; that is, it will only overturn the findings of the trial court if it can find no evidence in the record to support them. When the First Amendment and the clear-and-present-danger rule are introduced, the same issues cease to be questions of fact falling under the no evidence rule and become mixed questions of fact and law, since they involve the application of a constitutional standard to the facts. The Supreme Court, therefore, permits itself an independent review of the facts and will reverse the findings of the trial court if it feels that the weight of evidence considered as a whole falls differently than the trial court had thought it did, even though the trial court's findings are backed by substantial evidence. In the one instance, the weighing of evidence remains primarily with the trial court which will {132} only be overruled if none of the evidence in the case supports its conclusions. In the other, the Supreme Court undertakes an independent weighing of the facts and reaches its own conclusions. Thus, in normal criminal cases the fact finding rests more with the trial court, and when clear-and-present-danger is introduced, more with the Supreme Court. I do not think this is a particularly grave strain to put on the Supreme Court's capabilities in order to make the First Amendment operative, particularly in view of the Court's own, recent inclinations to allow itself more leeway under the no evidence rule.

It should also be noted that the reasonableness test makes similar demands on the Court. The notion that the state was entitled to reasonable regulation of at least the time, place, and manner of speech was a favorite of Justice Frankfurter, and often appeared as a rival to clear-and-present-danger in the forties. If this test is to be used independently and objectively by the Court, rather than as just another cover for judicial surrender, it requires the Justices to be familiar in the same way and to an even greater degree with local circumstances than does the danger rule. For if the Justices must decide whether it was reasonable to withhold a license from the Happy Valley Rambling Evangelists to parade on a Thursday afternoon down U. S. Grant St. in Little Falls, New Jersey, the Court will not only have to consider the risk of violence involved in such a parade as it would under the danger rule, but such things as traffic conditions, other events scheduled for the same place and day, the business or residential character of the street, the presence of schools, churches, cemeteries, etc., and anything else that might pop into the town fathers' minds as an excuse for getting the Happy Valley boys out of town quietly. I am not objecting to the reasonableness test on this ground; I am simply pointing out that the technical demands of the clear-and-present-danger rule are comparable to or less than those of the meaningful alternatives.

However, let us go on to the most wide ranging and, therefore, most difficult demands that the clear-and-present-danger test would impose on the Court's judicial capabilities. Professor Emerson puts the problem when he writes:

> If the Supreme Court had taken the factual issue seriously in the *Dennis* case, for example, and attempted to assess whether the utterances of the Communist Party actually constituted a clear and present danger, it would have been plunged into consideration of a mass of historical, political, economic, psychological and social facts concerning the position and influence of the Communist Party in the United States and abroad. This judgment {133} would have included both evaluation and prophecy of a sort no court is competent to give.[28]

It seems to me that Professor Emerson's example is nicely chosen to illustrate the considerable difference between the apparent and actual demands of the danger rule. If the Court in *Dennis* had been called upon to predict the chances of success for World Communism in the near future, it would indeed have been up against it. But the defendants in *Dennis* were not charged with speech contributing to Communist revolution in Czechoslovakia, Algeria, Timbuktu, and points south. They were charged with conspiracy to advocate overthrow of the government of the United States. The Court did not need to concern itself with whether there was a clear and present danger of revolution at any and all points of the compass. Just the U.S. would do. That is already a considerable cut in its load of political analysis. In fact, all the actual ramblings on the international situation engaged in by the various judges concerned in convicting Dennis were just excuses for sending men to jail under an indictment for a misty, ill defined crime without concrete evidence. Looking at it realistically, Dennis undoubtedly went to jail for what happened in

Czechoslovakia and elsewhere, not for what he did. We couldn't catch his friends who did it in those places, and we could catch him. But the danger rule is designed to prevent just this kind of international guilt by association.

Under the danger rule only one sort of international prognostication is required: whether the defendant's speech is connected with espionage or sabotage. In *Dennis*, there was not one shred of real evidence to suggest such a connection, nor does the indictment or anything in the record suggest such a connection, so that under the clear-and-present-danger rule the Court would not have had to do even this international analysis. And, again incidentally, it should be noted that if the courts were to be called upon to determine whether a given speech were creating a clear and present danger in the sense of being linked to espionage and sabotage, they would be doing no more than they would have to do in determining whether the government had met its burden of proof under a criminal charge of conspiracy to violate the espionage statutes.

In the final analysis, it must be held firmly in mind that what Dennis was charged with was conspiracy to advocate the overthrow of the *United States* Government *in the United States.* Under the clear-and-present-danger rule the only question for the Court would have been, did Dennis' speech create an immediate danger of overthrow of the U.S. government. I don't think that question required any extraordinary {134} range or depth of political and social analysis by the Supreme Court. Indeed, it was precisely because Hand and an overwhelming majority of the Supreme Court had no difficulty in completely agreeing that it was obvious that Dennis' speech did not create such a clear and present danger that everybody had to work so hard to sidestep or scuttle the danger rule in order to confirm his conviction.

That agreement suggests that the political judgments required by the danger rule in cases like *Dennis* are not nearly so subtle or difficult as they are sometimes made out to be. After all, what reliable observer would have had any difficulty then or now in determining whether the spouting of Marxist tracts at secret meetings—and that is all Dennis was charged with—created a clear and present danger of immediate overthrow of the American government by force and violence? The whole pitifully ineffective record of the Communist movement in America provides the key to the obvious solution to the problem. In order to apply the clear-and-present-danger rule to the speech of allegedly subversive groups, the Supreme Court must decide whether the specific speech in question is rendering the nation ripe for nearly immediate revolution. While that might seem a very difficult piece of analysis in the abstract or in the Congo, in practice it does not prove to be a particularly difficult task in the United States.

FREEDOM OF SPEECH

It is, of course, the factual analyses connected with clear-and-present-danger that make the most severe demands on the Justices' capabilities, and we have seen that these are not so severe after all. At the level of legal and moral philosophy, the danger test is one of the simplest of those available. In terms of legal principles, the Justices need only rely on the thought-action distinction which, in view of its traditional acceptance, is relatively easy to expound and defend. The clear-and-present-danger rule is completely neutral at the moral level. It is totally unconcerned with the question of whether the substance of the speech with which it deals is good or bad. This was, of course, precisely its appeal to Justice Holmes who wished to protect speech without involving the Justices in ideological judgments about its merits. It would be a Pyrrhic victory indeed if we saved freedom of speech from the clutches of the legislature only to turn it over to a set of nine Platonic guardians. More important for the purposes of our discussion here is the fact that, in a period in which there is no firmly fixed and universally acknowledged liberal-democratic political philosophy, the clear-and-present-danger rule allows the Court to avoid making judgments as to which of many rival philosophical pronouncements are correct or incorrect. {135}

In this sense, the clear-and-present-danger rule is the First Amendment formula most in accord with our current state of philosophical uncertainty. It forbids the Justices to undertake exercises in political philosophy which would at best seem incomplete and at worst naïve. It should be remembered that the market place rationale on which the danger rule partially rests need not be taken as implying that the free competition of ideas leads to truth, thus making the Justices somehow responsible for reaching truth. The foundation of the market place rationale for Holmes was his skepticism, which takes its more general form in modern systems of scientific and linguistic uncertainty. If we can never be sure that any statement is true—indeed, if the only thing we are nearly sure of is that no statement is completely true—then any government action preventing any given statement is illogical and arbitrary: illogical because the throttling of one statement as partly false implies that the government is in possession of a contrary statement that is wholly true, and there are no such statements; arbitrary because the government chooses to protect the partial truths favored by some citizens and to attack the partial truths held by others. And unscientific and unaesthetic because such government action tends to freeze the status quo mixture of truth and falsehood. The amorality of the clear-and-present-danger rule is thus designed to prevent the courts, and indeed all of government, from undertaking a task which is beyond the current capabilities of science and philosophy.

Thus, the clear-and-present-danger rule makes fewer demands on judicial capabilities than any test requiring them to rest their decision on the moral or philosophical merits of the speech in question. Under the danger rule the Justices need not decide whether the speech is correct or incorrect, good or evil, or how good or how evil, but only if it creates a clear and present danger of action that violates the criminal law.

Clear-and-Present-Danger and Our Next Problems

If the clear-and-present-danger rule requires the Justices to look a little bit into the immediate future, it might be best for us to do the same thing. Indeed, this is probably the best way to sum up some of the merits of the danger rule as well as to reach a realistic estimate as to what demands it will make on judicial capabilities.

Speech cases in the immediate future are likely to involve three sorts of situations and groups. It is always possible that some combination of {136} international and domestic circumstances will bring on a renewal of the Red scare, but by this time there are few overt Communists or obvious fellow travelers left to pick on. It will be necessary to do some very fancy imagining indeed to hang the Communist label on what little mildly leftist political sentiment remains in the United States. The clear-and-present-danger rule, by requiring a link between such sentiment and revolution, would direct attention to the weakest link in the argument of the hysterical rightists and effectively protect leftist speakers without putting undue strain on the Court's capabilities.

The second speaking group that is likely to end up in court is the extreme right wing of the neo-Fascist variety. The problem with groups of this sort is handling them in such a way as to avoid creating precedents for stifling political dissent, while at the same time thwarting their goal of creating situations of intergroup hatred and violence which might snowball into further support for extremism. In a general way this is the classic case that the clear-and-present-danger rule was designed to cover, for it will frustrate the urges toward censorship and other illiberal responses that Fascism often does, and indeed sometimes hopes to, bring on, while allowing the intervention of the law as soon as there is a clear and present danger of street violence. I do not underestimate the difficulty for judges in deciding just when the portents of violence become clear enough to justify intervention, but that is the inevitable problem which all responsible officials of a liberal democracy must solve when faced with antidemocratic groups seeking to goad them into antidemocratic action. The judgment of the courts is likely to make a nice counterbalance to the judgment of the police and other local officials. It must nevertheless be admitted that the clear-and-present-danger rule is not in and of itself completely adequate to deal with the hostile audience situations that might frequently arise when Fascist speakers are involved. Shortly, however, we shall look at some addenda that should make the rule fully applicable in such instances.

The third, and probably the most serious, First Amendment problem we are likely to encounter in the near future is now being incubated in Harlem and other Negro ghettos. The clear-and-present-danger rule is obviously so well suited to responsible Negro spokesmen that there can be little doubt of its use by the courts in the future. Surely we do not wish to stifle Negro claims and, just as surely, at certain times and places, under certain circumstances, allowing Negro leaders to voice such claims would be an invitation to massive bloodshed. The clear-and-present-danger rule allows a relatively independent and unentangled observer to decide when the threat of violence was real and when it was {137} used as an excuse for cutting off legitimately voiced but politically embarrassing Negro claims.

Opponents of the clear-and-present-danger rule sometimes argue that, even if it is applicable, local administrative officials, because of their detailed and direct knowledge of local conditions, are in a better position to apply it than are the courts. They certainly are in the best position to apply it initially, but not independently. It is, after all, the local official who is frequently the target of the speech. At the very least, the local official is often identified with the circumstances, or politically supported by the interests, denounced. Moreover, it is the local official who is immediately responsible for peace and good order, and the more seriously he takes his responsibilities, the more likely he is to be overzealous in quieting "trouble makers." Administrative expertise must be given its due, but administrative impartiality is likely to be most severely strained when speech denouncing the status quo is involved. The clear-and-present-danger rule allows the administrator full scope for his administrative knowledge and the speaker a necessary protection against the misuse of administrative discretion in circumstances where it is peculiarly likely to be misused.

Those, however, who are preaching doctrines of racial hatred present a much more difficult problem than the spokesmen for normal Negro political demands. When we were dealing with Communists advocating class struggle, the problem was not serious because class antagonisms are simply not strong enough in the United States for such teachings to threaten our political structure. Unfortunately, the racial situation is far more grave. Would it be possible to tolerate long-term, concerted, and widely effective advocacy of a philosophy of racial hatred and apartheid by black nationalist groups in Negro communities where social and political conditions might make the population peculiarly receptive to such doctrines? Are we for once faced with a situation where speech alone, unconnected with criminal action, might gradually so exacerbate feelings of social conflict that, long before the clear and present danger of an open outbreak, too much damage would have already been done to repair by the normal means of counter persuasion and practical political concession? It must be admitted that the racial question is the one issue in American life that has at various times proved unamenable to the normal workings of the political process and has broken through our general Lockian consensus to become a conflict of principle. Conflicts of principle are, of course, the one sort of conflict that a liberal democracy, whose life is compromise, cannot tolerate, for it is possible to compromise interests but not principles. {138}

If large numbers of American Negroes insist on immediate satisfaction of all their just claims and righting of all past wrongs, on principle and without regard to the interests of other social groups, and on the threat of violence—that is, if Negroes are unwilling to submit their claims to the normal complex and non-principled compromises of the political process —a great many of our liberties are going to go by the boards, and Americans are going to become familiar with all sorts of police state tactics that we have been fortunate enough to avoid in the past. It will be necessary to do something not only about the First Amendment, but also about the unreasonable search and seizure provisions of the Fourth, the due process clause of the Fifth, and the jury trial guarantees of the Sixth as well.

Under such circumstances, neither the clear-and-present-danger rule nor any other rule calculated to allow all speakers equal rights under the First Amendment is going to work, and we would inevitably have to resort either to balancing, to censorship techniques, or to some form of doctrine which would exclude racial agitation, as it now excludes obscenity, from First Amendment—and thus from clear-and-present-danger rule—protection. It is not difficult to imagine how a racial exception to the First Amendment and the danger rule could be formulated and defended in terms of the peculiar danger of racial tensions to our social structure.[29]

All this may seem to be a curiously dubious and depressed note on which to end a discussion of what I believe to be the efficacy of the clear-and-present-danger rule. My point is, however, that the clear-and-present-danger rule only need be abandoned if we actually do begin to encounter something close to a new civil war, and that in abandoning the rule we would be confessing that our democratic political process could not contain American racial tensions. So long as we are faced with Negro spokesmen of the more moderate variety, clear-and-present-danger will work. So long as Negro extremism remains a fringe element, the clear-

and-present-danger rule will operate, as it does with all extremist fringes, to keep it from stirring up the immediate violence on which extremism thrives and to allow us to rebut vicious philosophies in the market place of ideas without whittling away at the First Amendment. The danger rule and the ideas that lie behind it have the added advantage in this situation of constantly reminding the citizenry that everyone is free to engage in politics but no one is permitted to solve his political problems in the streets.

Before we begin to junk the democratic process in the face of racial unrest, we ought to be quite sure that the danger is grave enough to {139} warrant such extreme steps. It would be the most vicious form of racism to assume that American Negroes are not sufficiently endowed with American values and sufficiently amenable to the free competition of ideas to reject subversive ideas without the aid of a kindly white censorship. In terms of racial agitation, it seems to me that the clear-and-present-danger rule will suffice for the immediate future and, indeed, until such time as we are reasonably sure that circumstances have changed so markedly for the worse from their present condition that we cannot maintain both the integrity of our social and political structure and the full freedom of speech. That is, after all, as much of a life expectancy as can be granted to any constitutional doctrine.

The Eclectic Decade

This book is not intended as a complete survey of all the possible alternative approaches to the First Amendment. It might well be titled "Preferred Position and Its Enemies." But an analysis of preferred position exclusively in terms of its implementation through the clear-and-present-danger rule would not be completely satisfactory for two reasons. First, the clear-and-present-danger rule in and of itself is not sufficient for dealing with all the possible infringements on the First Amendment. In certain kinds of cases and factual situations, it must be supplemented by other judicial devices and concepts in order to effectively fulfill the special tasks of the Court in relation to speech.

Secondly, while this is basically a book of prescription not prediction, it must be recognized that the Supreme Court is now moving into a period of doctrinal flux. The marginal reintroduction of the clear-and-present-danger rule, plus the decline of balancing and the tendency to shift from a modest to a preferred position tone, promise a doctrinally eclectic judicial style for the immediate future. This tendency is reinforced by the general instability in Court attitudes caused by the presence of several new Justices and the very marginal strength of the libertarian alliance of Justices Black, Douglas, Warren, and Brennan—an alliance which cannot last indefinitely and may or may not gain new re-cruits in the future. Under such circumstances, no single doctrine, clear-and-present-danger or otherwise, is likely to emerge as the domi-nant tool of the Court, even if the Justices return to the role of protectors of speech envisioned by the adherents of preferred position. Indeed, the Court might achieve a rather confused but relatively effective return to preferred position through a medley of doctrines in which clear-and-present-danger was but a single contributing voice. {140}

Therefore, it is necessary to look at several additional doctrines and problems of First Amendment interpretation, both in order to complete the design of supplementary equipment necessary to make the clear-and-present-danger rule operate effectively, and to indicate other ingredients that the Court might well mix with clear-and-present-danger to imple-ment the preferred position philosophy.

Least Means, Narrowly Drawn Statutes, Vagueness, Reasonableness

It might be best to begin with a catalogue of left-overs from the forties and early fifties. The most important of these may well be the "least means" test, which can be used either independently, or as a supplement to clear-and-present-danger, or as a decisive element in balancing — par-ticularly when balancing is limited to determining the constitutionality of legislation aimed at some legitimate purpose but incidentally infringing on speech. The classic example of the test involved a local sanitation or-dinance forbidding the distribution of handbills. The Court struck down the ordinance on the grounds that the city could find other means of keeping the streets clear—for instance, a fine for littering—less restrictive of freedom of speech.[30] If we put our emphasis on "least," this is a ba-lancing test. The state is allowed some limitation on speech so long as it can demonstrate that it is the least limitation possible in order to achieve some other public interest. But in practice "least means" may easily be-come "no means." In most instances the Court will be able to envisage some means of achieving the state's purpose which does not infringe upon speech at all, and that, of course, would be the "least means."

This test allows the Court to handle realistically all sorts of excuses for governmental infringements on speech that are really not necessary to achieve the legitimate goals of the state. At the same time, it requires the Court to set itself up as a kind of general expert on governmental ways and means and, like balancing itself, it permits and will cover any deci-sion the Court wishes to make without requiring any particular judicial consistency. Justice Harlan recently wrote:

> This Court has repeatedly held that a governmental purpose to control or prevent activities constitutionally subject to state regulation may not be achieved by means which sweep unnecessarily broadly and thereby invade the area of protected freedoms. The power to regulate must be so exercised {141} as not, in attaining a permissible end, unduly to infringe the protected freedom. Even though the governmental purpose be legitimate and substantial, that purpose cannot be pursued by means that broadly stifle fundamental personal liberties when the end can be more narrowly achieved. . . . There are appropriate public remedies to protect the peace and order of the community which do not infringe constitutional rights.[31]

The least means test allows the more modest members of the Court to strike down invasions of free speech while still assuring themselves and the legislators that the Court will not cripple the power of the state. Such a test may help to protect the First Amendment now while committing the modest to no more than the case by case determination of when a government action infringes upon speech as little as possible in achieving its goals. At the same time the test asserts the special position of speech. It may then serve on occasion as a meeting ground for most of the elements on the Court.

Indeed, the least means test may be the most potentially libertarian speech formula available, one roughly equivalent to the old reasonableness test in the field of economic regulation which allowed the Court to strike down any statute that it found unwise. For, in effect, the least means test allows the Court to formulate its idea of which statutes would be wisest, which would fulfill social goals with least invasion of liberty, and then to strike down any statute that does not meet its views. There is already some indication that the Court is moving in this direction.[32] Closely related to the least means test is the requirement that statutes touching upon speech be narrowly drawn so that administrative officials may not use them to arbitrarily discriminate between speakers, or to infringe on freedom of speech when the statute is ostensibly for some other purpose.[33] This test merges gradually into the void for vagueness doctrine. Under the First Amendment, a statute touching upon speech must be worded with sufficient clarity to insure that the administrator cannot use it discriminatorily in favor of the exponents of some views at the expense of others, or as a means of prohibiting speech that could not be constitutionally prohibited.[34] Alternatively, a vague statute offends the First Amendment because the very uncertainty of what constitutes an offense will unduly intimidate potential speakers who will not be certain just what they are or are not legally permitted to say.[35] The Court has struck down statutes which condemned "sacrilegious" utterance[36] or "collections of pictures or stories of criminal deeds of bloodshed or lust . . . so massed as to become vehicles for inciting violent and depraved {142} crimes against the person."[37] It has also struck down statutes which provided no standards at all when vesting in administrative officials the discretionary power to license speakers.[38]

Like least means, this test too has recently been reemphasized by Justice White, a Justice not identified with the libertarian camp. In *Bagett v. Bullitt*,[39] a state loyalty oath provision was struck down for vagueness. As the dissenters (Harlan, Clark) point out, the language condemned by Justice White there as vague was strikingly similar to the language with which the Court had had no difficulty earlier in another oath case, and, indeed, to the language which is at the heart of the statute involved in the *Dennis* case. Void for vagueness seems to be a handy and flexible doctrine for protecting freedom of speech at the moment, without the sort of total commitment implied by the clear-and-present-danger rule. Like least means, it implies that the state can always find a better and constitutional way if it will keep trying. Also like least means, however, it can be useful as a rallying point for a kind of eclectic, ad hoc return to preferred position.

Closely connected with all of these tests is the old reasonableness rule for time, place, and manner ordinances. The notion is that so long as neither the ordinance nor its administration is directed against the content of speech, but is designed to deal with problems of traffic flow, noise control, commercial solicitation, etc., the state action is constitutional if it is reasonable. Basically the reasonableness test is inimical to both preferred position and clear-and-present-danger because it suggests that the state may do what it pleases to speakers if it acts reasonably. But as long as it is confined to time, place, and manner regulations, it maintains the crucial distinction between the control of thought and the regulation of action, and is compatible with a high level of protection for speech. When used negatively to find an infringement of speech unconstitutional, it too may serve as a meeting ground for various Justices who wish to protect speech in a given instance but do not share a common vision of what the Court should do in general about the First Amendment.

All of these tests are best suited to governmental action aimed at some other purpose which incidentally affects speech. Depending on their precise employment, all of them may be used either to approximate a balancing technique, which permits extensive limitations on speech in pursuit of other interests, or the clear-and-present-danger rule, which allows infringements only under pressure of dire necessity. In a somewhat unsettled doctrinal period all may be used to avoid commitment to either of these positions or as supplements to one or the other when {143} particular cases involve circumstances for which they seem particularly suitable. The actual impact of all these approaches, therefore, awaits their crystallization over time into aspects of or counters to a preference for freedom.

Procedural Objections

Next we turn to a technique of the fifties which has not crystallized. At the time of the maximum assault on alleged Communists and fellow travelers, the Supreme Court issued a great many decisions which did not go to First Amendment questions, but managed to keep the speaker out of jail by resort to finding some minor, and usually procedural, fault in his treatment prior to conviction. This approach has been erected into a whole new philosophy of judicial modesty, in which the role of the Court becomes one of wielding a suspensive veto. Where a statute is constitutionally dubious, the Court is to find some minor flaw so that it may be sent back to the legislature which will then have a chance to reconsider the constitutional question. Of course after reconsideration, if it still wants the statute, the legislature can repass it eliminating the minor flaw.[40]

In practice, while this technique has saved a few individuals from immediate punishment, it has been largely ineffectual as far as defending the First Amendment is concerned. Its principal virtue is also its debilitating vice. The legislature, or often only some administrative agency, often need only change a few words and we are back where we started with an infringement on freedom of speech. In more than one instance the very defendant saved the first time around received precisely the same punishment in the end after a few formalistic bows to the Court's procedural sensitivities. Nearly every one of the major procedural decisions has been followed by a second decision approving a slightly cleaned up version of the same governmental practice, which remains just as repulsive to the First Amendment as it ever was. A Court which constantly turns the First Amendment into an exercise in legal technicalities will eventually convince the public and the rest of the government that the First Amendment is simply a legal technicality. If all that stands in the way of a "good and necessary" governmental program, like making the world safe from communism, is some legal technicality, certainly the reaction of many Americans is going to be that all we need do is hire a good lawyer to get around the technicality for us and go right on with what we were doing. Long series of technical decisions do not necessarily husband the Court's strength for the big battle to come. {144}

They may materially reduce the Court's ability to win that battle by sapping its public position as guardian of the fundamental truths of the First Amendment which becomes obscured under a mass of technical ifs, ands, and buts. Indeed, no matter how careful the Court's wording, procedural decisions are likely to leave the impression that there will be no problem once the details are fixed, and so create an expectation that the basic line of legislative action will be declared constitutional at the next go round. Such an expectation further weakens the Court's position. If the Court constantly whispers "maybe" and never delivers a ringing no, people trained in the common everyday experience of life, instead of in the law schools, are likely to take the Justices as meaning yes. Certainly the Court's past record of procedural objections followed by constitutional surrenders would indicate that that is precisely what the Court has frequently meant.

Much of the Court's influence in American politics is derived from its ability to set the basic vocabulary in which communications on certain political issues are framed. One of the key advantages of the clear-and-present-danger rule and the preferred position doctrine is that, when sufficiently popularized by the Court, they force the discussion of political regulation into channels basically favorable to speech interests. Professor Bickel's vaunting of the "passive virtues,"[41] of which procedural opinions are one element, tends to neglect this fact. If pursued consistently, the policy of avoiding constitutional issues and invoking various technical grounds to return constitutionally unpalatable statutes to the legislature, without declaring them unconstitutional, in the hope that they will be corrected, robs the Court of its chance to create a vocabulary of freedom.

Professor Bickel's virtues become either virtues or vices, depending upon the basic attitudes of the judges and commentators who employ them. For the judicially modest, they are simply another means of deferring to the legislature without admitting that they are abandoning judicial review. For the activist they are a convenient device for avoiding the legitimation of invasions of freedom of speech *when and only when* the total constellation of political forces makes it politically unwise for the Court to attempt the direct confrontation with opposing forces that declaring a statute unconstitutional entails. The passive virtues, like most political tactics, are useful when they are wielded with sophistication and delicate timing to enhance the power of the tactician. But to achieve their purpose they must be employed as part of an over-all pattern in which the Court chooses at any given moment precisely that degree of activism or passivity which will best contribute to its own position and {145} the position of the interests it represents, both immediately and in the long run. In politics, there is always a time to run and a time to fight. Professor Bickel has shown us various procedural and jurisdictional methods of making limited retreats. Preoccupation with these methods should not obscure the fact that retreat must be viewed as a preliminary to advance, and that retreat prolonged indefinitely is likely to lead to final defeat.[42]

Indeed, I take this to be precisely the message of Professor Bickel's book, although he tends to obscure the basic activism of his approach in the language of Professor Wechsler's neutral principles of constitutional law.[43]

We can probably expect many procedural decisions in the future. In the first place, the real vice of some statutes infringing speech may be procedural. Certainly, where tighter procedures will in fact cure a statute's potential invasion of the freedom of speech, procedural decisions are in order, and eminently suitable for judges whose expertise, after all, supposedly lies in the procedural realms. For instance, the Court might well hold that the Post Office's practice of seizing allegedly "obscene" materials in the mails without a judicial determination of obscenity is unconstitutional because of the absence of sufficient procedural safeguards to insure that only obscene materials are seized. Some of the decisions employing least means or vagueness are suspensive vetoes of the Bickel variety, although it should be noted that many go further than this, by requiring that the state infringe less on the First Amendment, not simply infringe with greater nicety. In each instance one crucial question is going to be, does the opinion really force the state into respecting freedom of speech, or does it simply give the state a second chance to do the same thing all over again? A long series of procedural victories for speakers is one method of implementing preferred position for the movement but it is the least likely of all such methods to have any solid or lasting effect.

What Is an Infringement on First Amendment Rights?

One of the favorite expressions of the Supreme Court these days seems to be "[First Amendment] freedoms . . . are protected not only against heavy-handed frontal attack, but also from being stifled by more subtle governmental interference."[44] By and large, although sometimes sub silentio, the Court has come to accept Justice Black's long insistence that any sort of government connected deprivation motivated by past speech or association is a violation of the First Amendment.[45] Dismissals from public employment, disbarment, loyalty oaths, and the {146} withholding of tax exemptions now seem to fall within the First Amendment area, although they may still be subject to only rather weak First Amendment limitations.[46] The withholding of passports has moved somewhat in that direction.[47] It is now assumed that governmental breaches of anonymity in speech and association are infringements on freedom of speech, even when disapprobation by private citizens may be the only result. The Court has recently suggested that union members whose dues are used to further political causes to which they are opposed may have valid First Amendment claims.[48] It has held that litigation is a political activity protected by the First Amendment, and that a state law unduly interfering with the right of an association to litigate and aid others in litigation is unconstitutional.[49]

We have already noted that the *Thornhill* rule gives a special preference to freedom of speech by allowing one man's standing to plead the First Amendment rights of another, even when a statute as applied to himself would not infringe upon his speech. The rule thus allows the Court to strike down statutes that contain potential infringements on speech even before actual infringements occur. The *Thornhill* rule has recently found a very prominent place in Supreme Court decisions.[50]

Even the most vigorous enforcement of the clear-and-present-danger rule would provide but limited substance to the preferred position doctrine if the rights protected by the First Amendment were narrowly defined or only criminal punishments and formal prior restraints were considered infringements on those rights. Under the pressure of the increasingly elaborate range of tortures that have been invented for alleged subversives in the north and dissatisfied Negroes in the south, the Court has been moving toward a broader and broader concept of First Amendment rights and what constitutes infringement of those rights, even if it still sporadically tends to find excuses for those infringements.

The Newest Problem: No Evidence, Private Property, Hostile Audience

Racial agitation is not precisely a new problem for the Court, but it promises to play a newly important part in First Amendment litigation. The Court has recently been getting a considerable number of street and sit-in demonstration cases from the south. Several of them presented situations that the clear-and-present-danger rule would have easily disposed of. But to have employed the clear-and-present-danger rule would have been to admit that First Amendment rights were involved. For reasons we will get to in a moment, the Court did not wish to make {147} such an admission. Luckily, the southern prosecutors and trial courts had been obliging enough not to provide any evidence at all that the conduct of the speakers had actually threatened or created the disturbances of the peace for which they were convicted. The Court invoked the "no evidence" rule.[51] By means of this rule the findings of a state trial court will be reversed by the Supreme Court under the due process clause when there is no evidence in the record to support such findings.[52] In this particular instance, the no evidence rule acted as a kind of clear-and-present-danger rule without the First Amendment, the Court in effect holding that you cannot send speakers to jail unless there is a proven threat of substantial violence. However, the no evidence rule will not work when there is even a little evidence, and in the future prosecutors are likely to provide some. Like so many of the devices we have been assessing, the no evidence rule provides only a temporary and very self-limiting supplement to the clear-and-present-danger rule.

The no evidence rule will only work at all when sit-in demonstrators have been arrested for disturbing the peace. Quite a different situation arises when the arrest is for trespass since the speaker's presence on the scene plus the owner's protest provide some evidence. The sitter-in accused of trespass has three general lines of defense open to him. The first is that his arrest and conviction constitute state action in aid of discrimination violative of the equal protection clause. The issues here are very complex and, while a majority of the Court has been moving in the direction of this argument, its position is carefully hedged. The second is that the Constitution itself prohibits discrimination in places of public service and accommodation. Therefore, no trespass has occurred because the owner of, for instance, a restaurant has no right to forbid entrance to a Negro simply because he is a Negro. Here again the issues are complex, and it seems probable that a majority of the Court would prefer to let the new Civil Rights Act take care of the problem without going to the constitutional principle.[53] If the Court in the future affirms either of these two positions, or if the Civil Rights Act is fully effective, the third defense is less likely to be raised. It is a First Amendment claim. The sitter-in argues that his demonstration was a part of the freedom of speech protected by the First Amendment. His punishment under a trespass law would then be an unconstitutional infringement on freedom of speech.

So far most of the Justices have been unwilling to face up to this problem.[54] The only important precedent is *Marsh v. Alabama*,[55] a 1946 decision in which the conviction of speakers for trespass on the streets of a company owned town were found unconstitutional. *Marsh* {148} can today be read in any way you wish. Narrowly interpreted it means that the streets of a town which is in all respects like any other town except that it is privately owned are to be treated for First Amendment purposes like the streets of any other town. Alternatively, it can be read very broadly to suggest that the rights of the First Amendment extend to private property devoted to a public use or upon which the general public is customarily invited, or even to any property devoted to a commercial use or to which large numbers of people are admitted.

Only Justice Black, in a case which, significantly enough, found Douglas on the other side, has fully canvassed the issues, and it is worth quoting him at some length. In summing up the First Amendment position of the sit-in demonstrators he says:

> Their argument comes down to this: that . . . they had a perfect constitutional right to assemble and remain in the restaurant, over the owner's continuing objections, for the purpose of expressing themselves by language and "demonstrations" bespeaking their hostility to Hooper's refusal to serve Negroes. . . . Unquestionably petitioners had a constitutional right to express these views wherever they had an unquestioned legal right to be. But there is the rub in this case. The contention that petitioners had a constitutional right to enter or to stay on Hooper's premises against his will because, if there, they would have had a constitutional right to express their desire to have restaurant service over Hooper's protest, is a boot-strap argument. The right to freedom of expression is a right to express views—not a right to force other people to supply a platform or a pulpit. It is argued that this supposed constitutional right to invade other people's property would not mean that a man's home . . . could be forcibly entered or used against his will—only his store . . . which he has himself "opened to the public . . ." Legislative bodies . . . could of course draw lines like this, but if the Constitution itself fixes its own lines, . . . legislative bodies are powerless to change them, and homeowners, churches, private clubs, and other property owners would have to await case-by-case determination by this Court before they knew who had a constitutional right to trespass on their property. And even if the supposed constitutional right is confined to places where goods and services are offered for sale, it must be realized that such a constitutional rule . . . could as well be applied to the smallest business as to the largest, to the most personal professional relationship as to the most impersonal business, to a family business conducted on a man's farm or in his home as to businesses carried on elsewhere.

> A great purpose of freedom of speech and press is to provide a forum for settlement of acrimonious disputes peaceably, without resort to intimidation, force, or violence. The experience of ages points to the inexorable fact that people are frequently stirred to violence when property which the law recognizes as theirs {149} is forcibly invaded or occupied by others. Trespass laws are born of this experience. . . . The Constitution does not confer upon any group the right to substitute rule by force for rule by law. Force leads to violence, violence to mob conflicts and these to rule by the strongest groups with control of the most deadly weapons.[56]

It seems to me that Justice Black's position sticks squarely within the boundaries of the clear-and-present-danger rule and the distinction between thought and action that should lie at the heart of the Supreme Court's treatment of speech claims. Trespass is a criminal action which accompanying speech cannot excuse. When the state punishes a vocal trespasser, it punishes his actions not the content of his speech, and his actions are such as to have traditionally been considered criminal, all questions of desirable and undesirable speech aside. The employment of passive physical force is no more within the domain of freedom of speech than is that of active physical violence. The Court has recently gone out of its way to specifically declare that deliberate violation of valid traffic laws—that is, civil disobedience—is not itself a form of expression protected by the First Amendment but a form of action, even when such demonstrations are intended as a vehicle of protest.[57]

The final problem raised by Negro demonstrations is the old one of hostile audience. The clear-and-present-danger rule will handle most street demonstration cases, but there is a notable exception. If a concrete or tacit agreement can be reached with the police, groups hostile to a speaker may repeatedly create the appearance of a clear and present danger with the assurance that the result will be the arrest of the speaker and not themselves. The clear-and-present-danger rule will be circumvented if the police allow or encourage a real or staged clear and present danger to develop as an excuse for arresting the speaker.

Therefore, as a supplement to the clear-and-present-danger rule in such cases, the Court might employ a version of the least means test. Was the arrest of the speaker the measure least damaging to speech that could have been employed to prevent the substantive evil of rioting? Put another way, did the police take reasonable steps to protect the speaker and control the audience before resorting to the arrest of the speaker?

It must be admitted that such a test is far from automatically self-enforcing. What are reasonable steps? Must the police call out their reserves, station fire trucks at the intersections, and have their tear gas bombs ready before the imminent failure of these measures warrants arrest of the speaker? It would be tempting to sketch out ground rules, {150} but this seems to be one of those instances where the answer must really develop case by case, since there is an infinite number of possible situations, each in some ways unique. Certainly in *Feiner v. New York*,[58] where the speaker was arrested under the danger rule after one man accompanied by wife and child told a policeman that he would stop the speaker if the police didn't, there was an easily diagnosable abuse of the danger rule.

Negro demonstrators in the south and in many parts of the north, or white demonstrators in Negro areas, will pose more difficult problems.

But surely the Court can prevent charades in which police encourage or remain passive toward real or mock audience grumblings, and then take as their first step the arrest of the speaker. And surely there must be some independent review of the police measures taken to quell the incipient rioters rather than arrest the speaker if unpopular speech is not to be at the mercy of anyone who finds a friendly cop and says, "I'll yell and you arrest the speaker."

If the Supreme Court has the time to decide whether every movie a state censor dislikes is dirty enough to ban, it can surely find the time to assess whether the police are following the spirit as well as the letter of the danger rule. In close cases, it might be well to give the police the benefit of the doubt, and it should be remembered that the danger rule does not require that the police allow a riot to begin and then arrest the rioters before the speaker. Nevertheless, the right of free speech in public places would be a hollow one indeed unless the Court insures that the police have not actively or passively encouraged the danger which they then use to justify the arrest of the speaker.

Preferred Position Balancing

At the height of the balancing technique's popularity in the fifties it was possible to note a certain divergence of view between Justices Black and Douglas on the one hand and Warren and Brennan on the other. While Black and Douglas more and more openly rejected balancing, Warren and Brennan tended to pick up at least some of the rhetoric of the technique. They, however, attempted balancing of a more realistic variety than that of the modest, for whom balancing was simply a means of retreat before legislative pressure. Of course real balancing, unhampered by the prearranged results of modesty, is likely to find the speech interest more weighty and, consequently, the restrictive statute unconstitutional, at least some of the time. Indeed, since Justices Warren and Brennan felt that freedom of speech was an especially important {151} interest, it was likely to win most of the time. After all, Justice Frankfurter had felt just as strongly about the importance of freedom of speech, and he constantly assured us in his opinions that, but for considerations of modesty, he would have jumped to its defense. Stripped of that modesty, balancing, therefore, tends to become preferred position balancing—that is, balancing of interests with an especially heavy weight given to the claims of speech. Thus *Gibson v. Florida Investigating Committee* speaks of the need for an "overriding and compelling . . . immediate, substantial and subordinating state interest."[59] These "compelling interest" opinions now form one of the strongest lines of precedent in the case law of the First Amendment.[60]

Balancing could in the future be used over a wide range of First Amendment problems to implement the preferred position doctrine, or it could be used in only a few areas in which it seemed especially suitable, for instance where two First Amendment claims are in conflict with one another. It may well be that balancing will continue to be useful in some situations of this kind, where the clear-and-present-danger rule is not completely suitable, particularly when used in conjunction with the least means test and other similar devices. The intersection of the First Amendment claims of newspapers as speakers with their responsibilities as businesses under tax and commerce laws is one example that comes readily to mind.

Justice Black has continued to insist, with much academic support, that the Court ought to limit balancing to the purpose for which it was originally intended, situations in which a law aimed at action had some incidental effect upon speech.[61] Thus, in mass picketing and other mixed speech-action situations, where only the action not the substantive speech is regulated, incidental effects on speech would be permitted where a serious evil of action could not be met without some minor inhibitions on speech. In effect, balancing would be reduced to a cross between the reasonableness test for time, place, and manner regulations and the clear-and-present-danger rule itself. In this form it would be compatible with preferred position.

It is, from my point of view however, inadvisable to use the technique any more than is absolutely necessary, for reasons that have already been stated at sufficient length. It is significant that the First Amendment areas in which it continues to enjoy considerable favor are those in which the Court is faced with the problem of living with those past decisions which deny rights to Communists while beginning again to extend those rights to non-Communists. Balancing is a convenient way of reducing the precedential impact of the earlier decisions without repudiating them. {152} The Justices can always say that the balance is simply different today than it was then. The greatest weakness of balancing is precisely this failure to repudiate a past betrayal of the First Amendment, however well intentioned and required by political exigencies that betrayal may have been. However frequently the speakers win the balancing game in the near future—and I suspect they are going to win fairly often—the *Dennis* and *Barenblatt* precedents will remain, and the Court will be doing nothing to build up a solidly pro-speech doctrinal base from which to defend it against future assaults.

It seems probable that balancing will, in the immediate future, continue to serve as one of the principal weapons in the armory of a Court increasingly interested in protecting speech. But, as a matter of prescription rather than prediction, it would be best to reduce that service to an absolute minimum.

Prior Restraint

In the 1930s the Supreme Court hit upon the constitutional prohibition on prior restraints as a partial substitute for the then out of favor clear-and-present-danger rule.[62] Prior restraint is the prevention of speech before it occurs, rather than subsequent punishment via fine or imprisonment. There has been a steady trickle of decisions striking down statutes as prior restraints. If anything at all is clear about what the founders meant by the language of the First Amendment, it is that it was designed to prohibit prior restraints. Nevertheless, the modest have in the usual way argued that there is no absolute right against prior restraint, and that the prohibition on prior restraints when used to strike down statutes has been a mechanistic substitute for thought.

The notion that prior restraints are peculiarly obnoxious rests on several grounds. First, the public never gets to hear the speech and so does not know what it has been deprived of. Public opinion cannot, therefore, act as a check on governmental restriction. Second, censorship systems grant an arbitrary power to the censor to pick and choose what he wishes to enter the market place of ideas. This does not, by the way, seem to me a totally realistic argument for finding all prior restraints worse than subsequent punishment. Prosecutors, too, choose which speakers to subject to subsequent punishment and which to leave untried. In both instances the arbitrariness of the administrator can be much reduced by systematic statutory and administrative prescription of standards. But in any given instance, a system of prior restraint may give tremendous amounts of unrestricted power to the arbitrary decisions of {153} the censor if it is not carefully circumscribed, and in fact, it often isn't.

Thirdly, subsequent punishment, unlike prior restraint, allows speech unless and until the state intervenes. In the setting of liberal democracy at least, such intervention is likely to be sporadic and speech the rule, punishment the exception. Put another way, the government official must make a rather extraordinary decision to act. Administrative inertia and the tolerance of public officials, their willingness to let well enough alone, is, so far as it exists, on the side of speech. A censorship system, on the other hand, requires constant state supervision of speech. The censor is under a positive duty to judge each speech. Unlike the prosecutor, he cannot react by inaction in doubtful cases. Anything he does not disapprove, he must approve and thus take personal responsibility for. This must naturally lead to much more prohibition of speech than the supervision of a prosecutor who does not officially associate himself or the state with the speech he chooses not to prosecute. When in doubt the prosecutor permits, but the censor must condemn, for he cannot risk putting the state seal of orthodoxy on materials of doubtful quality. For this reason, historical experience has endlessly demonstrated the deadening and self-expanding effect of censorship on the propagation of ideas.

Any attempt to summarize the state of the Supreme Court case law on prior restraint would be largely useless, for the total number of cases is not very large and the decisions are spread out over a long time period that includes many Courts of many differing moods and purposes. On the whole, the doctrine has been used to supplement the Court's First Amendment conscience by giving the Justices an occasionally handy peg on which to hang speech decisions. There has never been an absolute prohibition on prior restraint as such, and what generally raises the Court's constitutional ire is not prior restraint per se, but the presence of one of the specific evils that I have just now briefly sketched or of some other attendant evil.

For instance, in *Thomas v. Collins*,[63] which involved a Texas statute requiring that outside labor organizers register their presence in the state, it was the problem of anonymity that actually seems to have led the Court to a finding of unconstitutionality on prior restraint grounds. Similarly, in *Kunz v. New York*,[64] a license to speak was denied a sidewalk evangelist, apparently because the police anticipated trouble in the street. The Court invoked prior restraint, but seemed basically to be concerned with preventing the police from circumventing the clear-and-present-danger rule by invoking the threat of street violence so far in advance of the actual speaking situation that no realistic assessment of their claim could be made by the courts. {154}

Where licensing or registration requirements have been struck down, it is generally because they left room for an arbitrary or discriminatory decision by government officials.[65] Not the prior restraint itself, but the vagueness or total absence of standards, which allowed an official to make decisions on the basis of his own attitude toward the content of the speech, was usually at the heart of the Court's objection.

Prior restraint claims have recently been concentrated in the obscenity area. Here again what happens to those claims depends upon the actual or potential infringements on speech that lie behind the prior restraint. The Court approved a New York statute that authorized preliminary court injunctions forbidding the sale of obscene materials.[66] The statute required a hearing before the judge issuing the injunction and provided for an almost immediate trial thereafter to finally determine whether the works were obscene. In two later cases where ordinances permitting seizure of obscene materials before trial lacked the rigorous procedural safeguards of the New York provisions, the statutes were struck down.[67] What matters then is not the prior restraint per se, but the opportunity for arbitrary limitation on speech before a full trial on whether the utterances were obscene and thus constitutionally subject to regulation.

In these obscenity cases the Court seems to be aiming at the evil of arbitrary advance censorship, but at the same time it seems to have overlooked another evil of prior restraint—that the public does not find out what has been withheld from it, since the material is seized before it reaches the public. There is, of course, the easy way out by arguing that obscene material is not entitled to First Amendment protection. In this light, the Court's demand for careful procedures eliminating arbitrary and discriminatory use of prior restraint powers is identical with its demand that obscenity regulation carefully avoid infringing on non-obscene materials. Once the prior restrainer is sure that the material is obscene, his prevention of its distribution is neither discriminatory nor an interference with the public's right to know what is being condemned because that right only extends to materials covered by the First Amendment. In other words, the normal arguments against prior restraint do not apply to obscenity because they are derived from the First Amendment and obscenity is not speech within the meaning of the First Amendment. I have already argued that the exclusion of obscenity from First Amendment protection is just a clumsy dodge to avoid the clear-and-present-danger rule, and that to consider obscenity regulation without considering the First Amendment is like playing Hamlet without the hero. If we continue to hold the First Amendment firmly in {155} mind, the fundamental evil of secret censorship remains a major feature of seizure before trial of allegedly obscene materials. We are not dealing simply with prior restraint in the abstract, but with one of the real evils behind prior restraint. It is true that since a trial eventually occurs, the public will get some idea of what is being withheld. On the other hand, all it will discover is the titles of works that it cannot read because they have all been seized. In such instances, unless the work is already well known, there is no possibility of an informed public opinion acting as a restraint on the would-be censors. Moreover, where periodicals are involved, an immediate seizure, even followed by an eventual finding of non-obscenity, threatens such serious economic loss that a good deal of self-censorship is likely to occur on the part of dealers and distributors, and self-censorship is the most secret of all.

All this leads us to one area of obscenity prior restraint that does pose a peculiarly vicious threat to freedom of speech—motion picture censorship. The evils of this already evil system are multiplied tenfold because of the peculiar nature of motion picture prints as a form of expression.

Censors rarely object to a film as a whole but only to certain scenes. If those scenes are excised, the film will be granted its license. The exhibitor is faced with the choice of losing a few scenes, a loss that will not prevent him from showing the remains at his usual prices, or getting himself involved in long and costly litigation so that in the end he may show the whole film at his usual prices. Moreover, in many instances he is faced with the choice of showing a cut version of a current film that is enjoying a spate of good reviews and publicity or the uncut version of same film in a couple of years when it has been forgotten. If he suffers the cuts he is not compelled to advertise that fact on his marquee, so, cut or not, he is likely to get the same size audience now but a much smaller one later. Faced with this situation, the economic pressure on the exhibitor to submit to the censors' demands, no matter how arbitrary and unreasonable, is extremely great, and the impact on freedom of expression enormous. And this is also the most secret form of censorship. If a book is withheld, some of the public will at least know the title of the work they are not being permitted to read. But when an exhibitor agrees to allow cuts in a film, neither he nor the city are likely to advertise the fact. The public sees the film and never knows that excisions have occurred. Motion picture censorship is the closest to *1984* we have so far gotten in this country.

In *Times Film Corporation v. Chicago,*[68] the Supreme Court decided that it would be premature to declare *1984* unconstitutional now. Chicago's film licensing ordinance was subject to a broadside attack by {156} an exhibitor who refused even to submit his film to the police, hoping in this way to force the courts to decide on the constitutionality of the system as a whole, rather than avoiding the issue by allowing their decision to turn on the actual obscenity or non-obscenity of the film itself or on some due process flaw in the procedures used. Five members of the Court were unwilling to say anything that might be interpreted as a general prohibition against film licensing, and so the censors won. In effect, the majority directed exhibitors to submit their films to the censor and then come to the courts if the censor incorrectly found the films to be obscene. Such a decision perpetuates precisely those features of prior restraint which are most damaging to freedom of expression. It preserves the all pervasive censorship of the state which has to assume direct and positive responsibility for the quality of every film. It maintains the economic pressures on the exhibitor to accept secret cuts that may affect his artistic but not his financial balance sheet rather than engage in costly litigation which, even if he wins, will probably reduce his box office.

The Court has recently chosen to reaffirm its approval of prior restraint of films, but to impose a set of conditions on such restraints that are designed specifically to meet many of the evils of the system. In

Freedman v. Maryland,[69] a decision striking down Maryland's film licensing law, the Court listed the following requirements for a valid film statute:

1. The burden of proving that the film is obscene rests on the censor.

2. Final restraint (denial of license) may only occur after judicial determination of the obscenity of the material.

3. The censor will either issue the license or go into court himself for a restraining order.

4. There must be only a "brief period" between the censor's first consideration of the film and final judicial determination.

In short, *Freedman* turns the censor into a prosecutor who, unlike a censor, is not in the position of having to say that he approves every film he licenses, but only that he licenses those films on which he does not think he can get an obscenity conviction in court. The exhibitor is guaranteed a quick judicial decision which reduces the economic pressures on him to make concessions to the censor. The judicial standard of obscenity is now so broad that the judge is bound to be the most liberal censor available. The necessity of court proceedings will bring somewhat more publicity to the whole process. {157}

Yet the basic evil of secrecy remains, since the result is that the supposedly offensive material will be excised before it reaches the public, rather than that the criminal communicator will be punished subsequent to public showing. *Freedman,* then, affirms roughly the same prior restraints on films as the Court allows on printed materials under the New York pre-seizure system. It confirms the Court's general tolerance for prior restraint at least in the area of obscenity, but it also sets up such rigorous constitutional standards that the Court will be able to knock down most existing statutes piecemeal as violating one or another of its requirements.

Such a piecemeal assault on prior restraint whenever it involves real infringements on speech would be one means of implementing the preferred position doctrine and an occasionally useful adjunct to the clear-and-present-danger rule. Where prior restraint is part of obscenity regulation, much of the task may be accomplished by continuing to narrow, either in principle or practice, the definition of obscenity. In both obscenity and other areas, the prior restraint doctrine may be useful for clothing judicial demands for stricter statutory standards and procedural safeguards to restrict the censorial whims of administrative officials and for statutes which achieve the states' legitimate goals through means other than those which restrain speech. There is nothing in the life and times of the doctrine, however, that suggests that the Court is likely to move to the position that all prior restraints on speech are per se unconstitutional. The prohibition on prior restraints is at best a small caliber weapon in the preferred position arsenal.

Obscenity and Libel

So long as the exclusion doctrine survives, it will, of course, be impossible to apply the clear-and-present-danger rule to obscene speech. Only Justices Black and Douglas currently oppose the exclusion of obscene expression from First Amendment protection. The Court has invented one formula after another to define what is obscene. Each is piled on the last, so that not only is each formula internally contradictory, but layer upon layer of definitions are built up, all of which are still supposedly valid and each of which contradicts every other. There would be little use tracing the history of this confusion except to say that the Court has gradually been moving toward a hard core pornography standard that extends First Amendment protection to any speech having any redeeming social importance or artistic merit. Such a standard {158} would, in effect, implement the preference for freedom for everything but the most dreary dirt.

The Court's latest pronouncement, *Jacobellis v. Ohio*,[70] is a step, albeit a confused one, along that route. I count one Justice moved all the way to hard core pornography (Stewart), two more traveling in that direction (Brennan, Goldberg), and two who would in effect support the regulation of only hard core pornography in the sense of opposing any regulation at all (Black and Douglas). Even Warren and Clark are not so much opposed to a hard core pornography standard as discouraged about pumping any more precise meaning into it than can be found in earlier Court efforts. Moreover, their insistence that deeds and circumstances, not the content of the work, are the crucial questions, in effect leads to a hard core pornography standard, since it is designed to catch only those who sell dirt for dirt's sake to those who buy dirt for dirt's sake.

It might then be concluded that seven Justices currently favor the narrowing of state regulation and consequent increase in freedom of expression suggested by the shift from obscenity to pornography. However, Justices Warren and Clark dissented in *Jacobellis* because they now generally prefer to allow state court findings of obscenity to stand unless the evidence is quite strongly against such a finding. The box score is then, I think, roughly seven to one (White uncommitted) for hard core pornography when cases come up from the states that themselves use a hard core pornography standard (including the center of publishing, New York); five to three when the state uses a broader obscenity standard; and probably eight to zero when federal regulation is involved, since Justice Harlan believes that the federal government should be held to a much stricter standard than the states. For practical purposes the Court seems to be willing to go fairly far in broadening freedom of expression over sexual matters.

This practical movement should not, however, be allowed to obscure the fact that obscenity is the one First Amendment area where the Justices countenance thought control instead of control of action, that they have gotten into this position by abandoning the clear-and-present-danger rule, and that the result is a judicial confession of confusion, intellectual impotence, contradiction, and divisiveness unparalleled in any other area of the Court's jurisdiction. One reading of that logical nightmare labeled *Jacobellis v. Ohio* should be enough to convince anyone that the Supreme Court is totally unequipped to undertake the role of grand moral censor that Professor Berns and others might wish {159} to assign it.[71] Indeed, the Court is presently so demoralized about the morality of speech that it seems useless to propose any new solution which, even if accepted, would undoubtedly be heaped on top of the old to add further confusion to the pile. For the moment we must be satisfied with the vague and imprecisely rationalized liberalization embodied in the movement toward a hard core pornography standard. Eventually Americans may come to recognize that control of sexual thought, like control of any other kind of thought, is basically incompatible with the First Amendment and the role of the courts in its defense.

We saw earlier that obscenity and libel are two areas of speech that were "excluded" from First Amendment freedom of speech as part of the attack on the clear-and-present-danger rule and the preferred position doctrine. Just as obscenity is being moved back into the fold through the hard core pornography standard, libelous speech too seems to be regaining its status as speech protected by the Constitution. In 1964 in *New York Times Co. v. Sullivan*,[72] the Court unanimously ruled that the First Amendment offered some protection to libelous speech directed at a public official's conduct in the performance of his office. Six justices ruled that an official might recover for false statements of this sort in a civil damage suit only if the statements were made with "actual malice—that is with knowledge that it was false or with reckless disregard of whether it was false or not."[73] Three justices viewed such statements as constitutionally protected, malice or not.

This opinion is, in effect, a compromise between the laws of libel and the preferred position of freedom of speech, which neither completely includes or excludes libelous speech from the First Amendment, but does strongly emphasize the priority of freedom of speech over some of the traditional social interests expressed in the libel laws.

FREEDOM OF SPEECH

Anonymity and Congressional Investigations

The right of anonymity seems in recent years to have become an accepted corollary to freedom of speech itself. Curiously enough, this right has been firmly imbedded in Supreme Court doctrine by the *Barenblatt*,[74] *Wilkinson*,[75] *Braden*,[76] and *Communist Party v. Subversive Activities Control Board*[77] decisions, in all of which First Amendment claims were denied. In each case, the four dissenters insisted that compulsory disclosure of past political advocacy, or membership in organizations engaged in political advocacy, violated First Amendment rights {160} and thus was unconstitutional. The majority agreed that First Amendment rights were being infringed but, using the balancing doctrine, discovered sufficient government interest in disclosure to constitutionally justify the infringement. So far as we can tell, all nine Justices affirmed that the right to speak and write anonymously and maintain anonymous membership in an organization engaged in political discourse is an integral part of the freedom of speech protected by the First Amendment.

The right of anonymity presents some serious problems stemming from the market place rationale. On the one hand, fear of disclosure, and the official and unofficial harassment that might follow, would discourage many purveyors of dissident and unpopular views from putting their goods on the market. On the other, the consumer certainly would benefit from knowing that the strictures on Japanese foreign policy he has just heard came from the Ancient and Honorable Company of American Tuna Fishermen. This paradox exists whether you believe that the market place is the best test of truth or the acknowledgment of human intellectual imperfection. A knowledge of the source of views would in many instances obviously help to establish their truth or falsehood. And one of the fundamental requirements of philosophies of uncertainty—which are, after all, rationalist philosophies—is to identify and label as many of the sources of distortion and imperfection in observation and communication as possible.

The difficulty of the problem can be seen in the decisions of the Supreme Court. It has approved exposure requirements for lobbyists engaged in face to face contact with Congressmen, while at the same time making clear that such requirements for lobbyists who seek to influence legislators indirectly by propagandizing the public would run into grave constitutional difficulties.[78] It has similarly approved the registration of speakers in the pay of, or controlled and dominated by, foreign powers whose speech is directed at furthering the interests of those powers.[79] But even Justice Frankfurter, in throwing the Communist Party into that category in *Communist Party v. Subversive Activities Control Board*,[80] strongly hinted that organizations without such foreign ties could not constitutionally be forced to reveal themselves.

Moreover, even when the Court has quashed convictions and declared statutes unconstitutional on the basis of a right of anonymity, it has usually hedged its bets. Thus, in the late fifties and early sixties in *N.A.A.C.P. v. Alabama*[81] and *Bates v. Little Rock*,[82] it struck down exposure ordinances aimed at the NAACP, but on the grounds that they bore no reasonable relation to a state interest justifying exposure. The NAACP decisions were in turn heavily relied upon in the recent and now {161} leading decision on exposure by legislative investigation in which the Court got no further than the following cautious statement:

> Nothing we say here impairs or denies the existence of the underlying legislative right to investigate . . . with respect to subversive activities by Communists or anyone else . . . and we hold simply that groups which themselves are neither engaged in subversive or other illegal or improper activities, nor demonstrated to have any substantial connections with such activities are to be protected in their rights of free and private association.[83]

Only in *Talley v. California*,[84] which struck down an ordinance forbidding the distribution of anonymous handbills, did the Court introduce the constitutional right without any ifs, ands, or buts. And even *Talley* is probably less an assertion of an absolute right of anonymity than some sort of variation on the least means test. In *Shelton v. Tucker*,[85] which involved an Arkansas statute that compelled every public school teacher to file an annual list of every organization to which he belonged or had contributed in the last five years, the Court was careful to preserve the right of the state to ask specific questions of specific teachers while condemning a blanket exposure that might excessively intimidate teachers from exercising their rights of association.

The Court has obviously been moving toward a constitutional right of anonymity on the same level with freedom of speech itself, but largely because of the paradox of anonymity discussed above and, of course, because of the always tricky problem of the Communist, it has continued to do a good bit of fence straddling. It is not worthwhile to attempt an elaborate analysis here of precisely what the previous cases mean, because they obviously mean that the Court is uncertain and is preserving its options.

Its principal method of rationalizing its uncertainty is the balancing technique. Indeed, the line of anonymity cases from *N.A.A.C.P. v. Alabama* in 1958 to the recent *Gibson v. Florida* is the principal current survival of balancing. If we are in a position where we wish to approve some kinds of exposure, like the registration of foreign agents, and condemn others, like the registration of the NAACP, balancing seems like a pretty good idea, but largely because it will allow us to do anything we please without worrying about consistency or real fairness. Moreover, the use of balancing in the *Subversive Activities Control Board* case to approve an invasion of anonymity was the high point of self-abortion in the use of balancing as a judicial technique. For there Justice Frankfurter stated more clearly than he ever had before that the only thing {162} the Court can do is balance, and that once Congress strikes a balance, the only thing the Court can do is gracefully accept it no matter how constitutionally repulsive it is.

It seems to me preferable to frankly acknowledge that we are confronted by a paradox, and acknowledge that it is not entirely soluble, rather than resorting to a balancing formula which is at best a smoke screen to hide the lack of a complete solution, and at worst a cause of judicial paralysis and a means of downgrading First Amendment rights. What most of us would really wish to say about infringements on anonymity is that when they are designed as punishments or intimidations they are wrong and when they simply provide additional, useful information, they are permissible. For instance, the federal legislation requiring the registrations of those directly lobbying Congress does give Congress more adequate means of assessing the truth, but is unlikely to cause any organization or interest group to cease lobbying—that is, it is unlikely to reduce the flow of ideas into the market place. To be sure, the persuasiveness of certain political pleas will be reduced when their source is identified, just as it would be lessened by counter argument, but this ideological rough and tumble is just what the market place requires. Similarly, the registration of agents of foreign governments may make their arguments less persuasive, but it will hardly coerce any of those governments into abandoning their claims to our attention. Such registration simply means that when Chiang Kai-shek urges us to invade China, he is also required to present the first argument that opponents of his position would make—that it is Chiang who is urging us on, not the Society for World Peace and Divine Brotherhood. On the other hand, certain exposure requirements are purely coercive and designed to drive the speaker out of the market by tacitly threatening him with the official and non-official harassment that would follow the breaching of his anonymity. Such obviously were the regulations involved in the NAACP cases.

So far, certainly, no balancing is required. Exposure statutes that give additional information about ideas, without narrowing the flow of ideas, are constitutional. Statutes designed to narrow the flow of ideas by opening speakers to various forms of harassment are unconstitutional. In this way the Supreme Court's decisions on lobbyist and foreign agent registration can be easily squared with its NAACP decisions. However, what of statutes that would give us more information, but at the cost of coercing speakers. Cases like *Talley* present the heart of the paradox of anonymity. Unsigned political handbills, particularly those disparaging candidates for office, can often be the most vicious exploitation {163} of the market place. They can offer shoddy goods that we would reject out of hand if we knew the identity of the seller, and they can offer them at crucial moments, like the night before elections, when there is no time for rebuttal. On the other hand, for individuals or groups holding popularly despised views, the anonymous pamphlet can be the one shield behind which they can speak safely. As I said earlier, paradoxes are not always subject to perfect solutions. If, however, the Court is to act as a special protector of speech, it must, where it can, resolve paradoxes in favor of speakers, particularly since other government agencies are likely to resolve them differently. Once it is admitted that breaches of anonymity that open the way to coercion and harassment of speakers are invasions of the First Amendment—and the whole Court has admitted this at one time or another—then preferred position and clear-and-present-danger can be used in connection with exposure statutes just as with any other statutes infringing speech.

Under the preferred position solution suggested here, the Court would seek to discover for each statute whether it had a coercive potential or not. Those that do not, do not violate the First Amendment, as it is not exposure per se that is unconstitutional. It is exposure that creates the potential for intimidating speakers. Where this is the obvious thrust of the statute, the statute is unconstitutional. There is no reason why the Court should not pierce whatever facade of legitimacy is thrown up by the state as it did in *N.A.A.C.P. v. Alabama* and *Bates v. Little Rock* in order to find a direct attack on the substance of speech. Such an attack is an obvious violation of the First Amendment, and so does not require the application of preferred position or clear-and-present-danger.

Where the state is seeking to further some legitimate purpose by its exposure, its actions should be governed by the same constitutional rules that ought to govern other state actions aimed at a legitimate purpose, but infringing on speech—the preferred position doctrine and the clear-and-present-danger rule. Thus, in cases like *Shelton v. Tucker,* but those purged of the obviously punitive motives of that particular instance, the state might be told that, in the interest of teacher qualification, it could require the disclosure of such speech activities by teachers as constituted a clear and present danger. On the other hand, its interest in an ideologically conforming body of teachers should yield to the preferred position of freedom of speech for all citizens including teachers.

Instances like *Talley*, where the paradox of the market place is really involved, are not so easily disposed of because there the state is, in effect, asserting one market place interest against another. Nevertheless, exposure so disfavors unpopular speech, as opposed to speech supporting {164} the status quo, that the Court's special duty to protect unpopular speakers, expressed in the preferred position doctrine, should take preference over the occasional improvements in ideological marketing conditions that exposure might bring. This is not a perfect solution. There is none. But it is a solution that recognizes the special duty of the Court to protect speakers from governmental and social coercion. There is, in a sense, a kind of balancing here because two internal values of the market place, and thus of the First Amendment, are in conflict with one another. But I do not think ad hoc case by case balancing is necessary, because I can imagine no situation in which an exposure statute which does coerce speakers could create so much added truth in the market place as to overbalance the harm to the market done by the coercion. If such a statute were to be found, it might be worth introducing a balancing doctrine to cover this peculiar instance of two First Amendment rights conflicting with one another.

Communist Party v. Subversive Activities Control Board,[86] decided in 1961, presents one of the most difficult of the market place paradoxes. Justice Frankfurter emphasized that the registration statute only applied to a foreign controlled and dominated organization. But the Communist Party was more than that. It was also a numerically substantial group of Americans espousing a political philosophy in which they personally believed. While a Wall Street law firm or a Washington lobbyist is not going to be substantially intimidated by a registration requirement from professionally representing the views of the Trujillo regime, some Americans are intimidated from expressing their own views by the registration requirements of the Subversive Activities Control Act. Indeed, it was obviously the intention of those who wrote the act to stifle Communist ideological activities by subjecting individual Communists to the social and material deprivations that would follow their exposure. This peculiar dual status of Communists, who are both agents of a foreign power whose views will always be known to us even if its agents have to register, and exponents of a domestic philosophy which may be cut off from the market place by exposure, precludes the kind of easy solution that exists when registration either exposes without coercing or coerces without exposing anything of crucial importance. Justice Frankfurter seeks to resolve the dilemma by balancing which, as he goes to great pains to admit himself, leads to a foregone conclusion because of his modesty. The preferred position doctrine would have led to the opposite conclusion by resolving the contradictions in favor of the speaker unless the government could demonstrate that the Communist Party constituted a clear and present danger. Since the statute does {165} coerce the Communists out of the market in their domestic capacity, the preference for freedom would require that it be declared unconstitutional even though it would not coerce the Soviet government out of the market. Again, such a solution is not perfect. Ideally we should know both what the Communists are saying and that they are saying it. But in the actual situation, and indeed in the intention of the legislators, the statute would prevent us from knowing what the Communists are saying by intimidating them. Only when a statute adds to our fund of information *without* cutting anyone out of the market is it any service to the First Amendment to find it constitutional.

Frankly, I see no prospect of a reversal of the *Subversive Activities Control Board* decision, but the key area for anonymity at present is that of legislative investigations which is currently in a very fluid state as far as Supreme Court decisions are concerned. Perhaps it will be possible to do better there.

It is necessary to begin any discussion of legislative investigations and anonymity with a firm understanding that exposure is now, and always has been, one of the chief purposes of legislative investigations. It has been intrenched into legitimacy by long usage, and is so intimately a part of nearly all investigations, whatever their other purposes, that a condemnation of all investigations involving exposure would in fact almost totally destroy the investigative power of the legislature. Unfortunately, when the Supreme Court first searched about for some constitutional means of limiting Congressional investigations, it hit upon the separation of powers doctrine in its most naive form, and reasoned that since Congress had only lawmaking powers, only those investigations in aid of making laws were constitutional. Conversely, investigations designed to hold wrongdoers up to public scrutiny, rather than gathering information on which to base legislation, were unconstitutional. Since this constitutional requirement was totally out of kilter with reality and would have required a Court crusade against the whole investigatory power to enforce, the Justices soon came up with a doctrine of presumption of legislative purpose for Congressional investigations. And since the Court was inevitably confronted with one case after another in which exposure was obviously an important element in the investigation, the presumption doctrine had to grow and grow until it outweighed all contrary evidence, for otherwise the Court would have had to admit that no investigation in reality met its fairy tale requirement of a legislative purpose and nothing but a legislative purpose.

Aside from providing a curious case of judicial pathology, all this would not have been important but for two effects it had on the First

{166} Amendment rights of witnesses. First, the legislative purpose and presumption doctrines created a situation in which the Court became accustomed to absolutely refusing ever to look at what was really going on in Congressional investigations because the first realistic glance would have always resulted in finding a violation of its unrealistic separation of powers requirement. Thus, the Court could not afford to entertain arguments that exposure in a given investigation violated a given witness' First Amendment rights. Once the Justices took the fatal step of realistically examining one investigation to see if exposure there violated the First Amendment, how could they avoid finding exposure in all the other investigations and having to nullify all of them because exposure always violates the separation of powers. An excessive and unrealistic, and thus unenforceable, constitutional limitation based on separation of powers had, as its only effect, the creation of pressure on the Court to ignore the possibility of creating a narrowly drawn and workable limitation based on the First Amendment.

Secondly, the presumption of legislative purpose, when combined with balancing and judicial modesty, inevitably had a disastrous effect on First Amendment claims. If exposure for exposure's sake, a secondary and often morally dubious power of Congress, had been thrown on one side of the scale and freedom of speech on the other, freedom of speech might have occasionally won. But because the Court had always to presume that Congress had a lawmaking rather than an exposure purpose, it was the most sovereign, most august, and most intimidating power of Congress—the lawmaking power itself—that was placed on the balance opposite free speech. Thus, free speech was necessarily always the good little man who inevitably loses to the good big man.[87]

The Court may or may not openly confess its error on legislative purpose in the future, but it is important for us to get clear of all the tangled logic and stereotyped arguments that stem from its initial error in order to make a sensible assessment of Congressional investigations in connection with the First Amendment. Beginning, then, with the fact that nearly all the Congressional investigations about which First Amendment claims arise will involve an element of exposure, it is necessary to add a second fact acknowledged repeatedly by a unanimous Court: that public exposure of speakers is an infringement on First Amendment rights. It therefore follows that nearly all investigations of speakers are unconstitutional; it follows, that is, if preferred position is substituted for the balancing that in earlier cases acknowledged that exposure created First Amendment claims, but then balanced them away in favor of {167} other interests. If exposure is a legitimate and routine part of Congressional investigations, then the exposure functions of Congress are strictly limited by the First Amendment, just as are its other legitimate powers. If Congress cannot pass laws abridging the freedom of speech, it cannot make exposures abridging the freedom of speech.

The stock reply to this proposition is that the investigatory power must be somewhat wider than the lawmaking power, for otherwise, how would Congress know how far it could constitutionally go in passing laws? This argument is, in fact, one of those mechanistic verbalisms that act as substitutes for thought, about which Justice Frankfurter so frequently complained. It deftly drops back into the assumption that investigations are for the purpose of gaining information on which to base legislation. But if an investigation is for the purpose of punishing a speaker by exposure, it is surely entitled to no more constitutional leeway than a Congressional statute punishing him by imprisonment. Why should a secondary and peripheral power of Congress, that of exposure, be less limited by the First Amendment than its principal power, lawmaking?

It might be argued that since exposure is at least an incidental part of all investigations, some infringement on First Amendment rights via exposure is a price we have to pay in order to allow Congress to gather the information it needs to legislate and which it cannot get without investigation and thus without some exposure. This is, in essence, the argument of *Barenblatt.* It is actually just another instance of the blind, but modestly convenient, presumption that Congressional investigations are designed to find facts on which to base legislation. In fact, we know that in investigations like those of the House Un-American Activities Committee all the facts necessary to sustain legislative recommendations are developed by the confidential investigations of the committee's zealous staff and the testimony of voluntary and highly cooperative witnesses. These facts, *after they have been developed*, are used to stage manage the public showings of reluctant witnesses who, at best, do little more than confirm what the committee already knows. It is out of these literally post facto hearings that First Amendment claims arise, so that neither the infringements on the First Amendment nor the purpose of those infringements have had any real relation to Congress' need to know in order to legislate. Indeed, viewing committee hearings in general as part of the legislative process, there is almost no information developed in public hearings that was not available to Congress in written, confidential reports, from published sources, or through law {168} enforcement agency or committee staff files. Public committee hearings, including investigations, are basically designed for dramatic and cathartic purposes, not to obtain needed information for Congress. That is precisely why the parades of witnesses, the exact content of whose testimony everybody knows in advance, are such a common feature of such hearings.

Several other points need to be made about the relation between anonymity and the informing function of Congress. Any recalcitrant witness who really wants to hide things from Congress can take the Fifth. So the addition of First Amendment claims is not going to change the ultimate balance of power between committees and witnesses. What it would do is end the nasty little device of purposely calling witnesses in order to force them into taking the Fifth because that is the only way they constitutionally have of protecting the privacy of their politics. Forcing speakers into testifying or taking the Fifth is, in fact, the most vicious sort of exposure infringement on the First Amendment. It punishes speakers by either exposing what they actually said, or falsely exposing them to a presumption of criminality if they take the Fifth to avoid exposure of what they said.

Once exposure is recognized as a legitimate function of Congress, limited as are all such functions by the First Amendment, Congress can continue to expose juvenile delinquency, organized crime, government corruption, and anything else that does not concern free expression. It is only speech that Congress may not investigate. Moreover, the normal distinction between thought and action can be applied here. The fact that sixty gangsters meeting in Chestnutfever, Nebraska, solemnly discussed politics for fifteen minutes before dividing up the western territory would no more bar their investigation than would the fact that a burglar merrily sang Salvation Army hymns as he wielded his jimmy prevent his arrest. Any time criminal activity is involved, Congress can investigate.

Finally, the clear-and-present-danger rule would apply in this First Amendment area as well as in others. Where the Congress has discovered a clear and present danger that it wishes to quash by exposure rather than by criminal statute, it is free to expose. Once again we will find the argument: How can legislators discover a clear and present danger if they are not free to investigate fully? To ask Congress to demonstrate a clear and present danger before it investigates is to ask it to prove the very thing the investigation is designed to discover. And again the reply is that this objection is purely a verbal trick. It is going to be a peculiar {169} clear and present danger indeed that will evade all the preliminary investigations of committee staffs, administrative agencies, and various levels of police and intelligence organizations, and then suddenly come to light in a public parade of hostile witnesses, all free to take the Fifth. Congress can find out whether a clear and present danger exists which would justify exposure before it holds the hearings that expose.

How close has the Supreme Court actually come to this position? Its latest major announcement on investigations and anonymity in general was *Gibson v. Florida Legislative Investigation Committee* in 1963. In its broad outlines, that case seems to be a return to preferred position balancing. It requires that the committee establish a "probable cause or . . . substantial relation between the information sought and a subject of overriding and compelling [or] immediate, substantial and subordinating state interest"[88] before it could invade the witness' right of anonymity. The crucial question in the future may well be: Just how probable a cause? Presumably, a Court relatively sensitive to First Amendment freedoms will demand a relatively high level of probability.

On the other hand, the Court makes so much of the argument that membership in the Communist Party may be exposed by investigation or registration because of the very special, subversive nature of the Party that *Gibson* may well be granting very broad rights of anonymity to everyone but the Communist Party. In short, like *Yates* it may be read as creating full First Amendment freedoms, but making a special exception for the Communist Party. In this light, *Gibson* could later be interpreted by judges so minded as a return to the clear-and-present-danger rule. Legislative committees may only expose membership of organizations that present a clear and present danger, for it is only in such organizations that the state has an "immediate, substantial and subordinating interest." Exposure of the Communist Party, it might be argued, has been permitted by past decisions of the Court because, in that one instance, the special nature of the Party warranted the substitution of presentness of organization for presentness of danger.

I am not predicting that the Court will actually adopt exactly this position in exactly this language. Indeed, only Justices Black and Douglas—and they not explicitly—adopted a clear-and-present-danger position when they argued that the membership for ideological purposes could not be constitutionally exposed, but membership in organizations involved in criminal activity could. Nevertheless, the Court, by employing very strict standards of probable cause, and by finding a compelling state interest only where criminal organizations are involved, could in {170} effect re-establish the distinction of preferred position and the clear-and-present-danger rule between speech and criminal action, whether or not it explicitly re-adopted the exact language of the danger rule.

It has always been fashionable in legal commentary to confuse what you want the courts to do with what they are doing. There is nothing more aesthetically and intellectually pleasing, particularly to minds trained in the common law, than to say this is what the courts ought to do, this is what the courts will do, and this is actually what the courts have been doing all along—if you hold the light just right. In calling for a return to preferred position and clear-and-present-danger, I do not think I am asking for a violent break from the Supreme Court's previous decisions. It would not be particularly awkward, in terms of the body of precedents, to return to those doctrines, either in identical or slightly altered language. Indeed, there is a considerable number of signs that the Justices are moving in that direction. On the other hand, it is unlikely that the Court will, in the immediate future, go beyond a mixture of preferred position and clear-and-present-danger with the approaches discussed above. How far this eclecticism will carry the Court toward the high level of protection for speech envisioned by preferred position and clear-and-present-danger will depend upon several unpredictable factors, particularly changes in personnel and the general emotional tone of American politics. In any event, the reader should look forward to a period in which each Court decision will have to be examined more as a contribution to the tone and movement of the Court as a whole than as a monumental pronouncement.

Viewed in this light, recent Supreme Court decisions give considerable cause for mild rejoicing. There has been a spate of First Amendment cases in the last few terms, most of them favorable to freedom of speech. In the *Lamont* case the Justices for the first time held a federal statute unconstitutional as an invasion of freedom of speech. Using the bill of attainder clause, the Court struck down a federal law making it a crime for a Communist to hold union office, thus tacitly overruling *American Communications Association v. Douds* which, it will be remembered, was the lead-off case in the assault on clear-and-present-danger and its replacement by the balancing formula.[89] The Supreme Court is again active and seemingly sympathetic in the First Amendment area.[90]

Conclusion

The crucial issues of the First Amendment facing the Supreme Court have not been those that revolve about the desirability of maximum {171} freedom of expression in American society. On that question there has, perhaps, not been unanimity, but at least there has been a substantial libertarian majority since the late 1930s. This substantial majority did not translate itself into a working majority in favor of speech because of a clash within that majority over what the proper role of the Supreme Court should be. I have tried to show that the position of the judicially modest is based upon a fundamental misapprehension about the nature of American politics. Once that misapprehension is swept away, it can be seen that American democracy as it actually operates not only permits but invites and requires a strong measure of judicial activism in defense of those interests which are not properly represented elsewhere. Since speech is one such interest, the Court has a special responsibility for its defense. With that responsibility acknowledged, most of the difficulties with which the modest have confronted themselves in the area of the First Amendment are swept away, and it is possible to proceed to an examination of the evolution of judicial enforcement of the First Amendment, without the false weight of the democratic guilt feelings that have too long burdened the discussion.

The central feature of that evolution has been, of course, the rise of the clear-and-present-danger rule and its partial replacement by the balancing of interests test. The clear-and-present-danger rule symbolized certain basic American beliefs about freedom of speech: that free communication of ideas was philosophically desirable and politically essential to the maintenance of the American system of government; that government might punish men for what they did, but not what they thought; and consequently, that the law might intervene when speech became so entangled with criminal action as to be an integral part of that action. Balancing has never been able—nor has it really tried—to refute these propositions, for fundamentally, balancing was not an articulated position on freedom of speech, but a rhetorical device to clothe a judicial modesty which is not about speech at all, but about the democratic role of the Supreme Court.

If the movement away from the clear-and-present-danger rule and its accompanying preferred position doctrine was inspired not by a declining attachment to freedom of speech on the part of the Justices, but by the modest hesitancy of many of them to act "undemocratically" in its defense, it should be possible to return to those doctrines once we have demonstrated to the modest that their hesitancy was founded on a misconception of American politics. In fact, the preferred position doctrine is basically a summary statement of the political justification for Supreme Court activism in defense of speech in terms of the very system of {172} American democracy which the modest are so anxious to uphold. Preferred position should then again become the dominant First Amendment doctrine of the Supreme Court. The clear-and-present-danger rule still provides a working method for implementing that doctrine, a method which rests on the long established principle of distinguishing thought from action, and is well within the capacity of the Justices to apply. After the balancing onslaught, however, it is unlikely that the Court will soon return to the nearly exclusive employment of the danger rule, even with the supplements necessary to cover those situations in which it cannot operate directly. Instead, we may expect a period of doctrinal multiplicity in which many formulas of varying effectiveness will be used to implement the preference for freedom, if indeed that preference is firmly re-established.

The Supreme Court has only declared one minor law of Congress unconstitutional as a violation of the First Amendment, although it has struck down state and local ordinances. Particularly if the Court should return to preferred position through the employment of a multitude of minor rules and ad hoc decisions, this fact should be borne clearly in mind. Neither the preferred position doctrine nor the clear-and-present-danger rule has ever enjoyed more than a fleeting majority on the Court. It may seem strange, after all the ink spilled over the First Amendment and its obviously crucial importance to the preservation of our system of government, but it is nevertheless true that the Court has committed itself less firmly to the First Amendment than to nearly any other of the individual rights specifically guaranteed by the Constitution. In recent years the Court has irreversibly enlisted itself in the enforcement of the equal protection clause, both in terms of Negro rights and electoral apportionment. It has taken similar steps under the Fourth and Fifth Amendments and the due process clause of the Fourteenth to protect the rights of those accused of crimes in regard to illegally obtained evidence and right to council. The notion that the Court cannot do big things has been destroyed by the big things the Court has done. Several of its decisions of the past decade are causing fundamental changes in the course of American politics and others are bringing about less far-reaching but nonetheless important reforms. A firm and vocal return to preferred position and clear-and-present-danger or their equivalents, rather than a sub silentio and marginal protection of speech through decisions of the moment, would institute a parallel movement for the First Amendment. It seems to me that the First Amendment is first enough to deserve one of the Court's larger steps toward constitutional liberty. When and if a majority can be obtained for the kind of {173} commitment to freedom of speech that the Court has undertaken for Negro rights and the rights of voters, it would be foolish to dribble away that opportunity with anything less than a full scale return to libertarian principles. We must now await the occurrence of such an opportunity.

NOTES to Chapter Four

1 354 U.S. 234 (1959).

2 *The Bill of Rights* (New York, 1960), p. 69.

3 301 U.S. 242, 263 (1937).

4 *The Governmental Process* (New York, 1959), p. 517.

5 *The Bill of Rights*, p. 69.

6 Frank, "Some Reflections on Judge Learned Hand," *University of Chicago Law Review*, vol. 24 (1957), p. 700.

7 *Ibid.*, p. 691.

8 *On Understanding the Supreme Court* (Boston, 1949), p. 108.

9 See McKay, "The Preference for Freedom," *New York University Law Review*, vol. 34 (1959), p. 1182. My use of the phrase "preference for freedom," above, is borrowed from Professor McKay.

10 268 U.S. 652 (1925).

11 *Dennis v. United States*, 341 U.S. 494 (1951).

12 *American Communications Association v. Douds*, 339 U.S. 382 (1950).

13 354 U.S. 298 (1957).

14 367 U.S. 203 (1961).

15 The exception is, of course, the Court's obscenity opinions which do apparently allow punishment of those who inspire certain thoughts. But thought control is allowed in this area, at least theoretically, because it does not fall within First Amendment freedom of speech.

16 *Political Freedom: The Constitutional Powers of the People* (New York, 1960); *Free Speech and Its Relation To Self-Government* (New York, 1948).

17 *Free Speech*, pp. 24-27.

18 *Id.*, p. 18.

19 "Toward a General Theory of the First Amendment," *Yale Law Journal*, vol. 72 (1963), pp. 910-11.

20 376 U.S. 254 (1964).

21 85 S. Ct. 1493 (1965).

22 85 S. Ct. 1634 (1965).

23 *Id.* at 1649.

24 *Abrams v. United States*, 250 U.S. 616, 627 (1919). See Robert McCloskey, "Free Speech, Sedition and the Constitution," *American Political Science Review*, vol. 45 (1951), p. 665.

25 341 U.S. 494 (1951).

26 Edward S. Corwin, "Bowing Out Clear and Present Danger," *Notre Dame Lawyer*, vol. 27 (1951), p. 342.

27 *Thornhill v. Alabama*, 310 U.S. 88 (1940).

28 "Toward a General Theory of the First Amendment," p. 911.

29 See *Beauharnais v. Illinois*, 343 U.S. 250 (1952). {174}

30 *Schneider v. New Jersey*, 308 U.S. 147 (1959).

31 *N.A.A.C.P. v. Alabama*, 84 S. Ct. 1502, 1314-15 (1964).

FREEDOM OF SPEECH

32 See *Aptheker v. Secretary of State*, 578 U.S. 500 (1964); *Lamont v. Postmaster of the United States*, 85 S. Ct. 1495, 1497 (1965) (concurrence); *Griswold v. Connecticut*, 85 S. Ct. 1649 (1965).

33 See *Staub v. City of Baxley*, 355 U.S. 313 (1958); *Niemotko v. Maryland*, 340 U.S. 268 (1951); *Hague v. C.I.O.*, 307 U.S. 496 (1939); *Cox v. Louisiana*, 85 S. Ct. 455 (1965).

34 See *Hague v. C.I.O.*, 307 U.S. 496 (1939); *Joseph Burstyn, Inc. v. Wilson*, 343 U.S. 495 (1952).

35 See *Baggett v. Bullitt*, 84 S. Ct. 1316 (1964); *Speiser v. Randall*, 357 U.S. 513 (1958); *Smith v. California*, 361 U.S. 147 (1960).

36 *Joseph Burstyn, Inc. v. Wilson*, 343 U.S. 495 (1952).

37 *Winters v. New York*, 333 U.S. 507 (1948).

38 *Hague v. C.I.O.*, 307 U.S. 496 (1939).

39 84 S. Ct. 1316 (1964).

40 See Alexander Bickel, "Forward: The Passive Virtues, The Supreme Court, 1960 Term," *Harvard Law Review*, vol. 75 (1961), pp. 40-79; and *The Least Dangerous Branch—The Supreme Court at the Bar of Politics* (New York, 1962).

41 *Id*.

42 See Shapiro, "Judicial Modesty: Down With the Old!—Up With the New?" *U.C.L.A. Law Review*, vol. 10 (1963), pp. 533-560.

43 See Gunther, "Subtle Vices of the 'Passive Virtues'—a Comment On Principle and Expediency in Judicial Review," *Columbia Law Review*, vol. 64 (1964), p. 32, who emphasizes the relation between neutral principles and passive virtues in Bickel's writing, although he does so in the context of what seems to me a naive apoliticism that Bickel has advanced beyond.

44 *Bates v. Little Rock*, 361 U.S. 516, 523 (1960).

45 See Reich, "Mr. Justice Black and the Living Construction," *Harvard Law Review*, vol. 76 (1963), p. 673.

46 See, e.g., *Slochower v. Board of Higher Education of New York City*, 350 U.S. 551 (1956); *Konigsberg v. State Bar of California*, 353 U.S. 252 (1957); *Baggett v. Bullitt*, 84 S. Ct. 1316 (1964); *Speiser v. Randall*, 357 U.S. 513 (1958).

47 See *Kent v. Dulles*, 357 U.S. 116 (1958); *Aptheker v. Secretary of State*, 84 S. Ct. 1659 (1964); but see *Zemel v. Rusk*, 75 S. Ct. 1271 (1965).

48 *International Assoc. of Machinists v. Street*, 367 U.S. 740 (1961).

49 *N.A.A.C.P. v. Button*, 371 U.S. 415 (1963).

50 See *Aptheker v. Secretary of State*, 84 S. Ct. 1659 (1964); *Freedman v. Maryland*, 85 S. Ct. 737 (1965). Technically it can be argued that neither of these decisions precisely employs the *Thornhill* rule, but in fact both do allow the same broad construction of standing where speech claims are involved.

51 *Barr v. City of Columbia*, 84 S. Ct. 1734 (1964).

52 See *Thompson v. City of Louisville*, 362 U.S. 199 (1960).

53 The Court has already neatly shifted the burden from the First Amendment to the Civil Rights Act once.

54 They neatly avoided it in all of the recent sit-in cases. See *Barr v. City of Columbia*, 84 S. Ct. 1734 (1964); *Bell v. Maryland*, 84 S. Ct. 1814 (1964); *Robinson v. Florida*, 84 S. Ct. 1693 (1964); *Griffin v. Maryland*, 84 S. Ct. 1770 (1964); {175} *Bouie v. Columbia*, 84 S. Ct. 1697 (1964); *Hamm v. Little Rock*, 85 S. Ct. 384 (1964).

55 326 U.S. 501 (1946).

56 *Bell v. Maryland*, 84 S. Ct. 1814, 1878-79 (dissenting).

57 *Cox v. State of Louisiana*, 85 S. Ct. 453 (1965). The opinion, however, was written by Justice Goldberg who has subsequently left the Court. The Court seemed to be going out of its way to warn those engaged in civil disobedience that they will not be able to successfully argue that deliberately breaking the law as a demonstration of protest is speech covered by the First Amendment. Rather, it will be treated as action, and thus punishable by the state.

58 340 U.S. 315 (1951).

59 372 U.S. 539 (1963).

60 The language was first used in *Barenblatt v. United States*, 360 U.S. 109 (1959).

61 See *Cox v. State of Louisiana*, 85 S. Ct. 453, 466 (dissent).

62 *Near v. Minnesota*, 283 U.S. 697 (1931).

63 323 U.S. 516 (1945).

64 340 U.S. 290 (1951).

65 *Niemotko v. Maryland*, 340 U.S. 268 (1951); *Hague v. C.I.O.*, 307 U.S. 496 (1939); *Schneider v. New Jersey*, 308 U.S. 147 (1939); *Lovell v. City of Griffin*, 303 U.S. 444 (1938); *Staub v. City of Baxley*, 355 U.S. 313 (1958).

66 *Kingsley Books, Inc. v. Brown*, 354 U.S. 436 (1957).

67 *Marcus v. Thirty-One Search Warrants*, 367 U.S. 717 (1961); *A Quantity of Books v. Kansas*, 378 U.S. 205 (1964).

68 365 U.S. 62 (1961).

69 85 S. Ct. 734 (1965).

70 84 S. Ct. 1676 (1964).

71 See Shapiro, "Morals and the Courts: The Reluctant Crusaders," *Minnesota Law Review*, vol. 45 (1961), p. 897.

72 376 U.S. 254 (1964).

73 *Id.* at 279-80. See also *Henry v. Collins*, 85 S. Ct. 992 (1965); *Garrison v. Louisiana*, 85 S. Ct. 209 (1964). I do not find this case as significant nor read its portents in exactly the same way as does Professor Kalven in his incisive piece, "The New

York Times Case: A Note on the Central Meaning of the First Amendment," *Supreme Court Review* (1964), p. 191.

74 360 U.S. 109 (1959).

75 365 U.S. 399 (1961).

76 365 U.S. 431 (1961).

77 367 U.S. 1 (1961).

78 *United States v. Rumely*, 345 U.S. 41 (1953); *United States v. Harris*, 347 U.S. 612 (1954).

79 *Viereck v. United States*, 318 U.S. 236 (1943); *Communist Party v. Subversive Activities Control Board*, 367 U.S. 1 (1961).

80 *Id.*

81 357 U.S. 449 (1958).

82 361 U.S. 516 (1960).

83 *Gibson v. Florida Investigating Commission*, 83 S. Ct. 889, 899 (1963).

84 362 U.S. 60 (1960). {176}

85 364 U.S. 479 (1960).

86 367 U.S. 1 (1961).

87 The above passages summarize an argument I have put forward earlier in *Law and Politics in the Supreme Court* (New York, 1964), pp. 50-75.

88 372 U.S. 539, 546, 551 (1963).

89 *United States v. Brown*, 85 S. Ct. 980 (1965).

90 It should be noted, however, that the replacement of Justice Goldberg by Justice Fortas, and Justice Black's occasional, and to my mind quite justified, movements away from the libertarian camp, make prediction very uncertain at the moment.

INDEX

FREEDOM OF SPEECH

TABLE OF CASES

FREEDOM OF SPEECH

FREEDOM OF SPEECH

About this Book

One of the great continuing disputes of American politics is about the role of the Supreme Court. Another is about the First Amendment and freedom of speech. This book is about both.

In FREEDOM OF SPEECH, Martin Shapiro offers a provocative challenge to those who uphold the judicially "modest" interpretation of the role of the Supreme Court and who would keep the Court inviolate from the political process. Each branch of the government, he says, represents specific clienteles and defends specific interests and beliefs. Shapiro argues that one of the Supreme Court's unique functions is to defend those interests which can find no defenders elsewhere; those speakers whose methods we may not be able to countenance, whose ideologies we may deplore, whose objectives we may fear.

From this original analysis of the role of the Supreme Court *within* the American political system, the author goes on to challenge the Court to use its powers of judicial review to fulfill its special responsibility by maintaining a "special preference for freedom." Shapiro affirms the cause of judicial "activism" and clears the way for the Court to make a more militant defense of our most cherished right.

About the Author

Martin M. Shapiro is the James W. and Isabel Coffroth Professor of Law at the University of California at Berkeley. He has taught in the political science departments at Harvard and Stanford Universities and at UC Berkeley, UC Irvine, and UC San Diego. He joined the Boalt law faculty in 1977 and has been a visiting professor at Amherst University, Yale, Ecole des Hautes Etudes in Paris, Universita degli Studi di Milano, and the Summer Institute of the European Group for Public Law in Greece. He received his PhD from Harvard in 1961.

Shapiro is past president of the Western Political Science Association, past vice president of the American Political Association, a trustee of the Law and Society Association, and a member of the American Academy of Arts and Sciences. He has been a Jean Monet Fellow at the European University Institute in Florence, Italy, and a research scholar at the Institute for Judicial Research in Bologna, Italy.

In addition to this book, Shapiro is the author of *Law and Politics in the Supreme Court; Supreme Court and Administrative Agencies; Courts: A Comparative and Political Analysis*; and *Who Guards the Guardians: Judicial Control of Administration*. His publications also include "The Politics of Information: U.S. Congress and the European Parliament," in *Lawmaking in the European Union* (1998), and "Judicial Review, Democracy and the European Court of Justice," in the *Israel Law Review* (1998).

In 2003, Shapiro received a Lifetime Achievement Award from the Law and Courts section of the American Political Science Association.